The Radical Invitation of Jesus

The Radical Invitation of Jesus

How Accepting the Invitation of Jesus Can Lead
to a Living Faith and Fulfilling Life for Today

Duncan S. Ferguson

WIPF & STOCK · Eugene, Oregon

THE RADICAL INVITATION OF JESUS
How Accepting the Invitation of Jesus Can Lead to a Living Faith and Fulfilling Life for Today

Copyright © 2019 Duncan S. Ferguson. All rights reserved. Except for brief quotations in critical publications or reviews, no part of this book may be reproduced in any manner without prior written permission from the publisher. Write: Permissions, Wipf and Stock Publishers, 199 W. 8th Ave., Suite 3, Eugene, OR 97401.

Wipf & Stock
An Imprint of Wipf and Stock Publishers
199 W. 8th Ave., Suite 3
Eugene, OR 97401

www.wipfandstock.com

PAPERBACK ISBN: 978-1-5326-8321-3
HARDCOVER ISBN: 978-1-5326-8322-0
EBOOK ISBN: 978-1-5326-8323-7

New Revised Standard Version Bible, copyright 1989, Division of Christian Education of the National Council of the Churches of Christ in the United States of America. Used by permission. All rights reserved.

Manufactured in the U.S.A.   JULY 2, 2019

Jesus said to him, "I am the way, and the truth, and the life."

(JOHN 14:6A)

Also by Duncan Ferguson

Biblical Hermeneutics: An Introduction

Making the Bible Your Book: Content and Interpretation

New Age Spirituality: An Assessment (Editor)

Called to Teach: The Vocation of the Presbyterian Educator (Coeditor)

Exploring the Spirituality of the World Religions: The Quest for Personal, Spiritual, and Social Transformation

Lovescapes: Mapping the Geography of Love

The Radical Teaching of Jesus: A Teacher Full of Grace and Truth

Mindful Spirituality: The Intentional Cultivation of the Spiritual Life: A Book of Daily Readings

This book is dedicated to those who volunteer to help people in need and work for peace and justice.

Contents

Preface | xi
Introduction | xvii

Section 1—The Difficult Questions: How Do We Access the Invitation? | 1

1 The Nature of Historical Inquiry | 3
2 Starting Points for the Inquiry | 17
3 The Range of Interpretations | 34

Section 2—The Difficult Teachings: What Are the Components of the Invitation? | 55

4 The Ethical Demands | 57
5 The Nature of the Kingdom of God | 74
6 Dealing with the Realities of Conflict | 93

Section 3—The Difficult Events: What Are the Implications of Accepting the Invitation? | 113

7 The Birth Stories and the Calling | 115
8 The Teaching, Healing, and Prophetic Challenge | 134
9 The Last Week | 156

Section 4—The Difficult Decisions: How Do We Respond to the Invitation? | 187

10 The Place of Knowledge, the Place of Faith, and the Place of Action | 189

Bibliography | 207
Index | 213

Preface
The Invitation of Jesus

I HAVE BEEN LEARNING about the life and teachings of Jesus since my years in high school. I had little exposure to Bible stories as a child. But in my high school years, I was given some basic information and invited to make a commitment to the Christian faith and become a part of the church family. In a simple way, I did. I began to understand Jesus as both a savior (although unsure what that meant) and a model for a way to live my life. I became involved in the community that formed around him, both in youth groups and the church. It was an appropriate context in which to nurture my new faith.

In my years as a university student, I went beyond the faith-centered views of those who taught me in youth groups and the church community, and began to explore other views. I then went to a moderately conservative seminary and was exposed in detail to some of the complexities of understanding the life and teachings of Jesus. I began to deepen my understanding from within a thoughtful orthodox frame of reference. Though my teachers integrated the two dominant perspectives, critical history and thoughtful faith, I was gradually becoming more aware of the differences between the Jesus of history and the Christ of faith, and began to wonder if and how the two could be integrated.[1] I also began to wonder if I had made the right decision as a high school student to accept the invitation to follow Jesus with so little knowledge and understanding. I started to ask questions and joined Socrates in his questioning method as a way of life, hoping and believing

---

1. See the early efforts to integrate the historical Jesus and the Christ of faith, for example, in the book by Forsyth, *Person and Place of Jesus*, published in 1909, and the book by Kähler, *So-Called Historical Jesus*, first published as an essay in 1896. By the mid-twentieth century, the issue of discerning between the Jesus of history and the Christ of faith was clearly recognized and shaped the study of Christian origins.

that questions were welcomed in the Jesus movement. Generally they were, although not always by my most conservative colleagues and friends.

The years of graduate education in religious studies, in a disciplined and demanding way, increased my awareness that if I were to work in a church context or teach at the university level in religious studies, I had better continue to expand and refine my understanding of the issues surrounding the life and teachings of Jesus. I would also need to study in depth the creedal statements of the church. In these endeavors, I not only became better informed about the issues of faith, but also more aware of additional questions, and I was exposed to the direct challenges of being a person of faith in the Christian family and the church. Across my career in both settings, church and academy, I have continued my inquiry through teaching, preaching, research, and writing. These endeavors have been an important and life-giving dimension of my life, although not always a comfortable one.

I have read the well-reasoned literature that questions the traditional foundations of the Christian faith (or any faith, for that matter). I have also read much of the literature written by those within the Christian faith community who raise questions about many of the creedal statements of the Church. For example, I have read several books by John Shelby Spong, a biblical scholar and bishop in the Episcopal Church, whose recent book is entitled *Unbelievable: Why Neither Ancient Creeds Nor the Reformation Can Produce a Living Faith Today*. In *The Radical Invitation of Jesus*, I want to turn his theme around and address the subjects about which he writes in a more positive way. I want to take the heritage of the church, and more particularly the invitation of Jesus, and reframe it in a way that is credible and persuasive. I do respect Bishop Spong's work and have learned from it; he raises important issues, and the majority of his writing is positive in its outlook. Yet I am persuaded that it is possible to alter his negative thesis that many Christian beliefs are unbelievable. Bishop Spong's title may have the tendency to lead people away from faith. I would rather state his concerns in a positive way that invites thoughtful people to endorse an honest faith with integrity and believability. This shift is fundamentally a matter of interpretation, one that preserves the truth in the ancient statements, yet restates them in ways that take into account a contemporary way of understanding reality.

As I matured and became better informed, I sensed that I had a desire to try to put my questions and views, often in flux, into writing. It became clear to me that the subject of the life and teaching of Jesus was of great importance. After all, Jesus is certainly one of the most important people who ever lived, and Christians have given him divine status. Yet I remained reluctant to write on this subject because I was afraid that I might not be able to do it justice. I also knew that there were a great many excellent books about every aspect of the life, teaching, and identity of Jesus, and perhaps another one was unnecessary.[2] In addition, the settings in which I worked did assume that their ministers and professors would have faith commitments based on the church's guiding creeds and statements of faith, although allowing a diversity of expression. I was cautious about articulating a point of view that might challenge the more orthodox belief systems held in the settings in which I worked.

As I reached retirement age, I finally felt adequately prepared in terms of my scholarship, available time, and my faith orientation to write at the book level rather than at the level of public lectures, articles, and book reviews. I began with a volume entitled *The Radical Teachings of Jesus* with the subtitle of *A Teacher Full of Grace and Truth: An Inquiry for Thoughtful Seekers*. In this volume, I focused on the Jesus of history, and I spoke of Jesus as a charismatic teacher, a compassionate healer, and a radical prophet. I am grateful that well-informed seekers and believers have read the book and expressed appreciation for it. In addition, I have appreciated the many kind readers who have also asked why I didn't treat the "hard subjects" more fully. I replied that there was a need for a second volume, one that would address the sayings of Jesus that are difficult to understand, such as the way that he may have believed that the kingdom of God would be fully realized in his generation. And there is the ever-present question of how we might articulate the identity of Jesus. I also wanted to answer the questions of whether my faith had integrity and could be defended. I wanted to know whether I should continue to say yes to the invitation of Jesus to follow his way of understanding the will and way of God and stay in the Christian family. I wanted a credible and believable faith, not an unbelievable faith.

These dear friends who had read *The Radical Teaching of Jesus*, some of whom knew more than I did and many who had alternative views, were pleased when I said that a second volume might be possible. In their judgment, the first volume, written for educated readers, emphasized those aspects of the teaching of Jesus that are relatively well-known and generally affirmed, certainly in a Christian context but also by a wide range of people outside of the Christian faith. They wondered why I didn't say more about some of the quite difficult parables, the eschatological dimension of the teaching of Jesus about the kingdom of God, the complex issues regarding his identity, and why it is so difficult to say yes with integrity to the radical invitation of Jesus. Did he really heal those who came to him, perform

---

2. The three-volume study of the life, teaching, and meaning of Jesus by N. T. Wright, given the inclusive title of *Christian Origins and the Question of God*, is one of the most comprehensive (approximately two thousand pages) and persuasive treatments of the subject that integrates the Jesus of history with the Christ of faith.

miracles, and strongly oppose some of the teaching of the Pharisees? What about the central teaching of the New Testament authors regarding the resurrection of Jesus? Did he really "die for our sins"? In what sense might we think of Jesus as divine? All good questions! I won't be able to address them all in a second volume or in a lifetime, and choices will have to be made. There will be times when I will simply have to say, "I don't know, but it will be very stimulating as I try to understand."

This second volume will more fully acknowledge and address the challenging and difficult questions and suggest possible directions for interpretation and understanding. It will also speak, at least indirectly, to the creedal statements that have developed in the life of church, many of which are based on the assumptions of a premodern frame of reference and worldview. Some of these creedal statements are difficult to believe, and it is not easy to find ways to understand and interpret them in a way that provides a solid foundation for a persuasive and contemporary faith. I want to find a credible way to accept the invitation of Jesus in order to live a life of love and compassion and to seek justice and peace.

In section 1, I will review the reasons why accessing the life and teachings of Jesus is so difficult and how we can proceed to gain adequate information for good judgments and decisions. The next three sections will address the difficult teachings of Jesus and the events of his life that are hard to understand. We will also explore the resulting and perplexing choices we must make regarding his identity. On occasion, as some of the creedal statements of the church are directly related to Jesus, I will suggest other ways to reframe them so that they will provide poignant insights into contemporary life. Integrity in reference to these challenges of interpretation is critical to me as I continue to say yes to the invitation of Jesus and remain in the church community.

I will exercise some caution about going into excessive detail and try to address these concerns in a way that invites the thoughtful reader into a general understanding. I will review the major directions of scholarship and the range of views across history, both within the believing Christian community (the Christ of faith) and with those whose primary goal is to understand Jesus as a first-century Palestinian Jew (the Jesus of history). My hope is that the book will invite the reader to move toward a well-informed and life-giving understanding of the life and teaching of Jesus. I will suggest ways to say yes to his invitation to a life of love and remain in the family of faith with both integrity and commitment.

I will primarily use and quote from the New Revised Standard Version of the Bible, although I will on occasion select another translation that may speak more directly to the subject being discussed. In addition, there is a study guide for each chapter and a list of books that may be useful in the quest to better understand the life and teaching of Jesus.

Introduction
The Context of the Invitation

The Quest for a Credible and Nurturing Faith in Our Time

MY MOTIVATION FOR THIS writing comes both from what is going on inside of me and what is happening all around me. As I have implied in the preface, I have been on a faith pilgrimage, a journey toward a well-grounded faith and one that is nurturing, honest, and that "works" in the context of the contemporary world. As I look back upon the journey, I find myself reflecting on the context in which I traveled, how I managed its challenges, and why I ended up as one who has chosen to stay in the Christian family in my later years. Because of the length and intentional character of this journey, I think a further description of it may be helpful to others.[1] Therefore, at the risk of some redundancy, I want to add a few more comments about this faith pilgrimage, one that I traced briefly in the preface.

As I implied in the preface, I did begin my pilgrimage with some innocence. I was still in the garden and had not yet eaten the fruit from "the tree of the knowledge of good and evil."[2] I also remember that I was curious and somewhat needy in this state of innocence. My family had some dysfunctional dimensions because of alcohol, which created a good measure of insecurity. When I came home from school or approached the weekend, I was never quite sure what to expect. Added to the insecurity was the feeling of anxiety; I was worried about what the future might bring and whether I

---

1. See the book by Gushee, *Still Christian*, for a personal account of a changing perspective in a spiritual journey. The book by Airey, *Descending Like a Dove*, has a similar theme.

2. Gen 2:17.

could cope without a healthy family structure. I often hid these feelings of insecurity and anxiety because I was ashamed of them and too shy to talk about them. I went into each day wanting the stability that I thought would come if I were accepted and popular, not ignored or rejected. I smiled a lot and studied hard, which ironically led to a certain amount of loneliness. I didn't know how to express my feelings, nor did I know to whom I might turn. I did love my parents and appreciated the good life they provided for my older brother and me, but unfortunately they struggled with life as well. Now I better understand their struggle, can love them in my memory, and wish that they might have had a better life. Early on, I began to feel somewhat like a parent with the responsibility for creating some order in the occasional chaos in our family life. My role and the role of my parents were slightly reversing.

Perhaps I was not unlike any other teenager trying to find my way. It wasn't an easy period in my life. It was at this time that I was introduced to the invitation of Jesus and hoped there would be some answers. In fact, there were some answers. In the context of the youth group and summer camp experiences, I did feel like I was understood and belonged to a community of acceptance and love. There were caring people who in a variety of ways said to me that I was okay and even might have some gifts of leadership that could be cultivated.

I also felt that I was now in sync with a part of my culture. It was the accepted norm of the fifties to be in a church community, and I now felt that I belonged. It was the age when the majority of the population was Catholic, Protestant, or Jewish in the United States, and I thought I should belong to one of these religious traditions. I now realize that my need to belong was motivated by this social reality. I look back and now realize that I was engaged in extensive social learning from this context. We easily accept the cultural norms and beliefs of our setting and form values and beliefs from them. I now know that I was engaged in a long process of growth and development.

It was just a bit later during my university years in the late fifties that I began to wonder if my high school faith was believable. During these years, my courses did invite me to answer the question of how I really know. I did get one answer in some of the campus ministries in which I participated. It was that we know "because the Bible tells us so." But the courses in philosophy and religion pressed me to understand the Bible as a merely book of great wisdom and a human product, rooted in a particular time and place in history and not free from error. I did read some fine apologetic works such as C. S. Lewis's *Mere Christianity*. But I also bumped into David Hume, Friedrich Nietzsche, and Bertrand Russell. I began the lifelong quest for a faith that had intellectual and scholarly integrity and was emotionally satisfying.

In addition to the intellectual challenges to my faith, there were also the cultural challenges. I became aware of the way the culture changed during the transition from the fifties to the sixties. I was a young adult in the sixties, and many of the norms of traditional belief and behavior were questioned. Whole worldviews were now up for debate. Vietnam happened, Nixon resigned, the Kennedys and Martin Luther King Jr. were assassinated, there was music at Woodstock, and a persuasive counterculture filled with questions appeared. I wondered once again about whether my Christian faith had intellectual integrity and could sustain me as worldviews were changing.

I fell in love with the German word *weltanschauung* ("world outlook"), and sensed that my outlook was limited and framed in a particular time and culture. I asked myself, was what I believed exclusively relative to my time and place in history? Were there some universals? For the next several years, while still a part of the Christian community, I plunged into an intellectual search for defensible answers. I suspect that this search led me away from serving a parish and nudged me toward a career in higher education. The church did provide a life-giving community, although the academy was more my intellectual home. I straddled both worlds and sought a believable and sustaining faith to guide me.

Gradually, across the decades, I became the person I am today. I am a global citizen, living in a postmodern era. I have learned to accept those who are different from me, people from other parts of the world, those with other religious traditions, those with a different sexual orientation, and especially to accept the equality, full liberation, and affirmation of women. I care deeply about the extraordinary challenges of a deteriorating environment and global warming. I care about failing states, poverty, and the concerns of world hunger. I read about the suffering of immigrants, sense the inequalities of a consumer economy, wonder if there are risks inherent in a digital age, and observe with sadness the suffering caused by war and violence. I remain within the Christian family and struggle with ways to make my faith germane to my world, even in the small ways of my own service. I do know that my faith must be honest,[3] intellectually defensible, engaged in reducing human suffering, and offer guidance on how to believe and act in this world I inhabit. I want my faith to reflect and offer insight on the complexity of my world and give me comfort, guidance, and wisdom.

3. See Newbigin, *Honest Religion for a Secular Man*, which calls the church in Newbegin's generation to become more intellectually honest. See as well Robinson, *Honest to God*.

It can only do so if it sheds light on transcendent reality, guides us in the existential realities of life, empowers us to live with compassion, and wisely works toward a more just and humane world. My Christian faith, and indeed the faith commitments in other religious traditions, must respond in belief and practice to the new world being born in our midst. I cannot speak to all the issues and concerns that I imply in my comments, but perhaps I can address some ways that we might restate Christian beliefs that will help us be more inspired in doing our part in the movement started by the life and teachings of Jesus.

As I reflect on the traditional beliefs and creeds of the Christian Church, I find myself wanting to rethink and interpret them in a way that enables them to speak more poignantly in today's world. The church, in its wisdom, has nearly always strived to do so, although not without resistance to change. But across history, the Christian community has tried to make its faith relevant to the contemporary world. It is not heresy to do so, though these endeavors are nearly always challenged. Jesus, too, was challenged in this way. The goal of this writing is to study and gain insight on the invitation of Jesus, and then to follow a way of life that leads to maturity and a commitment to the common good. To arrive at these goals, we must turn to the challenge of gaining access to the life and teaching of Jesus.

As we go along, we will examine with some care a few of the creedal statements that directly intersect with our understanding of Jesus. Most of them address important concerns, but may be expressed in the categories of a premodern era that make them less applicable to our world and only credible to those deeply rooted in the Christian tradition. We cannot speak to all of them, but we will explore and attempt to restate a few of the foundational statements of faith.

SECTION 1

The Difficult Questions

How Do We Access the Invitation?

IN MY PREVIOUS VOLUME, *The Radical Teaching of Jesus*, I did address many of the reasons why it is difficult to access the life and teaching of Jesus. I stressed that the historical records that we have, and especially the Gospels in the New Testament, are central although filled with challenges for the interpreter. Among the challenges are that the Gospels were written many years after Jesus lived and that the authors of the Gospels and other New Testament writings did not write as critical historians, but with the purpose of nurturing and guiding the new Christian community. I also noted the complex challenges of interpreting the literature in that we start with preconceptions and assumptions that shape how we interpret the historical record. In section 1, we will briefly review some of these challenges.

In chapter 1 of this section, I go directly to the task of reviewing the many difficulties of getting back to the Jesus of history. We will need to keep them in mind as we attempt to understand what Jesus did and said. In chapter 2, we will explore the approaches and historical methodology that play a significant role in our goal to understand Jesus. We will examine how our use and understanding of history shape our views, and how to ensure an appropriate reading of the ancient documents. In chapter 3, we will seek to find the best ways of reading history, and will look particularly at hermeneutics, the art and science of interpretation. We will then review the many ways that well-informed interpreters have understood the life and teachings of Jesus.

> "The Jesus of Nazareth who came forward publicly as the Messiah, who preached the ethic of the Kingdom of God, who founded the Kingdom of Heaven upon earth, and died to give His work its final consecration, never had any existence. He is a figure designed by rationalism, endowed with life by liberalism, and clothed by modern theology in modern garb."[1]

---

1. Schweitzer, *Quest for the Historical Jesus*, 3.

1

The Nature of Historical Inquiry

An Example of a Complex Passage: The Christmas Story

IT IS POSSIBLE TO imagine being present as one hears and experiences the stories of the birth of Jesus at the Christmas season. The stories, the sermons, and the hymns, often with creativity and beauty, place the narrative in the idyllic setting of Bethlehem. It was a rural setting in which people lived a simple life, dealt with the realities of poverty, and navigated a confusing, layered, and unjust governmental system. The literature and carols do not place the birth "of the newborn king" in an elegant castle or a modern hospital. Jesus was born in a stable, and even the stable becomes somewhat idealized as we listen, read, and sing. The story of the birth of the child, his mother Mary, and his father Joseph becomes an iconic narrative with great power. There is drama, innocence, and a humble setting all pointing to divine intervention into history with implications not just for the simple family in Bethlehem, but for all of humankind.

I recently traveled to Bethlehem, visited the Church of the Nativity, and was once again moved by the Christmas story. I was also quite inspired by its power as I observed scores of visitors who knelt, prayed, wept, and worshiped. For so many faithful Christians, the story of the baby Jesus has led them to the Christ of faith.

Later, as I reflected on the experience, I was amazed again by the narrative's message that God had spoken in the child and in the life of the teacher and prophet from Nazareth. I feel informed and guided by the message of Christmas and the larger story of Jesus. It has given my life meaning and direction. Yet the years of study in Christian origins and thought have motivated me to squarely face the historical questions.[1] For example, regarding the Christmas story, I noted that several reputable scholars place the birth of Jesus in Nazareth instead of Bethlehem. Many thoughtful people as well have maintained that there was no virgin birth, just the birth of a baby with Mary and Joseph as parents. Other questions about the birth story arise. Was there really a star overhead that guided the three magi to the manger in Bethlehem? Did Herod have all the male children in the region of the birth who were two years old and under slaughtered because he was insecure about the birth of a new king? Were there angels that sang? And what about the differences between the two birth stories, the one in Matthew and the other in Luke?[2]

These questions and many others have suggested to me that the iconic narrative might be best understood as a beautiful and powerful story, a saga with great insight and meaning although not a fully accurate historical description of what happened. Yet something must have happened; Jesus was born, lived in Galilee, and had a distinctive mission. But the stories we have about his life are filled with premodern assumptions that are integral to the beliefs of the storytellers and the writers. Is it possible to accurately recover what he did and said? Inevitably, one begins to wonder whether it is possible to believe the literal account and primary Christian interpretation of the story. It may be easier to accept the account as a story filled with profound insights that point to God's loving approach to humankind. But the questions do not easily go away, even with this metaphorical interpretation. We might still ask whether to accept the accounts in Matthew and Luke as foundationally true. Is it wise to base my faith on the metaphorical truth of the legend? Is it really possible to base one's religious commitments to the grand truth of God's love for humankind on the simple story? How might this story become believable? How might I continue to say yes to the invitation to follow the way of Jesus?

The Nature of Historical Work

The Christian church has been busy answering these questions listed in the previous paragraph and many others across the centuries. There have been many attempts, some well-researched and persuasive, and others more

---

1. There are many books that deal with the history of the birth of Jesus. I'll mention two excellent ones at this point: Brown, *Birth of the Messiah*; Ratzinger, *Jesus of Nazareth*.

2. Matt 1:18—2:25; Luke 2:1–40.

difficult to accept from the perspective of a critical historical reading.³ We may assume too easily that history is an exact science and that we can gain an accurate record of what actually happened if we are just careful with the records we have and then check our assumptions and understanding of the past with these records.

There was a time in the early development of critical history when historians did say it was possible to find out what truly happened.⁴ As the discipline developed, this understanding of history started to be questioned by the historians themselves. They began to realize that history is hard work done by people who may be well-trained and informed, yet bring to the task a range of attitudes and assumptions that shape the outcome of the historical account.⁵ Historians do bring assumptions that influence what they write; complete objectivity is no longer assumed in the writing of history. As we do our historical work in reference to the life and teaching of Jesus, we need to be conscious of the way our presuppositions are shaping how we understand the past and what we write about it. As we do the historical work in accessing the life and teaching of Jesus, it is wise to keep the following in mind:

1. The best historians do attempt to stay as objective as possible in the reading of the records of history and in their writing. These historians learn as much as possible about the subject of their work. This may require the use of very refined methods of historical inquiry, including language study and a comprehensive review of the context in which the historical event or flow of events occurred. They need to be aware that history is more than a simple recording of what happened, although some basic facts are a good starting point. But soon there is a need for an interpretation of what happened. As historians engage in the work of interpretation, they need to be aware of and sensitive to their own historical context and the beliefs and assumptions they bring to the task. It will inevitably shape the content, character, and tone of their writing.

---

3. A. E. Harvey, in his important book *Constraints of History*, notes that historical access to Jesus is necessary and important, but cautions us about assuming that we can use a historical method as our access and gain a complete and reliable account. Our method of historical inquiry and the history surrounding Jesus will not enable us to arrive with full knowledge; there are constraints.

4. German scholars led in the development of critical history, and the phrase "as it actually happened" was often used in reference to the goal of history.

5. Many excellent books have been written about the nature of history and historical work. A classic is Collingwood's *Idea of History*.

2. They also need to be aware of the purpose of the writing. The historian, not unlike the scientist, starts with a thesis that is demonstrated to be accurate by a careful study of what occurred. The task is to inform and also to demonstrate a point of view. Likely the historian of American history will want to say that George Washington was the first president of the United States, but this observation is usually followed by an assessment that he was a great president and his influence was profound and lasting. There is fact, judgment or point of view being employed, and purpose in the writing.

3. When it comes to religious history, as in the case of the life of Jesus, religious beliefs and assumptions begin to shape the writing of the history. For example, a historian who holds the conviction that God enters into human history may say that God was present in the life of Jesus and empowered Jesus to perform miracles and to rise from the dead. Most current historians would more likely say that the part about God's presence in the life of Jesus is the domain of the pastor and theologian. But history cannot prove it. It is the task of history to record events in terms of sequences of cause and effect and precedent. The historical statement would say that Jesus thought he was being guided and empowered by God, as did his followers. The modern historian would likely say that history couldn't prove that the resurrection of Jesus happened, but that there were circumstances that caused his followers to believe that it occurred. It is an isolated and original event, one that has no pattern of the flow of events in the cause and effect of history. Therefore, all I can say is that the followers of Jesus believed in his resurrection, and this belief caused the formation of the new Christian community called the church.

In short, there are many ways to write very good history, but it is not possible to write totally objective history.

Attempts to Find a Credible Account of the Life and Teaching of Jesus

The church, keenly aware of the constraints of history and also deeply rooted in the belief that God enters human history, has had to find thoughtful ways to tell its story and guide the Christian community. Note that Christianity is based on historical events, not exclusively on a religious or philosophical outlook or argument. Generally these attempts have fallen into three categories.[6] One category might best be labeled the traditional view, which may be defined as the decision to accept on faith the essential biblical account. The traditional interpretation is generally based on a particular view of the Bible, although reasoned argument and firsthand religious experience are occasionally used as well. But as a starting point, there is usually a reference to God's oversight and the Spirit's guidance in the formation of the biblical stories. Frequently the term "inspiration" is used, and the biblical verse in 2 Timothy 3:16 is quoted, where the word "inspired" appears in reference to Scripture. "All scripture is inspired by God and is useful for teaching, for reproof, for correction, and for training in righteousness." The Greek word, translated as "inspired," has the meaning of "God-breathed," and those who adhere to this view of the Bible maintain that the biblical accounts are inerrant because the Spirit of God superintended the process of writing. In the Roman Catholic tradition, and to some extent in the Orthodox and Protestant traditions, there has been the complementary belief that the Spirit of God has continued to inspire the interpretation of the biblical account as it takes shape in church doctrine and creedal statements.

With the rise of the challenge to church authority in the Enlightenment, the emergence of the scientific understanding of the world around us, and the development of critical historical methods applied to the Bible in the nineteenth and twentieth centuries, the traditional view of accepting the inerrant and literal account of the Bible was forcefully questioned.[7] Let me suggest some of the issues raised by those who find it difficult to accept the Bible as inerrant and advocate the literal interpretation of the Bible.

The first is that to quote the Bible in order to defend it is to resort to circular reasoning and therefore invalid reasoning. Other grounds must be found to sustain the argument. Yet defenders of this approach often continue to claim that the Bible is inspired and inerrant by quoting the Bible in defense of their view. Incidentally, the quote from 2 Timothy 3:16, often used to sustain this point of view that speaks about the Scriptures as being inspired, is likely a reference to the writings in the Hebrew Bible. It is not a reference to the writing that gradually and much later became the New Testament.

---

6. Of course there are many subtle and detailed differences in these accounts, and there is some risk of distortion in bunching them all into three categories. But perhaps suggested types of response rather than detailed accounts of the individual responses will be helpful.

7. Two excellent accounts (and there are many!) that trace the discussion of the Bible's character and authority are: Reventlow, *Authority of the Bible*; Rogers and McKim, *Authority and Interpretation of the Bible*.

In addition, there are a number of accounts in the Bible that contain conflicting statements of what occurred. For example, in the Gospels, there is inconsistency in the order of events in the final week of the life of Jesus. John places the overturning of the tables of the moneychangers at the temple in Jerusalem early in the ministry of Jesus, while the other Gospels place it at the end of the ministry of Jesus. Many other examples could be given.

Further, a large number of sources were used in the development of both the Hebrew Bible and the New Testament. A careful study of the formation of these documents reveals a pattern that lasted over long periods of time and the use of a wide range of oral traditions and unrelated sources and writings to piece together the biblical documents. It is hard to defend the process of the many years of development of the Hebrew Bible and the New Testament as anything more than a precritical attempt to write the story of the Hebrew people and the account of the life, teaching, and meaning of Jesus.

It is also apparent in the reading of the biblical documents that there are clear points of view that are defended by quoting passages from the Hebrew Bible. In some cases, they are used in a somewhat awkward and strained way to suggest that what is being described has been predicted in earlier documents. It is not uncommon in the Gospels, and perhaps in Matthew especially, to see a passage drawn from the Hebrew Bible to maintain that what has happened was foretold in one of the books of the Hebrew Bible. Matthew is quite intent upon understanding Jesus as linked to King David and as the new king of Israel. In chapters 12 and 13, Matthew uses quotes from Isaiah (12:18–21 and 13:14–15) that may illustrate his point, although are not easily interpreted as predicting what he describes.

And there is the larger question of whether a premodern understanding of reality that speaks easily of God's intervention in the world in many miraculous ways can be defended. For example, there is the description of the miraculous intervention of God as the Hebrew people cross the Red Sea in the Exodus. Can this account be defended as an actual occurrence in which God moved the water away? Or is it a premodern description of the movement of the tides and the crossing at the point where the water was shallow and filled with reeds? Such passages are often "deconstructed" to separate fact from opinion.

There are scholarly and thoughtful people, those with deep faith and integrity, who defend the traditional outlook. Their defense takes several forms.

On occasion, they may maintain that the original biblical documents, especially those of the New Testament, were without mistakes about what happened and not in conflict with other accounts. Unfortunately many of these original documents were lost and all we have are copies, ones that have been changed slightly across the years of translation and the process of forming the New Testament. This point of view is used in reference to the Hebrew Bible as well. These documents come from many sources across hundreds of years and would be in harmony if we only had them in their original form. What we need to do in our practice of source criticism is to find those closest to the originals.

Those who hold the traditional view would also maintain that there are a great many passages in the Old Testament that do accurately predict the coming of Jesus the Messiah and even point to the events of his life and his death. As one hears the *Messiah* sung at Easter, one senses that Jesus was truly the long-expected Messiah. There may be a coherent and defensible way to bring the Testaments together.

Those with the traditional view would have no difficulty in explaining certain events in terms of miraculous intervention and divine power. The Exodus did happen, freeing the Jewish people from the tyranny of Egyptian rule. Jesus did heal in a miraculous way, and he did rise from the dead in victory over evil and death. The argument is that we need not be bound by the worldview of "scientism" that says, for example, that the natural law of cause and effect is always present as we attempt to read and understand history. The rise of science has helped us to understand the world and improve our way of life. But this scientific outlook and critical history need not become an exclusive worldview. It is also possible to have and maintain a faith perspective. It is acceptable to believe that there was the intervention of God into human life, the patterns of history, and the dynamics of the cosmos. This perspective may answer some of the *why* questions, although not always the *how* questions, which we should leave to critical history and science.

Another and second category of understanding the Christian narrative is to focus on the occurrence of Jesus in history and to view the Bible as a reliable witness to the life and teaching of Jesus. The challenge is how best to interpret the coming of Jesus from the records we have. This point of view would speak of the biblical record, and in particular the account of the life and teaching of Jesus as normative for the Christian faith, although without the necessity of a belief in an inerrant Bible and the need for a literal interpretation of it. In the case of interpreting the life and teachings of Jesus, the New Testament provides the basic factual information about Jesus and the authoritative witness to the meaning of his life, his teaching, his death, and resurrection. In the mid-twentieth century, this view was referred to as neoorthodoxy, an outlook that affirmed the essential message of the New Testament and the account of the life and teaching of Jesus in the Gospels, but did so in a way that did not require a commitment to the inspiration of Scripture that demanded a belief in an inerrant Bible. The movement had great diversity, although there was a consensus that the Bible need not be understood as God's word in every detail. Those in this frame of reference spoke of God's Word as John's Gospel declares in chapter 1; the true word of God is Jesus, not a book. "In the beginning was the Word, and the Word was with God, and the Word was God . . . And the Word became flesh and lived among us, and we have seen his glory, the glory of the father's only son, full of grace and truth" (John 1:1, 14). The Greek term, *logos*, translated as Word, means more than a simple word; it points to the full expression of God who is creator, redeemer, and sustainer of all that is.

There are different interpretations between the many Protestant and Catholic theologians of this era and how the "happening" of Jesus might or should be understood. Theologians and scholars such as Karl Barth, Rudolf Bultmann, Karl Rahner, Hans Küng, Paul Tillich, and Reinhold Niebuhr read the event in quite different ways, but agreed that it happened and points to God's loving intervention into human history. Bultmann, the renowned New Testament scholar of a previous generation, took the more extreme point of view and said that we can know only a little about the Jesus of history, but we know that God spoke in him and we can make this "speaking" our own with an existential decision of faith. We need not accept the premodern mythology of the biblical authors and should demythologize their views. But the essential message of the gospel remains as we do this difficult work.

In many ways, the work of Bultmann and the earlier work of Albert Schweitzer and Wilhelm Wrede pointed to the third dramatic shift in the way that the life and teaching of Jesus is interpreted and understood. This outlook and scholarly endeavor, begun in the nineteenth century, fully blossomed in the early twentieth century and continues in the early years of the twenty-first century. It might best be understood as a return to the quest to understand the Jesus of history from the framework of his time. There were many inspired and noble efforts to write the life Jesus in the nineteenth century. I have read several of these works, and I am sure they capture a measure of truth and the spirit of the ministry of Jesus.[8] As I read them, I do have in the back of my mind the pointed criticism of Albert Schweitzer's book, translated as *The Quest for the Historical Jesus*. In this volume, he makes the persuasive case that so many of the so-called "lives of Jesus" were idealized accounts filled with the values of the author and

---

8. For example, the book by Farrar, *Life of Christ*, and the one by Edersheim, *Life and Times of Jesus*, written in the late nineteenth century, were widely circulated. Ernest Renan's *Life of Jesus* presents Jesus as entirely human. It is a more critical account.

the time in which they were written. Jesus undoubtedly lived an inspiring life, but it wasn't one guided by nineteenth- and early-twentieth-century western European thought and values. Jesus was a first-century Palestinian prophet shaped more by his understanding of the Hebrew Bible and Second Temple Palestinian Judaism. In Schweitzer's classic work, he underlines that Jesus may have thought that the kingdom of God would become a reality in his time. Schweitzer notes that Wilhelm Wrede's account of Jesus in the Gospel of Mark was not a biography, but more of an essay using illustrations from the life and teachings of Jesus that culminate in his redemptive death and resurrection.

In the first half of twentieth century, New Testament scholarship turned its attention in many and complex ways to a new quest for the historical Jesus.[9] Following the work of Schweitzer, there was a reluctance to continue the quest to write a full biography of Jesus. Within the church community, there were those who used the Gospels as they were intended to be used: to inform and nurture the Christian community with reference to the events of the life of Jesus. New Testament scholars, however, were cautious in that they were doubtful that there was enough information for any sort of biography. Little was known about the early life of Jesus. There was even less access to his personal life, and the accounts of his ministry in the Gospels were written to guide the new church community that was forming, not to present a historical account of his life. As we have mentioned, it was Rudolph Bultmann in the first third of the twentieth century who maintained that there is not much we can know about all the events of the life of Jesus.[10] What we can know is that he gave a great deal of attention to the kingdom of God and understood this concept as eschatological in character. At mid-century, there were scholars who did take Bultmann's caution about writing a biography seriously, but who were inclined to say that there is more that we can know about life and teaching of Jesus.[11]

The criticism of Bultmann's point of view has taken many forms, but in general these scholars have maintained that it is possible to know a great deal about Jesus if we use a range of historical methodologies. They have found their way with these approaches, and a multitude of books about

9. There are excellent accounts of this movement; for example, Dawes, *Historical Jesus Quest*; Tatum, *Quest of Jesus*; and Theissen and Mertz, *Historical Jesus*. The small volume, written by James Robinson in 1959, *A New Quest of the Historical Jesus*, captured the spirit of this new trend.

10. See Bultmann's book translated into English in 1934, *Jesus and the Word*.

11. Hans Conzelmann, a student of Bultmann's, was an important voice in delineating a new point of view in Jesus studies. See his modest book, *Jesus*, an essay that was originally published in a German encyclopedia in 1959.

Jesus and Christian origins began to appear. In many ways, it was the dominant theme of New Testament studies in the second half of the twentieth century. The general thesis of these writings affirms that God has entered into human history as recorded in the biblical record. But it is what the record points to, God's gracious presence, not the inerrant record that is the heart of Christian belief.

Those on the more conservative side have maintained that not having a fully trustworthy account allows for Christian belief to be determined subjectively. They argue that the interpreter's own frame of reference, shaped by historical circumstances, the beliefs of a particular church traditions, and the idiosyncrasies of the historian determine the outcome. The general response to this criticism is that the same issue is present for those who believe in a divinely inspired Bible that should be interpreted literally. The interpretation still needs to take place, and the belief system of the interpreter leads to a somewhat-subjective outcome. Further, those who say they can't accept the error-free Bible argue that it is vitally important to be honest with the realities of the biblical literature. It is a wonderful guide, but a human product.

Many within both of these traditions do add and value the great creeds and statements of faith that have been developed across history. While these documents are not thought of as Holy Scripture, and are not therefore an absolute standard for correct belief and practice, they nevertheless represent the best statements of faith for the generations that developed them. While rooted in a time and place in history, they often rise above the particularity of their time and speak eloquently and wisely to other generations.

This third broad category of understanding of the life and teachings of Jesus, international in scope, is now in full bloom within the Christian community, although often on its edge. It might be called progressive liberalism in the sense that each generation of Christians must be willing to reassess their faith and to interpret it within the context and needs of their time and place in history.[12] In nearly every era and setting of Christian thought, this inclination has been present. Even those within the more conservative side of the church have spoken persuasively about the need to speak about faith in ways that are germane to the realities of their life and circumstances. Church history, from the beginning, was filled with discussion and debate. There were differences between Paul and Peter, and there has been a continuation of this trend for the two thousand years of church history. Peter did not want to change his faith orientation in reference to the

---

12. One thoughtful expression of this movement within Christian thought is Ottati, *Theology for Liberal Protestants.* From a Roman Catholic perspective, see Sonderegger, *Systematic Theology.*

continuation of Jewish practices. Paul said that the new gentile members of the Christian community do not need to follow Jewish practices having to do with circumcision and the purity of one's diet. Origin (185–254) and Arius (256–336) argued for alternatives to the accepted views of their time. The Reformation occurred as Martin Luther (1483–1546) and John Calvin (1509–64) argued for a change in belief and practice within the church. Today there are many who argue for a restatement about faith and practice in the church, acknowledging that the work of biblical scholarship and theology is never done. There is space for just a few examples of those who are not comfortable with traditional orthodoxy or an earlier version of theological liberalism. Let me mention just some of these characteristics of this current trend.

Many of these people and movements are inclined to say that they are not moving fully away from the Christian faith held by the more conservative traditions and the liberalism of an earlier generation. They are often grateful, inclusive, and indebted to those who have gone before. Many still hold the great insights of earlier forms of Christian thought but are less traditional in their language and practice. They want their faith to speak to their circumstances: the rapidity of change, the global context in which they live, the liberation of people of color and women, the need for social justice, and the overwhelming challenges they face with climate change. There is no shortage of issues to which they want their faith to speak and inform.

This new expression of Christian faith is keenly aware of the ways in which the Bible is central and the values inherent within the Christian tradition need to be affirmed. But the argument should not really be about an inerrant Bible interpreted in a literal way. It will only lead to the protection of the status quo and divisions within the church. The issues about the nature of the Bible may not have been fully resolved, but there is the more important and immediate challenge of the new world being born in our midst. However one reads the Bible, its message is still clear: we are called to care in a wise, courageous, and compassionate way for this new world.

This trend affirms the Christian faith, but expects it to be integrated with and applied to the extraordinary and overwhelming problems of the earth. It takes into account the rapid expansion of knowledge and the new understanding coming from the digital revolution and the new discoveries and outlooks in the sciences, the social sciences, and the humanities. It is a Copernican moment, and the church should not stand over against the new and holistic understanding of the world. Rather it can draw upon the work of people such as Pierre Teilhard de Chardin and those who are revising and restating his point of view.[13] There are those who are working hard to develop a view, often called panentheism, which understands God's presence within the cosmos as not totally separate from it and entering into the cosmos in miraculous ways from the outside. The emphasis may need to be more on the goodness of the original creation rather that issues of sin, atonement, and redemption. Jesus died because of our sins more than for our sins, and we seek to follow him and to worship God. This point of view would speak about the goodness of the created world and how this generation of caring people must care for the earth and for the sacred universe. Thomas Berry argues that this care is "the great work" of our time.[14] As we care for the sacred universe, we care as well for all who dwell in it, not just those whose culture, way of life, and even religious beliefs and practices are like our own. There is a compassionate universalism, interfaith understanding, and humility before the mystery of the divine rather than an insistence that all must believe and act as I do. Together we must seek the common good.[15]

A Summary of the Development of the Quest for the Historical Jesus

We have said that access to the life and teaching of Jesus is difficult, and we stressed three observations about why it is difficult. We underlined that it is difficult because the materials we use, primarily the Gospels in the New Testament, were written many years after Jesus lived, with the first one, the Gospel of Mark, being written at least thirty years after the time of Jesus. The Gospels were based on oral tradition and some written documents or units that were circulated (called a pericope or a logion) among the new communities of faith. There may have been some eyewitnesses still alive to assist in the writing, although this resource was quite limited.

It is also true that the Gospels were not primarily historical accounts of the life and teachings of Jesus.[16] The primary purpose was to provide

---

13. See, for example, the writings of Ilia Delio, such as *Making All Things New*.

14. See Berry, *Great Work*; and Berry, *Sacred Universe*.

15. Ken Wilbur, in his most recent book, *Religion of Tomorrow*, provides a developmental framework for what he calls a Holistic-Integral outlook that moves well beyond the magic and mythic outlooks of more orthodox traditions (Wilbur, *Religion of Tomorrow*, 534–79).

16. The writer of Luke's Gospel does say he is attempting "to write an orderly account."

information and guidance to the early church community. In some ways, the Gospels are more like extended sermons than historical accounts.

The authors of the Gospels lived prior to the understanding of critical historical study. They were not as apt to check the historical viability of the sources available to them and the oral accounts that were circulating. And they came to the task with a premodern understanding of how the world works and assumed that events could be explained by postulating the miraculous intervention of God or spirits. We will say more about this perspective in the next chapter when we speak about our worldviews and ways of understanding reality.

In short, they did not write what we now know as critical history using a critical-historical methodology, but were careful and devoted in writing from their perspective of faith. It was not until the end of the eighteenth century and more into the nineteenth century that the writing of critical history developed. It wasn't long before the important subject of Jesus, his life, teachings, and identity became a subject for critical historians. There were many who in a dedicated way spoke of Jesus as a noble and gifted teacher who suffered and was crucified because of his courageous life. In the later part of the nineteenth century and well into the twentieth century, historians challenged the accounts of Jesus in the Gospels and maintained that what was recorded about his miracles and healing could not be substantiated. What we have are premodern descriptions of events that were described and explained within a premodern worldview.

Gradually, historians of the Bible and New Testament scholars in particular began to develop a variety of historical approaches that would enable them to provide a more accurate historical account of the life and teaching of Jesus.[17] This endeavor has gone through several stages, and we now turn to these new approaches in historical study that will help us understand Jesus.

Study Resources

Discussion Questions

1. What are the primary difficulties in accessing the Jesus of history?
2. What are the differences between the Jesus of history and the Christ of faith?

---

17. See, for example, Grant, *Jesus: An Historian's Review*, as an effort to use the best methods of historical study to describe the life and teachings of history,

3. What are your views of the Bible, and especially its account of the life and teachings of Jesus?
4. Do you think the birth of Jesus took place as it is described in the Gospels of Matthew and Luke? If so, how do you account for the differences between them?
5. What would you take into account if you were to write a book about Jesus?

Terms and Concepts

1. Inspiration: In reference to the Bible, the term describes the way the biblical authors were guided (God-breathed) by the Spirit of God to write their accounts.
2. Myth: A term similar to saga or legend that tells a true story in a metaphorical way rather than a historical way.
3. Orthodox: Religious beliefs conforming to the established doctrines of the church.
4. Liberal: A term often used to describe beliefs that are altered in order to match accepted contemporary views of reality, similar in many ways to the way the term progressive may be used.
5. Premodern: A way of viewing reality with assumptions accepted prior to the rise of science and critical historical study.

Suggestions for Reading and Reference

Bultmann, Rudolf. *Jesus and the Word.* Translated by Louise Pettibone Smith and Erminie Huntress Lantero. London: Collins: Fontana, 1934.
Conzelmann, Hans. *Jesus: The Classic Article from RGG Expanded and Updated.* Translated by J. Raymond Lord. Philadelphia: Fortress, 1973.
Ferguson, Duncan S. *The Radical Teaching of Jesus.* Eugene, OR: Wipf & Stock, 2016.
Grant, Michael. *Jesus: An Historian's Review of the Gospels.* New York: Scribner, 1977.
Renan, Ernest. *The Life of Jesus.* London: Watts, 1935.

2

Starting Points for the Inquiry

The Demanding Work

It is not necessary that every Christian and those who have a profound interest in the life and teaching of Jesus must become scholars of history and theology. However, nearly all people who have either accepted the radical invitation of Jesus or who are considering it want to do so with the assurance that what they are accepting is credible and trustworthy. They need to have confidence in those that do the hard scholarly work in Jesus studies. Those with a special calling or the vocation of teaching must do the difficult work of careful study and research on behalf of others who may be called to contribute to the common good in another way. As the apostle Paul says to the often confused but gifted new church in Corinth: "Now there are varieties of gifts, but the same Spirit; and there are varieties of services, but the same Lord; and there are varieties of activities, but it is the same God who activates all of them in everyone. To each is given the manifestation of the Spirit for the common good. To one is given through the Spirit the utterance of wisdom, and to another the utterance of knowledge, according to the same Spirit" (1 Cor 12:4–8).

Most of us want to know that our faith is well-founded and that there are reasonable grounds for accepting it. This is especially the case in a faith tradition with a foundation that rests upon people and events in history as Christians do. Across the years, I have sensed the calling to teach. While I have not always done it well, I have spent the better part of my professional life in the role of a teacher with the goal of assisting others to better understand their faith and its place in the world. I have also done administrative work and provided pastoral care, and while these things are satisfying in many ways, I have always returned to the role of teacher-scholar.

The subject of great interest to me in my calling has been the person of Jesus and his message and mission. As I have engaged in this work of understanding Jesus, I have had to directly face the inherent challenges in this quest to understand his life and teaching. In chapter 1, we have noted that there is difficulty in accessing information about Jesus, although there is certainly no shortage of writing about him, which adds a whole other dimension to the task. In summary, we said there are three primary challenges in getting back to the first-century Jewish teacher and prophet.

One is that the written material we have, primarily the Gospels of the New Testament, were written many years after he lived. It is likely that there was some material (the Q source) and an earlier oral tradition that provided information about him that was preserved and circulated before the Gospels were written.[1]

We said as well that the authors of the Gospels lived before the development of the discipline of critical historical work. So the emphasis in the Gospels is not on the preservation of a historical account or to write a well-researched biography of Jesus. The Gospels do contain some factual information, but their purpose is more about helping the new Christian community find its way in a complex world. A narrative is written for this purpose.

We then noted that the Gospel writers had a clear point of view and purpose that shaped the writing of the material. The Gospels were written to inform readers about Jesus. Three of the Gospels, Matthew, Mark, and Luke, are called the Synoptic Gospels because they have many similarities and have only a slightly different perspective about the life and teachings of Jesus. The Gospel of John is different from the other Gospels and more theological in character. All four, however, were written to encourage the new Christians and the developing Christian church to commit to and live a way of life based on faith in what Jesus said and did.

To understand Jesus, then, we must do the demanding work of interpreting the records we have about him. This requires that we know as much as possible about the history of his time, the culture in which he lived, the languages spoken, the government structures, and the branches, beliefs, and practices of first century Judaism. As we do this work, we must explore the possibility that there was a Jesus of history who to some extent stands behind the Christ of faith written about in the Gospels. We access this Jesus

---

1. The Q source is a reference to other written documents about Jesus that appear to be used by the authors of the Synoptic Gospels but have been lost. Q is shorthand for the German term *quelle*, meaning "source."

with humility because of the difficulty of the work and access, and with the best critical-historical methods available to us.

In addition to the historical work, we come to our task with our own assumptions and points of view, even as the authors of the Gospels did. In this chapter, our goal is to describe the historical methods that will help us, at least partially, to get back to Jesus. As we do, we need to be self-aware about our worldview, outlook, and purpose as we bring Jesus forward and use the example of his life and teachings to guide the present generation. It is important to be fully open about the assumptions we bring to the task of describing Jesus; only then will our interpretation of Jesus have integrity. We do this work for those who follow him as Christians and those who simply want to understand this extraordinary Palestinian Jew who was a charismatic teacher, a compassionate healer, and a radical prophet.

Brief Summary of the Quest to Understand the Jesus of History

We will start with a brief description of the way history has been practiced to gain access to Jesus. There was a long period of time when historians and biblical scholars attempted to understand Jesus by doing the basic work of history. It might best be characterized as the precritical period existing before the nineteenth century, a time in which the biblical account was largely accepted as an accurate account. Historians and biblical scholars did their language study (Greek, Hebrew, and Aramaic), examined the contours of the culture in which Jesus lived, reviewed the religious setting (Judaism) in which he participated, and placed first-century Palestine within the larger context of the Roman Empire. Careful attention was given to the nature of the small village of Nazareth situated in the region of Galilee. There were descriptions of the influence of Mary and Joseph and the call of Jesus to leave his family and travel south to be with his cousin, the prophet John the Baptist. There was a review of his public life, the selection of disciples, the teaching about the kingdom of God, and the healing ministry. There was special scrutiny of the way Jesus interacted with the religious leaders and especially the Pharisees. And, of course, there was sensitive and careful examination of the final week of his life. This historical work had great value and informed biblical scholars, teachers, and pastors in the church, and the wider public. There were differences among the historians, thoughtful debates, and whole schools of thought in different regions of the world. This historical work was done with care, although it was more descriptive than it was a critical assessment of whether the records that were available—i.e., the

New Testament and histories of the time and region, were accurate.[2] It was accepted, for example, that Jesus did heal the leper and calmed the storm on the Sea of Galilee. The events of his life and the account of his teaching described in the Gospels were viewed as a true description of what occurred and what it meant. In addition, there were numerous attempts to integrate the slightly different accounts in the Gospels.

Toward the end of the eighteenth century and into the nineteenth century there was the rise of critical history. Fundamental questions began to be asked. Among them was whether the ancient records could be trusted. There were certainly discussions about the value of the records prior to the rise of critical history and alternative judgments concerning what the records reveal about the past. This give and take was sometimes accepted and valued, in other cases at least tolerated, and in some cases there were divisions in the church because of alternative interpretations. In reference to biblical history, there was the increasing motivation to examine the accepted orthodox views of the church regarding the nature of the Bible. Scholars did take some risk in challenging the belief that the Bible was altogether accurate and authoritative, and a price was paid by some who questioned the long held views of the church. But question they did.[3]

One of the first directions of historical scholars was to study and question traditional views about the formation of the New Testament and the Gospels in particular because they contained the account of what Jesus said and did.[4] Did the historical information handed down essentially in the Gospels come to us as an early unified whole, much like what we read in our Bibles? Or did it have a fairly long process of formation? The answer was that it took about three hundred years to put the New Testament in its final form. In addition, as it reached its nearly final form, the question was raised about which of the many manuscripts were the most reliable and how this judgment should be made. There was an extensive examination of both internal and external evidence. The internal evidence came from within the text itself, focusing on what was claimed by the author, the author's aim in the writing, the consistency of the presentation, and the nature of the literature.[5] The external evidence had to do with placing the documents within the larger historical context of the time and place in which it was written.

2. In the next chapter, I will provide a summary of the views of Jesus that were products of this precritical era.

3. A good summary of this challenge is Grant and Tracy, *Short History*.

4. The Judaism of the Jewish people was carefully studied as well from a critical historical perspective.

5. This careful historical work was called historical criticism and literary criticism, and it generally preceded some of the more specialized methods of study.

What emerged from this more general work of critical history were the historical methods of textual criticism, a method that was focused on determining the best possible text from among the many that were available. Complementing textual criticism was source criticism, which attempted to discern what sources the author used in writing the document. The goal of the historians was to find manuscripts that were the closest to the original writings and which contained material that described what actually happened.

There were four primary criteria for making this judgment. The first was to determine which of the manuscripts were the oldest and, therefore (in time, at least), the closest to the original manuscripts. This criterion was not followed in every case, because it became apparent that even some of the oldest manuscripts were altered through translations to be supportive of a particular theological point of view. So, in addition to age, the manuscripts were judged in reference to a relatively clear picture that was emerging of what Jesus did and said. Those that varied greatly from the consensus view, regardless of age, may have been altered to fit a particular theological perspective. At times, however, a description that stood out as unlike others was judged to be a valuable source because it may not have been altered to fit a particular point of view. In fact, it was often included as authentic rather than discarded. Third, there was a careful study of the sources from which the manuscript developed. For example, it became apparent in the Synoptic Gospels in particular that there was a common source, now lost, from which material was used. The common source, called Q, was identified but not found. Fourth, there was also the discovery of the interdependence of the Synoptic Gospels, with Mark likely being the first to be written. It is apparent that both Matthew and Luke used Mark as a major source of information. With careful sifting and sorting, New Testament scholars found the most reliable texts. At the end of this careful process, there was still the most vexing question: Did Jesus really do and say what the text records?[6]

In the early twentieth century, in part out of the motivation to get as close as possible to the life and teachings of Jesus, another methodology was developed called form criticism. It was a sort of a "hybrid of historical and literary criticism."[7] The observation was made that a particular biblical verse or paragraph may have a history of its own and was inserted into a

---

6. John T. Carroll, in his recent book *Jesus and the Gospels*, provides fine summaries of the ways that scholars have used to answer these questions. For example, he provides the criteria for assessing whether Jesus said and did what the Gospels report (Carroll, *Jesus and the Gospels*, 25).

7. See the article written by Carl Holladay on biblical criticism in *Harper's Bible Dictionary*, 132.

larger section. The insertion may have been part of an oral tradition or even a written document, and it was used in a particular way to serve the needs of a congregation. It might be quite early and have had a particular function in a community of believers, but was slightly changed as it was passed on to other groups. The goal of form criticism was to discern its role in the life of a community of believers and assess whether it reveals an accurate account of some aspect of the life and teaching of Jesus.

Partially growing out of form criticism was another historical method, redaction criticism, which is the effort to discern the way a particular text or passage may have been edited or a section eliminated, perhaps with an insertion to make the passage more clear or to express a point of view. Within the Synoptic Gospels, the largest and obvious redaction is the set of closing verses (16:9–20) of the Gospel of Mark.

In the second half of the twentieth century, there were two additional historical methods applied to the Gospels in order to discern what may be an authentic recording of what Jesus did and said and how it might be understood. One method, comparable to parts of literary criticism, was narrative criticism. For many years, there was the general strategy of reducing the size of a passage by breaking it down into smaller units. This method had merit with the study of key words and small units such as the aphoristic statements of Jesus, like the Golden Rule. It was determined that these small units were used and circulated, and to study them in terms of their function was a valuable method to discover the authentic teaching of Jesus. However, longer passages carried a story or narrative that could be missed if you only studied one small logion. For example, if all you studied were conclusions, as for example in the parable of the Good Samaritan, "Go and do likewise," you would miss the full message of the narrative (Luke 10:37). Jesus often used a story (parable) to teach, and the authors of the Gospels often developed a narrative or point of view with a lengthy text. Narrative criticism developed as a way of grasping the theme and teaching of a longer section.

In addition to narrative criticism, there was the further development of examining the Gospels from the point of view of a social scientific methodology. In general, the Gospels had always been read from the perspective of the discipline of history, with an understanding of history as part of the social science family. In the later part of the twentieth century, other social sciences were increasingly employed and used alongside of the historical quest. For example, John Dominic Crossan, a noted New Testament scholar, used the categories of sociology in his work, *The Historical Jesus: The Life of a Mediterranean Jewish Peasant*. He speaks of Jesus as coming from a particular social class (peasant), from a particular region (small village in Galilee), and explains the life and teachings of Jesus partly from this perspective. It is a compelling treatment and has some similarities to the larger movement known as liberation theology. Liberation theology has at its foundation an understanding of Jesus that portrays him as a radical prophet calling for and working toward social justice. The use of a social science perspective undergirded the movement of liberation theology in which Jesus was understood as one who prophetically advocated for the welfare of the poor, stood in solidarity with them, and sought to make the structures of society more just.

W. Barnes Tatum traces the development of critical historical methods and how they shaped New Testament scholarship in a helpful way. He provides the following list regarding the historical scholarship about Jesus:[8]

1. Period 1: Pre-criticism before the nineteenth century
2. Period 2: Source criticism (nineteenth century)
3. Period 3: Form criticism (early twentieth century)
4. Period 4: Redaction criticism (mid-twentieth century)
5. Period 5: Narrative criticism and social scientific criticism (late twentieth century)
6. We might add a Period 6: The Religious World of Jesus and Second Temple Judaism (late twentieth century and early twenty-first century)

Books can and have been written about these various historical approaches used to access the life and teaching of Jesus. Each one was helpful in providing a particular perspective and adding to the accumulation of credible information about Jesus. Dr. Tatum also provides a list about how the quest for the historical Jesus evolved and developed:

1. Pre-quest (before 1778): Accounts based on the Gospels
2. Old quest (1778–1906): Biographies or the "lives of Jesus"
3. Limited quest (1906–53): Awareness that it was quite difficult to write a biography of Jesus because of limited historical information
4. New quest (1953-1985)
5. Third or renewed quest (since 1985)
6. We might add a seventh point to this list in that there have been many changes and developments in Jesus studies in the early part of the twenty-first century. For example, there has been the use of

---

8. Tatum, *Quest of Jesus*, 11. In some cases I have changed Dr. Tatum's language slightly.

sociological analysis of the context of Jesus and the further study of Second Temple Judaism.

Again, it is difficult to find one category to describe them all. Most of them, however, have focused on the research placing Jesus in his time and place in history. There is the conviction that Jesus is best understood in reference to his historical and religious circumstances. Critical scholars have been cautious about using contemporary categories to describe his life, teachings, and identity, although in the context of the church, there continues to be a hermeneutical method that seeks to bring Jesus into the present to comfort and guide those who seek to live a Christian life.

Each of the categories in regard to historical criticism and different historical strategies are of great interest and importance as we seek to understand Jesus. They have helped us see how complex the effort to find the historical Jesus has been. In addition, these historical strategies have provided information and insight for those of us who continue to engage in Jesus studies, and also for those pastors and lay people who continue to guide the Christian community. Essentially the studies of the life, teachings, and meaning of Jesus from the past two centuries guide us away from uninformed perspectives and enable us to understand Jesus in a trustworthy way. There has been a profound search for a plausible Jesus.[9] These studies have given authenticity to our personal understanding and to our ministry in the name of Jesus. The also call us to be aware of and sensitive to our starting points and assumptions in that the Jesus who emerges from our studies often reflects our presuppositions. We turn now to a brief exploration of the best starting points for accessing Jesus of Nazareth and gaining the assurance that it can be done carefully and with integrity.

Theological and Historical Starting Points for Understanding Jesus

One of the observations that stands out in the demanding work of writing about Jesus is that one's comprehensive worldview about the nature of reality inevitably shapes the way one reads history. It raises the never-ending question of how much we create Jesus in our own image and out of our own needs. Perhaps it is impossible not to impose our prior assumptions onto the reading of history, although an effort to be as objective and careful

---

9. See Theissen and Winter, *Quest for the Plausible Jesus*, for a careful study of the ways historians have sought to describe the life and teachings of Jesus with care and integrity.

as possible in writing about Jesus is an essential starting point. However, we do the work of making sense of the past, and especially the part of the past that has shaped the beliefs and values of our lives, with an outlook that influences what we read and how we frame it.[10]

In my years of graduate study at the University of Edinburgh, I became acquainted with and informed about the concept of preunderstanding. I had studied the philosophy of Kant, who maintained that it is next to impossible to understand a particular object or historical event in itself. He noted that we supply the categories of understanding through our thinking and use of language. I had also been exposed to the ways our particular backgrounds and place in history shape our views of reality. It was in the translation of a German word used by Rudolf Bultmann, *vorverständnis*, in his study of the New Testament, and in particular his study of Jesus, that provided an invaluable insight to my study of Christian origins. It became so important to me that I used the concept as the primary subject of my dissertation. I observed that there were other words or expressions such as presupposition, preconception, assumption, outlook, and frame of reference that might be used as well, although with slightly different shades of meaning.

The definition I used for preunderstanding was "a body of assumptions and attitudes which a person brings to the perception and interpretation of reality or any aspect of it."[11] In a recent reading of N. T. Wright's three-volume comprehensive treatment of the life, teaching, and meaning of Jesus, I was very pleased to see that he begins his work with a careful examination of his starting points and goes on to attempt to understand Jesus within this framework.[12] What I have learned in my research and broad reading is that we all have a frame of reference as we receive and make sense of the world around us. To be self-aware about the categories of understanding and selective and wise in our choice of them is the best strategy. If they are hidden from us, we are likely to distort the material we are using, which in turn would inappropriately shape our theme or the subject in our writing.[13] I want to briefly describe my preunderstanding as a way of being self-aware and intentional concerning the approach I am taking in writing about what

---

10. In Richard J. Bernstein's book, *Beyond Objectivism and Relativism*, he underscores that the goal of being totally objective and detached as we study history is not possible, and that we need to find other ways to have integrity in historical work.

11. Ferguson, *Biblical Hermeneutics*, 6.

12. Wright, *Christian Origins*, 31–80. He does the same in his definitive study of Paul. He frames his understanding of Jesus and Paul with terms such as worldview and narrative and draws charts in order to demonstrate the structures of the work of Jesus and the thought of Paul.

13. This topic will lead us into a treatment of hermeneutics in the next chapter.

Jesus did and said. Perhaps it can be an example of how we all start with assumptions. In what ways do I receive and make sense out of the historical material?

I begin my approach to understanding Jesus from within the Christian faith, and therefore use my outlook within my faith tradition as a guide in framing my understanding of Jesus. I follow Augustine and Anselm in affirming *credo ut intelligam*, or "I believe in order to understand." The Christian faith is my worldview. For the most part, it has been an advantage to be on the inside of the Christian faith with an informed and good understanding of the material I am reading and interpreting. I am fully aware that an insider's perspective might be a disadvantage in reading the material with objectivity; almost automatically, I read it in a positive way and affirm its truthfulness and value. I want to stress that to be an insider doesn't guarantee a well-reasoned and defensible understanding. It would be difficult for me to count the number of conversations with Christians who have maintained that their view and understanding of the Christian faith is the absolute truth. Yet in many cases these conversations have revealed a lack of understanding and an inordinate dependence on a narrow tradition in a particular historical moment. Often the view articulated was quite sectarian in description, and even less acceptable as it morphed into a judgmental outlook on all those who had a different outlook, or who might view the complexity of Christianity with more humility.

I am inclined to view my understanding of Jesus and the Christian faith as helpful, and to begin with a positive outlook as I approach the careful study of the life and teaching of Jesus.[14] I do so with some humility and an eagerness to learn more and understand better. In this spirit, I find my outlook to be of great value in helping me to continue to learn and deepen my understanding. I know that certain sections of the Gospels and the larger biblical account will continue to be difficult to understand and fully accept. Even with this caveat, I take the position that being open and eager empowers me to hear and understand in a more subtle and nuanced way. My worldview helps rather than hinders my growth and understanding.

I enter into this study as a progressive Christian in the sense that I am not narrowly bound by traditional and orthodox belief systems, and I remain open to alternative ways of understanding Jesus.[15] There may be

---

14. I became especially sensitive to this insider-outsider issue as I taught courses in the world religions. I was reminded from time to time that my understanding was not sufficiently subtle or nuanced, as was the views of those who were insiders. It was especially true, for example, in my teaching of Buddhism and Islam.

15. I am aware that the use of the term "progressive" will raise some eyebrows, but it is a word in common usage to describe those within the Christian family who are open

times when it is wise to defend or protect the Christian faith, but more frequently I find that I defend and protect less and remain open to new ways of understanding more. Part of what helps me to stay in this frame of reference is the way I attempt to internalize my faith and live congruently with its teachings and values. I continually remind myself that my current understanding will influence my views and be transformative as I receive and make sense out of new insights and information. I also try to remain fully aware of how my assumptions might inadvertently distort what is there for me to see.

As a progressive within the larger Christian family, I am also a Protestant in the Reformed Tradition living in the United States in the first half of the twenty-first century. I have an obligation to try to understand how these dimensions of my Christian beliefs have shaped and continue to shape my outlook. I view them as a positive presence in reading the accounts of Jesus, although there are times when my beliefs must be held in check or changed. One fundamental value of my tradition is that it is the responsibility of Christians to work for a just, peaceful, and compassionate society. As I apply this outlook and these values to the social and political realities in which I live, I must ask how they may give me a basis to judge whether current leaders and governments are truly seeking the common good. In addition, my convictions may give reason to move toward challenging an excessive nationalism and a consumer-oriented society. As I understand what is going on, it guides me toward judgment and action. I ask myself if I should have a prophetic outlook seeking change, or should I be careful and better informed in order to be fair, rather than so critical that I miss what is really happening? As a general rule, I try in some cases to be supportive, and in other cases I need to challenge the policies of the government. The federal government of the United States gives me abundant material and a frame of reference for thinking about a more compassionate and just society.

I am a progressive within the Reformed Tradition, and therefore feel led to challenge the status quo. I am guided by and look with great appreciation for the way that the life and teachings of Jesus comes to us (the narrative). I seek to find ways of understanding that are most likely to be accurate about what he said and did. I look for ways to understand how the narrative may be enabled to jump over centuries, apply its teaching for the common good, and move the human family toward a better future for a threatened planet. It is from the narrative that I begin to shape my life goals. There is a gradual flow from the worldview to a progressive outlook and then on to action.

---

to change in framing beliefs and practices.

From within this larger frame of reference, I receive guidance about how I want to live my life. I begin to reflect on the goals and values of Jesus as he interacts with the people he encounters and how he acts in relationship to them. I try to discern the aims of Jesus and the deep values that guide him in these encounters. I then look at what stands behind the encounters to the social systems that are in place. I sense that he was profoundly concerned about injustice, poverty, people with illness and disabilities, and all who suffered. He addressed these concerns by helping these individuals and by challenging unjust ways, such as that the social order protected the privileged and powerful and neglected the suffering of the poor. This was his strategy for mission. It is within this frame of reference that I read the historical records. I read with a Christian worldview, as a progressive open to change, with attention to the narrative in the Gospels and a strategy for my life in harmony with the goals and values I sense were those of Jesus.

I become motivated by three major themes in the narrative, the three themes that guided my writing of *The Radical Teaching of Jesus*. On reading the narrative, primarily in the Gospels, and then reading many commentaries and interpretations of the life and teachings of Jesus, I gradually began to understand Jesus in reference to how he acted and how his contemporaries began to understand him. I started first with his teaching and how he taught. The descriptive category that came immediately to mind was that he was a charismatic teacher. By this category, I wanted to emphasize that Jesus was gifted. He taught in an insightful way that was transformational for his followers. He provided great insight into life, drawing often upon his familiarity with the Hebrew Bible and the immediate world around him. He seldom just provided factual information, although there was accuracy as he drew upon his Jewish faith and observed his environment. Yet he did not stop just with information, but also invited his followers to pause and ponder, to reflect on a story or answer a question about what was being said and then apply it to their lives. He had the spiritual gift (the *pneumatica*) of teaching, one in whom God's Spirit took his words and made them personal and meaningful for his listeners. Transformation took place through his teaching.

I then moved on to a second category with no judgment about the importance of one descriptive category over another. The second category I use, in reference to the grand narrative of the Gospels, was that Jesus was a compassionate healer. As one reads about the healing ministry of Jesus, there is usually a question about how he did it without the benefit of modern medicine. I do address this question in *The Radical Teaching of Jesus*, and will give it more attention in chapter 8. At this point, I want to stress that he approached the ill people whom he encountered with great compassion. Compassion is that capacity to identify and live in solidarity with those who suffer from illness and disabilities, to come close to them, speak with them, and (when appropriate) even touch them, as he did with the leper. Compassion is also an effort to relieve the suffering of people with illnesses and disabilities.[16] Time and again, Jesus reached out to heal those with skin disease and who were crippled or blind. Compassion is also expressed by addressing the circumstances of those who are ill or disabled. For example, he counsels the leper to speak with the authorities and to have his status as an outcast from society changed from isolation to inclusion (Mark 1:40–45).

The third category I used to describe Jesus was that he lived his public life as a radical prophet. I understood this role of radical prophet as one who challenged the unjust structures of the social system and called attention to those norms in the social system that discriminated against the poor and disadvantaged. Jesus spoke the truth boldly and clearly about unjust social systems to those in power. He challenged the norms of his culture. In many cases, he not only spoke clearly about hypocrisy and injustice, but also acted courageously in ways that illustrated the unjust social systems. The action of overturning the tables of the moneychangers when he was in Jerusalem, while not everyone agrees on exactly how it should be interpreted, illustrates his bold actions on behalf of the poor and his challenge to the inherent lack of integrity in the religious practices in the temple (Matt 21:12–13).

I may begin my reading of the Gospels with a point of view that assumes too much and runs the risk of imposing categories onto the historical narrative. On the other hand, to have a carefully constructed Christian worldview, a progressive outlook that is open to change and make application to the present, an intimate familiarity with the historical narrative, and a desire to follow Jesus and live in harmony with the values, aims, and goals that appear to be present in Jesus is a good place to start. I do understand the difficulties in accessing the life and teachings of Jesus, and therefore I do so with an openness to learn and change. I am aware that I have imposed more contemporary categories onto the literature and that I represent a viewpoint that is not the same as many other Christian traditions. I nevertheless think that what I have done has enabled me to come close to understanding Jesus and his teaching. I have confidence in accepting his invitation to live a life of love and compassion.

---

16. At times, I used the expression "loving kindness," an important concept in Buddhism as well as Judaism and Christianity.

A Place to Begin: A Summary of Basic Facts

What do we need to take into account as we begin to piece together a believable account of the life, teachings, identity, and meaning of Jesus? There are some very obvious answers. We must find good ways of using the records we have and the Gospels in particular. It is wise to review the history of the accounts of the life and teachings of Jesus, most of which have been written by competent and thoughtful people. It is an almost endless resource. We need to make use of the best resources of historical study and immerse ourselves in the history of the context of the life of Jesus and the languages spoken. Increasingly, other social sciences such as sociology and anthropology may reveal insights that add to our knowledge. It may also be wise to be self-aware about our own frame of reference; it will influence our view as well. For example, I believe that having a positive outlook on the material opens my eyes; it fills my mind and my heart. I am careful with this dimension, yet sense that it empowers me to see better and hear with more depth and understanding.

As we conclude this chapter on starting points for understanding Jesus, I thought it might be wise to provide a brief account of his life. A simple factual framework will guide us as we look in more detail at his life and teachings. As a way of providing a brief sketch of his life, I will turn to the classic questions and hope our brief answers to them will enable us to begin our work on the hard teaching and events of the life of Jesus. The questions are who, what, when, where, and why (at times, we may need to add the question of how)?

I start with this question: Who was Jesus? As we begin with the question of the identity of Jesus, we will first move toward some facts about his life and address the larger questions about his identity in the final section of the book. To begin, then, we might identify Jesus as a first-century Palestinian Jew. Note the three identifying labels: first-century, Palestinian, and Jew. Jesus was born in approximately 4–6 BCE. As one examines the birth stories, we learn that there were events such as Herod serving as the ruler and a census that would inform us that the Common Era date, based on the birth of Jesus, was a slight miscalculation. He was Palestinian in the sense of living in the North of Israel, in the region of Galilee in the small village of Nazareth. He was Jewish rather than what we might now call Arab, although he lived among a diverse people rather than in the center of Jewish life in Jerusalem. His native language was Aramaic, and there is some evidence to suggest that he also spoke Hebrew and had some familiarity with Greek. His family included his mother, Mary, his father, Joseph, and it is likely that he had siblings. As he grew up, he joined his father in the work of carpentry.

He later left his family, traveled south to be with his cousin, John the Baptist, and prepared himself for his new calling.

The brief description of who he was gives us a base from which to add more information, especially about his public ministry. We will then review what he did. As a boy, he joined with the family in the simple life in the rural village of Nazareth. As he grew, he joined his family in the work of the household, perhaps learned Hebrew and about his faith in a synagogue, traveled to Jerusalem and engaged in conversations with religious leaders, and returned to Galilee to join his father as a carpenter. We do not know the exact date, but we know that his father died while Jesus was still quite young. As he reached the approximate age of thirty, he made the decision to act on his Jewish faith and the values inherent in the Torah. He went to Judea to learn from John the Baptist, the prophet. Following his own retreat in the wilderness, he began his work as teacher, healer, and prophet, a period that lasted from eighteen months to three years.[17] He was initially well received by the people in his region. But in time, in part because of his actions and direct teaching, he faced opposition from the religious leaders, traveled to Jerusalem, and was crucified with the sentence of treason against the Roman Empire.[18]

As we turn to the question of when, we note that it was a time of unrest in Palestine. The people felt oppressed by the different levels of government: the Roman, the Herodian, and the Jewish. The alien Roman government had placed a governor in charge, and we know the one that ruled during the public life of Jesus. His name was Pilate, the fifth governor of the Roman occupation, serving from 26–36 of the Common Era. The Roman government selected regional government officials to take care of the responsibilities of government business, and Herod, an Idumean, was selected and ruled until 4 BCE. When Herod died, his sons were appointed to rule the various regions in which Jesus lived and entered into his vocation. The Jewish leaders considered the Herods as only partially Jewish, somewhat suspect, and unjust in their policies. The Jewish government was based in Jerusalem and largely took care of both the public and religious life of Judah.[19] The government system was complex, and there were the problems of injustice and

---

17. There continues to be some discussion among scholars about the length of the public ministry of Jesus. The Gospel of Mark suggests a shorter period than the traditional view of three years.

18. The sentence of the Romans was based on the assertion that Jesus was the king of the Jews, and therefore a threat to Roman rule.

19. It was called the Sanhedrin and consisted of seventy elders from various branches of Judaism. It had authority over both the social and religious life of the Jewish people.

resulting poverty. The people of the region longed for relief and the removal of the alien government. Jesus lived in a turbulent time.

The place (the question of where) was in this small Roman province of Palestine, perhaps more important in terms of Roman affairs than its size and resources would suggest. The Romans saw it as a crossroads, linking Rome to the eastern and southern part of their empire. It was their access to what we now think of as the Middle East and Africa. The where question is also important in our inquiry in that it is the place in which Jesus lived and where he entered fully into his vocation. As we understand the where, we increase our knowledge of our next question: the why.

As we move to the question of why, we address both the historical question of why and the theological question of why. The historical question has to do with why Jesus chose to leave the region of Nazareth and Galilee, go to the wilderness of Judea to learn from his cousin, John, and then return to his own region and begin his public ministry. Our abbreviated answer, which we will later expand, is that he returned to address the needs of the people of his own region for whom he had great compassion. It was also a region in which he knew many people and had life experience. In addition, it was a region in which the social structures were unjust. There was poverty and suffering, and he knew that he not only had to help and heal the individual people of Galilee, but to go the source of power to address the injustice inherent in the social system which caused their suffering. The theological question of why is answered by addressing how the Jewish people had lost their way, strayed from the covenant, and needed redemption and restoration. We will return to this part of the why question shortly.

So we have some starting points for our quest to understand the life, teachings, and identity of Jesus. We are beginning to understand his invitation to follow his way. We now turn to how we interpret what we know and are able bring it into the present for transformation and into the future for guidance. We turn to the discipline of hermeneutics.

Study Resources

Discussion Questions

1. What is meant by the term "historical-critical method," and how is it applied to the Bible and the Gospels in particular?
2. How would you describe your assumptions as you try to understand Jesus?

3. Is it possible or necessary to be objective in your study of history? In what ways does being objective assist or limit your study of the life and teachings of Jesus?
4. Do you think it is appropriate to think in terms of the historical Jesus and the Christ of faith? In what ways are these terms different?
5. How much confidence should we have in the accounts of the life and teaching of Jesus in the Gospels?

Terms and Concepts

1. Preunderstanding: A body of assumptions and attitudes, which a person brings to the perception and interpretation of reality.
2. Worldview: A way of understanding reality and the world around us.
3. Progressive: In a religious context, the word means that one is willing to challenge the status quo and suggest new ways of understanding more in keeping with a contemporary outlook.
4. Redaction Criticism: The ways in which one studies a historical document to determine if it has been edited or had a section eliminated or inserted.
5. Textual Criticism: A term describing how it is that one attempts to ascertain how to find the most accurate text from among the many which are available; in reference to the Gospels, it is a way to find the text or manuscript that most likely provides the best description of what actually happened or what was said.

Suggestions for Reading and Reference

Carroll, John T. *Jesus and the Gospels: An Introduction.* Louisville: Westminster John Knox, 2017.
Crossan, John Dominic. *The Historical Jesus: The Life of a Mediterranean Jewish Prophet.* San Francisco: HarperSanFrancisco, 1991.
Dodd, C. H. *The Founder of Christianity.* London: Collins, 1971.
Harvey, H. E. *Jesus and the Constraints of History.* Philadelphia: Westminster, 1982.
Tatum, W. Barnes. *In Quest of Jesus.* Rev. ed. Nashville, Abingdon, 1999.

3

The Range of Interpretations

The Lingering Problem: Gaining Access

WE HAVE BEEN EXPLORING ways that will help us find a measure of both comfort and security in understanding the radical invitation of Jesus. We have noted the difficulties of gaining this confidence because the access to the life and teaching of Jesus, which is essential in understanding the Christian invitation to follow his way, is somewhat difficult. As one might expect, many biblical scholars have addressed this concern, written about it, discussed it in scholarly meetings, and made their views known in a variety of ways. For some within the Christian community, this endeavor has had great merit because it has helped to define the way the church should assure its members that its beliefs have integrity. A good case can be made that the central mission of the church is to teach about what Jesus said and did and then invite people to endorse this message and live in accord with it. If we have this accurate historical foundation, one that may be understood and trusted on the basis of sound biblical scholarship, then we can more easily commit to a life of faith, even if its expression questions or reframes some of the orthodox beliefs of the church.

There were others within the church that maintained that the critical historical endeavor went too far in that it questioned the authenticity of many of the accounts in the Gospels that tell the story of what Jesus said and did. In response to these efforts to defend traditional and orthodox views, there were those who argued that the accounts may not always express the actual words and the precise detailed accounts of the deeds of Jesus, but they were still a trustworthy report that provides a firm foundation for the

Christian message. They maintain that the Gospels are trustworthy in that they express the full intent and spirit of what Jesus said and did. And of course there are extreme views in both sides of this discussion about the reliability of the New Testament; those who may essentially change the Christian message and others who may force it into a narrow framework and judge others who dare to offer alternative views.

In 1985, a group of biblical scholars led by Robert W. Funk formed a movement known as the Jesus Seminar.[1] As the movement took shape and developed, fifty biblical scholars and one hundred laypersons became involved. The goal of the Seminar was to determine which of the sayings attributed to Jesus, as recorded in the Gospels, and indirectly the additional lost source (Q), were actually spoken by Jesus. Those in the Seminar, as a result of their inquiry, also gave attention to whether all of the activities of Jesus recorded in the Gospels took place. The initial emphasis, however, was more on the sayings of Jesus. These sayings and accounts were divided up into four categories: (1) parables; (2) aphorisms; (3) dialogues; and (4) stories.

The members of Seminar met frequently in different locations as they began their work. Phase 1 of their work was to list the passages in the Gospels in which Jesus speaks. They also kept an eye on which of these passages likely came from what they called the fifth gospel (Q). The list came to 1500 segments. The leaders of the Seminar also developed a way of grading these passages in terms of whether they were authentic expressions of what Jesus said and did. They used four categories and voted with different colored beads:

1. Red (likely authentic)
2. Pink (somewhat likely)
3. Gray (somewhat unlikely)
4. Black (unlikely authentic)

As they discussed and diligently worked on these 1500 passages over an extended period of time, they felt they could cast an informed vote. The outcome was that 82 percent of the passages were judged as unlikely authentic. This vote was shared with the public, and there was some affirmation of the Seminar's work, but also some profound criticism. For example, I served in a center for spiritual life at Eckerd College in the first decade of this century, and one of my responsibilities was to arrange for guest speakers. From time

---

1. See Robert W. Funk's thoughtful book entitled *Honest to Jesus: Jesus for a New Millennium*. In this book, Dr. Funk attempts to search for the true voice and activities of Jesus and makes the case for a faith based on the Jesus of history.

to time, I was able to get representative scholars from the Jesus Seminar to speak, and I was surprised by how many people came to the lectures. Many were quite supportive of the work of the Jesus Seminar and participated in it, believing that the work gave them a more reliable basis for their faith, which they carefully articulated as to "worship God and follow Jesus." In addition, I spoke with several others, including local church leadership, who said that they felt it was unwise to have speakers that questioned the authenticity of the Bible and the foundational statements of the church that affirm the Christ of faith.

What I have discovered across years of being engaged in Jesus studies and Christian origins is that it is possible to make a good case for both the Jesus of history and the Christ of faith and to find ways to integrate them. My approach has the following four dimensions. One is the conviction that there is wisdom in not becoming overly ideological or fanatical in one's views and to remain open to other viewpoints. There is always more to learn. A second is that I have also come to the conviction that there will be some diversity in the Christian church, depending upon one's background, history, language, culture, and tradition, and that this diversity need not be threatening and can be enriching and informative. In addition, I have found that I learn a great deal from others who have a different outlook on issues of faith and belief, and that to build a relationship of trust and honesty with them is both the Christian responsibility and richly rewarding. Further, I have learned that we often end up in our orientation to issues of faith and belief close to where we started, although cultivating a more mature outlook along the way. This process has invited me to think more deeply about hermeneutics, the careful process of how we interpret history and literature of the past and bring its lessons and learning into the present.

The Hermeneutical Task

Hermeneutics has been traditionally defined as the locus and principles of interpretation, particularly as it is applied to the interpretation of ancient texts.[2] If we apply this definition to the Bible, we might restate the definition just slightly and say that it is the careful method of reflecting on the time and the events in the Bible in order to make them applicable to our present situation. It is the way we take the events recorded in and teachings of the Bible and make them personally and socially meaningful in our context. The hermeneutical task is to find ways of enabling the material from the Bible to jump over centuries of history, culture, and language and speak to

2. Ferguson, *Biblical Hermeneutics*, 4.

us in ways that are true to the original text, carefully articulated, and that provide understanding and guidance for our lives. As we do this work, we are finding a good way of understanding and accepting the radical invitation of Jesus. As we define hermeneutics in this way, we are underlining three essential points.

One is that we are careful to determine what is being said in the ancient text. We try to understand what the author intended to say and then explain what it meant to the people who read it in the time that it was written and circulated. We then move beyond this explanation to an understanding of how the message or story of the Bible may be understood within our lives, giving us meaning and guidance for our present context and direction for our future. Some scholars in the field of hermeneutics take the inquiry one step further and say that we read the biblical literature in a way that takes us beyond explaining, and even personal understanding, and points us to the truth.[3]

The quest in biblical studies for those committed to a religious life becomes a quest to probe the mysteries of ultimate reality through language. The ancient text gives us a truthful foundation and allows the past to inform the present and point to the future. I might say at this point that hermeneutics over the past several decades has really been about finding an appropriate methodology, one that leads to a philosophical inquiry about our search to understand the truth, and it crosses many disciplines.[4] It is an academic field in itself, one that is deeply rooted in epistemology, the study of how it is that we can know.

The Role of Preunderstanding in Hermeneutics

There is that tendency at this point to say that the science of hermeneutics enables us to be detached and objective in our interpretation of the Bible. There is a point to be made by this inclination in that we too easily make the ancient text say what we want it to say in order to justify our point of view and to meet our needs for both security and power.[5] Within the field of hermeneutics there is the intention to practice the "hermeneutics of suspicion" in order to discern what might be a hidden motivation in the process

---

3. Gadamar, *Truth and Method*, 73–90.
4. See, for example, the work of Palmer, *Hermeneutics*.
5. The concept of deconstruction is a method that points to the way that interpretations of history and literature are demonstrated to defend a point of view or political power. These motivations have been challenged, shown to be self-seeking, and represent a bias against certain groups of people.

of interpretation. We do want to be free of these negative influences and tendencies, have some objectivity, and do careful scholarship that will assist us in finding the most accurate interpretation. We want to be taught by what it says, not what we distort it to say out of ignorance and in order to meet our needs. But we do receive the material as human beings and not as a computer. We receive the text as who we are, with our values, our heritage, our culture and language, and our worldview. The goal is to be sufficiently self-aware and receive it as persons who want to be taught and guided. We want the truth to enter into our lives and guide us. We want accurate information from the text and to understand it in a way that empowers us to apply it to our lives and the circumstances in which we live. We want to have a sense that what we are doing is linked to the truth of God's will and way.

In an earlier book, I spoke about the types of preunderstanding with which we come to the text and the way these preconceptions function.[6] Let me briefly summarize this analysis. I noted initially that the task of interpretation does not cease; it is neverending in the sense that we come to an understanding of the text and then return to it with a new perspective that may alter our initial view. This phenomenon is called the hermeneutical circle, and it is ever-present in the work of interpretation. We maintained that there are four primary types of preunderstanding:

1. Informational: We receive the text with information that we already have in reference to the material that we are reading and interpreting. We naturally give this new material meaning out of our frame of reference and out of what we already know. We make sense of what we are reading from the information that we possess and place it in our categories of understanding.

2. Attitudinal: A second type of preunderstanding might be termed attitudinal in the sense that we have opinions and feelings already in place about what we are reading and interpreting. We have a predisposition that we bring to the subject, or perhaps a bias or a fully formed outlook that will take the information and apply it in a particular way. We read the material (biblical text), give it a sense of order, and use it within our personal frame of reference.[7]

3. Ideological: A third type of preunderstanding might be called ideological in the sense that we may already have developed ideas about

---

6. See Ferguson, *Biblical Hermeneutics*, 13–20.

7. In Dale C. Allison Jr.'s excellent book, *Constructing Jesus: Memory, Imagination, and History*, he devotes an entire chapter to the ways that our ideas and attitudes shape how we read the material we have about the life and teaching of Jesus (Allison, *Constructing Jesus*, 1–30).

the subject of the text. We receive it with a worldview or a horizon of understanding. We try to make it fit in with already-formed ideas about truth and reality. We may inadvertently shape the material to fit our outlook on life, and we must be self-aware about this possibility and guard against distorting the material.

4. Methodological: A final type of preunderstanding is the way we approach the material and model or construct it in a way to apply it to one's personal life and responsibilities, and the circumstances of one's life. It is to say, for example, "The way I look at this text (e.g. the Golden Rule) is that it fits in with my way of relating to people and teaching my students." The Sunday sermon, based on a text, is often shaped around the goals of the worship service. There is a method we use in preparing the sermon.

In addition to the types of preunderstanding, I also speak about the various functions of preunderstanding in our interpretation of an ancient text, as I have already implied in speaking about the types. We are especially concerned about function as we deal with a biblical text in that it will often serve a particular purpose, as to inspire a congregation with a sermon, for example. Below are some of the ways that our preconceptions might act or make changes when the text is heard and assimilated.

The preunderstanding may act in either a positive or a negative way when a biblical text is heard and explained. The negative way is more readily apparent as we force a biblical text to say what merely advances our point of view or meets our particular needs. This may occur if we use a text to advance a narrow political point of view. It may not carry the message of God. On the other hand, with an open mind and heart, the text might expand our outlook and give us life-giving perspectives that can be shared with others in our interpretation for preaching, teaching, or counseling. It contributes to making us more loving and responsible people.

The preunderstanding may influence our reading in a comprehensive or limited way as we interpret a biblical text. For example, we might take the teaching about loving our neighbor as a call to love all people, and especially those who are victims of war, disease, and injustice. We become a responsible world citizen. We believe that God "so loved the world." Or it may function only in a more limited application and be seen as a call to love our family or those who are ill or live in poverty in my region of the town in which I live. These people are our neighbors. Both ways of functioning are acceptable, but the first about becoming a planetary pilgrim may be missed, especially if we have some fear of those who are different from us, the other.

The preunderstanding may function as we hear a biblical text in either a conscious way or unconscious way. For example, our preunderstanding might cause us to interpret a text that addresses the needs of poor people. We may partially resist this obligation in part because of our preconceptions that being poor is essentially the fault of the poor. Unconsciously we may assume that they are poor because they have not sought a good education or a good job with an adequate wage. We neglect their needs. Or we might have an outlook based on Scripture that maintains that all people are subject to the influences of their environment, and that poor people need to have the social system changed in a way that improves their circumstances and gives them a better quality of life. We engage in the cause of social justice. Or we might not know, for example, that we are prejudiced against the full empowerment of women, resist their full empowerment, and speak, for instance, about their place in the home. Most prejudices by their very nature are unknown to us. Or, when we hear a biblical text being interpreted about the role and place of women, fully conscious that it may be expressing or at least hint at a bias of a previous time in our culture, we should challenge it.

Further, our preunderstanding may function in a major or minor role, guiding us as we read a text and attempt to apply it to our lives. A text on the responsibility to care for the environment may only impact us in a few situations, such as our choice of an eco-friendly car, or it may shape our understanding and actions in the political life of our nation. At the very least we vote, but we also engage in the political process in a way that seeks the common good rather than defends the power of a particular social class or political party.

Still another way that a preunderstanding might impact us is whether we tend to be rational in the application of a text, finding a good way to apply it, or irrational, and turn our interpretation of a text into an extreme view that may cause harm. For example, an irrational fear may cause us to be prejudiced against people who are different from us, such as Muslim immigrants. On the other hand, we may view all people as being children of God and seek justice for everyone, regardless of their religion or country of origin.

We could speak of other ways that our preunderstanding might influence the way we read a text, but perhaps the ones listed will provide a frame of reference within which to work. I might also acknowledge that my selection of illustrations about function suggest my progressive outlook. My point is a relatively simple one, namely that we need to be self-aware and recognize that there will be times when we have a bias or a prejudice when we approach a text in the Bible. This may distort the intent of a text that we are interpreting. Or it may help us to be informed in a way that enables us to bring in forward to inspire us and apply it to our lives. This in turn may cause us to be better human beings and join with others in seeking the common good.

Historical Samples of the Interpretation of the Life and Teachings of Jesus In the Testaments

Some brief examples of the way the Bible has been interpreted across history will help us see and appreciate the variety of ways that people have attempted to understand and apply the teachings of the Bible.[8] We might begin with the way in which the authors of the New Testament interpreted the Hebrew Bible. The authors of the Gospels were committed to understanding Jesus in continuity with the narrative of the Hebrew Bible. A new book could be written, and many have been written on this subject. In terms of our goal to understand the difficult actions and sayings of Jesus, let me suggest two groups of interpretation within the Bible that are especially pertinent: one in the Gospels and the other in the writings of Paul. In light of our subject concerning Jesus, one way in which the Gospels interpret the Hebrew Bible is by describing the way that Jesus radicalizes the ethical norms and guidelines of the Hebrew Bible. Generally, Jesus is portrayed in the Gospels as having great respect for the Hebrew Bible, as it was his Bible. We have in the Gospels an account of the way that Jesus challenges not the text of the Hebrew Bible, but the ways that the ethical teachings of the Hebrew Bible were interpreted by the religious teachers of his time. Matthew, for example, uses the construct of "You have heard it said . . . but I say unto you." The author of Matthew, especially in the Sermon on the Mount (Matt 5–7), portrays Jesus as questioning the current norms of understanding of the Hebrew Bible and calls upon his listeners and followers to make the principle of the teaching more personal and a life commitment. The Gospel of Matthew has Jesus saying that the fundamental principle behind the teaching is what is important and needs to be incorporated into one's life. He speaks about the law (Torah), anger, infidelity, oaths or promises, the love of one's enemy, prayer, fasting, and the use and abuse of wealth, and teaches that the principles that undergird these teachings must be internalized and practiced. The author of Matthew then says: "Now when Jesus had finished saying these things, the crowds were astounded at his teaching, for he taught them as one having authority, and not as the scribes" (Matt 7:28–29).

---

8. There are several good introductions to this history of biblical introduction. One that I have found helpful, although somewhat dated, is Jasper, *Short Introduction to Hermeneutics*. I have already mentioned Grant and Tracy, *Short History*.

The apostle Paul, very familiar with the Hebrew Bible as a Pharisee, used it extensively in his teaching. He exercised a certain measure of freedom in his hermeneutical approach. One of those was to see the way that the Hebrew Bible prefigures a major principle, one which may now be used to illustrate a way of life for new Christians who have just accepted the invitation of Jesus and are just beginning to understand the Christian way of life. For example, he speaks of Abraham as being a person of deep faith as he leaves his homeland and undertakes a journey, "going without knowing" (Rom 4). This is the model of faith for the Christian. He speaks of the way that Jesus is the new Adam giving humankind a fresh start. He teaches that the law given by Moses has now been completed in the coming of Jesus, and the new way of faith has superseded the more legalistic understanding of the law (Rom 7).

The Developing Church

The early Christians were given the challenge of how to preserve the Hebrew Bible and began to integrate it with what was developing in Christian teaching and appearing in documents that would later become part of the New Testament. A concern in this endeavor was to eliminate the more tribal and cultic dimensions of the Old Testament. For example, one Christian teacher, Marcion, in the early second century of the Common Era, proposed doing away with all of the Hebrew Bible forming a new guide with Luke's Gospel and some of the letters of Paul. Two other quite influential teachers of the second century, Irenaeus (130–ca. 200) and Tertullian (160–ca. 220), articulated the hermeneutical principle that the Christian church must preserve the Hebrew Bible and integrate it with the new literature that was in the process of being formed as the New Testament. Tertullian also challenged the gnostic movement that was claiming that they had a new and special knowledge, either gleaned from the first apostles or directly from God. Tertullian insisted that the church must preserve the Hebrew Bible as foundational for its faith.

For the next two centuries, the church would attempt to frame its major beliefs about Jesus, no small task and one filled with the challenges of interpretation. Part of the challenge for the developing church was to find a consensus about how to understand the presence of the divine in the human first-century prophet and teacher who they now called Jesus Christ. There were a number of voices, some emphasizing the humanity of Jesus and others emphasizing the divinity of Christ. Again, books have been written about this fascinating period of time in the development of the Christian church.

But for out purposes, we can only hint at the importance and complexity of the conversation and argument. There were those whose voices were clear and profound about this vital concern, and over time these positions began to be acknowledged as a consensus point of view with some authority.

The way in which the church at least partially resolved these questions and concerns was by bringing the leaders of the church in various sections of the world in which it had grown and developed to a council. Many were held, and we might mention two that were especially important in understanding Jesus. One was called the Nicene in the fourth century, and the other called the Chalcedonian Creed in the fifth century, both named after the locations of the councils. A number of issues were discussed and forcefully debated; some members of the councils were even excommunicated because of their views. Two major concerns were more or less resolved, based to a large extent on hermeneutics. The first, the Nicene in 325 CE, basically settled the question of how Jesus had within him both the qualities of being human and being divine for many centuries. Drawing upon Greek philosophy, they employed the hermeneutical principle of using ideas and concepts from other sources, usually foundational for the way the culture understood the truth. They agreed that Jesus had within him both the substance of being human and the substance of the divine, which came together in one person.[9] Later, in fifth-century Chalcedon, the issue of the Trinity was essentially clarified, again using concepts from the cultural worldview of Greek philosophy.

From among many who had a profound and lasting influence on the church prior to the Enlightenment and the modern period, we should also pause to consider the views of Augustine (354–430) and Thomas Aquinas (ca. 1225–74). With some risk of oversimplification, let me underline their hermeneutical starting points as they attempted to bring the Bible into their life and times. Augustine taught that the interpretation of Scripture is not an easy undertaking, in part because we begin with a sinful or misguided outlook on life. He stressed the need for us to be transformed by the Holy Spirit and come to the Bible renewed and open to being guided by God's Spirit as we read. From this starting point, Augustine maintains that we must do the basic work of understanding, carefully studying each word and what it may have meant to the biblical author, and what it might now mean for his contingency. He says that we need to grasp the literal meaning of the text, but even as the New Testament does, it is acceptable to move on to figurative or allegorical interpretations. It was a direction Augustine took when he

---

9. The Greek philosophers—and especially Plato—maintain that every object in the world has a fundamental substance that identifies it.

spoke about the presence of sin, figuratively expressed in reference to Adam. One further dimension of Augustine's hermeneutical orientation, already implied in his view of the way we need to be empowered by the Spirit of God, is that the reading of the Bible is a spiritual practice, one that requires openness to the presence of God and a willingness to hear the voice of God. For Augustine, experience is the great teacher, a conviction he underlines and illustrates in the *Confessions*.

It is a substantial jump across the medieval period from Augustine to Thomas Aquinas (1225–74), although our goal is not to write the history of the interpretation of the Bible, but to illustrate different approaches. I mention Thomas Aquinas in part because he taught and wrote toward the end of the scholastic movement, which lasted hundreds of years. He was, in many ways, its most significant interpreter. The scholastic movement may be understood as a period in which the Christian church engaged in two major endeavors, carefully articulating the tenets of the Christian faith in rational and understandable ways and devoting themselves to living the Christian life with dedication and deep spirituality. It was the time that many Christians came together in monastic communities. While their views and way of life are admirable, they did not differ significantly in their understanding of the Bible and the life and teachings of Jesus from earlier church teaching. Often the scholastics would emphasize the need to come to the Scripture with a quiet and devout spirit; for them, the reading of the Bible was a profound spiritual experience. What Thomas added and emphasized was not so much a new method, but an outlook that affirmed the place of reason. His emphasis on human reason differed some from that of Augustine, who stressed that humans must be empowered to fully understand the revelation of God. Thomas Aquinas did not discount the place of empowerment, but he maintained that our minds are the gift of God and that our reason can be used to find and follow God's will and way.[10]

Modern Views and Methods of Hermeneutics

The Enlightenment, a European movement beginning in the fifteenth century and flowering in sixteenth century, created fundamental shifts in understanding and outlook.[11] In the next three centuries, this new outlook would have a profound impact on the Christian church and the way it understood and used the Bible. There were at least three major historical changes that

---

10. See Jasper, *Short Introduction to Hermeneutics*, 45–48.

11. There are many excellent books on the Enlightenment. See, for example, Holmes, *Florentine Enlightenment 1400–50*, and Johnson and Percy, *Age of Recovery*.

occurred that altered the way that the Bible was interpreted. The first was the way that individuals felt emancipated from traditional views of the church and felt free to challenge the church's authority. There were many societal changes that contributed to this sense of freedom, including the change in the economy that in turn altered the structures of society. A middle class began to form, and there was the rise of extensive trade, which meant that people were exposed to many cultures.[12] There was also the rediscovery of ancient Greek civilization with its literature, art, and way of life. This period is generally called the Renaissance, or the rebirth of classical culture.[13] These movements invited freedom of thought and the celebration of the values inherent in this classical culture. These changes and many others gave permission for people to challenge the teachings of the church and, indirectly, the teaching of the Bible. It basically gave autonomy and freedom of thought to the people.

A second fundamental shift was the rise of the scientific method, and with it came the Copernican revolution, which challenged the view that the earth was the center of the universe. With this revolution came the scientific method, a way of seeking the truth by calling for a hypothesis that could be defended by the careful accumulation of evidence. It was a method that was inductive rather than deductive. It wasn't long before this methodology was applied to the Bible. Gradually the Bible began to be seen from a historical point of view. It was not enough to accept the Bible as the word of God based exclusively on the authority of the church. Further, literate people could read the Bible as it was translated and became available. It should not be the exclusive domain of the clergy who passed down its message to laypeople, who were in turn told to live in obedience to the church's understanding of the Bible's content. In time, a methodology similar to the one in science emerged for historical inquiry into the formation and content of the Bible.[14]

This became the third major shift in thinking that altered the way people viewed and interpreted the Bible. It became what was later to be called the historical-critical method of studying the Bible. The Bible, not unlike other books and literature in general, could be analyzed in terms of how it developed across hundreds of years. Careful study revealed that the Bible was dependent on a variety of sources and was written by human authors subject to the same limitations as authors of any other books. The outcome of these historical developments for approximately three centuries

12. A classic study of these changes is presented in Weber's *Protestant Ethic*.
13. See the classic work by Burckhardt, *Civilization of the Renaissance*.
14. This development was a significant contributor to the Reformation.

was that the Bible could be viewed as human book, lacking the authority of being the literal word of God. Many felt that the Bible could not be defended as inerrant solely by the authority of the church, although the church continued to exercise its authority for believers. The hermeneutical method of interpreting the Bible went from accepting the authoritative view of the church about the Bible to seeing it as a human book that could be studied as a human product with a history of development.

By the eighteenth century and on into the nineteenth century, biblical scholars, theologians, and historians began to look at the Hebrew Bible and the New Testament from a historical perspective. It wasn't long before the main subjects of the Bible, such as the Torah and the life and teachings of Jesus in the Gospels, were addressed without the presupposition that what was read in the Bible must be accepted in a literal way or because it is the teaching of the church. The biblical authors could now be viewed as having the same human frailties of any author, though in many cases what they produced was profound and had great value. It is important to note at this point that the majority of these endeavors did honor the church and attempted to be faithful to the church's teaching. Most biblical scholars remained quite orthodox in their views, but others ventured out and used their newly found freedom to reinterpret the faith and to reexamine the church's teaching about Jesus. A multitude of interpretations began to appear. It is not within our purpose to examine them all, but it may be helpful if we look at three primary types of the interpretation of the life and teachings of Jesus that to some extent stem from the changes in outlook that occurred in the Enlightenment.

The first one we might call the biographical, or the endeavor to learn enough about the history and culture of Jesus and couple it with the Gospel record in an attempt to describe Jesus as an extraordinary human being, one that can be an example of how all people should live. Many of these "lives of Jesus" were written, some with great care and insight, and others from a more devotional or sectarian perspective. Jesus was often described as a loving person who was a great teacher, one who cared for the sick, and a prophet who worked for a more peaceful and just social order. As these biographies began to appear, readers discovered that there were many ways to describe the life and mission of Jesus. Critical reflection on these attempts to write a biography revealed that the Jesus of the "lives of Jesus" movement looked less like a first-century Palestinian Jew and more like a nineteenth-century liberal and benevolent European or American. In time, there was a consensus that a biography of Jesus is next to impossible to write because of the lack of and the nature of the material available.

By the end of the nineteenth-century New Testament scholars, many who honored the teaching of the church and who had great respect for the fine scholars who attempted to write a life of Jesus were persuaded that the biography of Jesus could not be written from the base of critical history. Those deeply rooted in the faith of the church continued to write and teach about Jesus, and did so by drawing upon the biblical record and the church's teaching. The new direction in New Testament scholarship, however, for many thoughtful Catholic and Protestant scholars, was to take into account the findings of New Testament scholarship and write a more limited account of what Jesus said and did. This second basic shift in outlook, following the assessment that a full biography of Jesus was not possible to write, sought to find other ways of interpreting the life and teaching of Jesus. This second quest to search for the historical Jesus took into account the limitations of writing a biography, but it did not stop them from dealing with smaller units of the life and teaching of Jesus. These accounts, amassed over much of the twentieth century, produced a vast array of scholarly writings that gave us an informed outlook on specific components of Christian origins. It is hard to summarize this vast accumulation of fine scholarship; I have lived with it across my career and been informed and shaped by it. What has emerged for me in my exposure to this literature is that it has been driven by four principles, not present in every book, but which, when taken together, describe the hermeneutical principles present in this vast literature. They are as follows:

1. It has been undergirded by careful scholarship. Not every book has the benefit of this fine scholarship; there were extreme and fanciful exceptions, but the larger movement had great integrity. Many of the church's finest scholars gave themselves to this new quest, and much of what they wrote is now a treasure for our generation.

2. It has been largely driven by the belief that a modern rational approach, rather than an earlier supernatural outlook filled with miracles and the intervention of God into human life, is the best outlook and strategy. Those with a faith perspective have contributed greatly to the movement, but much of their scholarship reflected a point of view that did not easily accept all of the healing miracles of Jesus and his resurrection.[15] The Jesus of history was more the subject than the Christ of faith.

---

15. Some of the church's finest scholars, such as Karl Barth of a previous generation and N. T. Wright in the current generation, are exceptions. Many Catholic and Orthodox scholars could be mentioned as well.

3. It was undergirded by a deep spirituality. There was the example of the spiritual life of Jesus and his sense that God (Abba) was with him as he used the Hebrew Bible in his teaching. So the need to approach the Bible with a deep spirituality has been present in a variety of ways in the endeavor. Many scholars speak of Jesus as the model for the almost universal quest for a deeper spiritual life that is present in nearly all parts of the world.[16]

4. The fourth quality present in this extraordinary scholarship across the twentieth century has been that we can continue to learn more about Jesus by using other disciplines in addition to history, such as sociology and anthropology. It is possible to keep on learning more about the Jesus who has been the world's teacher and model. Fundamental to this endeavor is that what we have learned can teach us the lessons of the good life and be applied to the overwhelming problems of our world.

This last observation points us to the postmodern era and the ways that Jesus is being understood and interpreted as a guide to the great changes that are occurring in our world. A new direction, current in the continuing search for ways to understand Jesus and bring his life and teaching into the present, is to attempt to understand him and what he said and did in reference to our postmodern world, filled with complex and overwhelming problems.

Postmodern Perspectives

Once again, our goal is not to comprehensively trace the history of hermeneutics or the ways Jesus has been understood across history. Our goal is rather to suggest types of interpretation and to learn good methods and strategies that will help us understand his life and teaching. Again, I would like to suggest two major types of contemporary interpretation of the Bible in general, and of what Jesus said and did in particular. It is from these perspectives that we begin to understand the radical invitation of Jesus. Perhaps the primary approach is to understand the teaching of the Bible and Jesus in reference to his particular religious world. Jesus was a deeply spiritual person and learned from the religious ideas that were current in his time. Although a radical who challenged many of the religious beliefs and practices, he was nevertheless shaped by them. One common phrase used

---

16. Many people acknowledge that Jesus is but one of many women and men who are models of spirituality. Buddha, for example, is often placed side by side with Jesus.

frequently is that the dominant Judaism of his time was Second Temple Palestinian Judaism.[17] The phrase of course refers to the way Judaism developed following the Babylonian captivity (586 BCE) and the return of Jewish leaders to Judah. There were several challenges for those who returned. It was a time of having to reconstruct a new social order. Religious faith of course continued to be central in this effort. It meant that the returning Jews had to reconnect with those who were not exiled to Babylon and build a way of life together that honored Yahweh. We might summarize the dimensions of this endeavor as follows:

1. It had to draw upon and return to the foundation of beliefs and practices of the Jewish tradition; it wasn't a time to start a new religion. There was sacred history, deep beliefs centered in the covenant with God, a priestly segment of society, a range of spiritual practices, and a strong moral code. In short, there was a creed (beliefs), a code (ethical practices), a cult (a way of worship), and a community (a sense of belonging and identity).

2. It required putting together an infrastructure that would facilitate a way of life that honored God, ensured justice for the people, and cared for those in need. A new temple, the symbolic center, had to be constructed, and an inspirational and dedicated way of practicing religion had to be established. Many prophets called for a deeper commitment to this ideal, John the Baptist among them.

3. Third, and fundamental to the dominant mood of the people, was to instill a measure of hope in the future. The people were discouraged, given how their way of life had been disrupted and how they continued to be controlled by alien governments. The religious outlook became apocalyptic in nature, which is to say that the people longed for God to enter into their history and create a new way of life for them based on faithfulness to the covenant. It also had to be one that would free them from foreign rule and enable them to establish an ideal kingdom, not unlike the one that existed in the time of David. Part of this hope hinged on the coming of a Messiah who would lead in this emancipation and reconstruction of the social order. Many wondered if Jesus might be that promised Messiah. This search for a more dedicated and profound faith was integral to the life and teachings of Jesus.

One part of the contemporary effort to understand what Jesus said and did is to place Jesus within his social and religious world and see how it may

---

17. See, for example, Murphy, *Religious World of Jesus*. See also White, *From Jesus to Christianity*, 95–142.

have shaped his life and teachings. This might be thought of as the explanatory phase of current Jesus research. The other half of current interpretation of Jesus is to discern how the example of his life and his teachings in his context might be brought forward from his time into our time, and be used as guidance for our present challenges and hope for our future. Hermeneutics involves both of these endeavors. There are many themes and practices that have been brought forward into our time from the reading about Jesus in the Gospels. Perhaps the dominant one that has been present for centuries, but given new life in these past several decades, is the way that Jesus sought peace, social justice, and liberation from foreign rule for his contemporaries. It is not that the theme of personal faith in the Christian way that brings peace and purpose to the believer's life has not been emphasized. It has, but what is in many ways a more unique interpretation is to see how his life and teaching went beyond personal renewal and suggested radical transformation of social structures. It has been a worldwide movement, starting in some ways with the first writing and prophetic actions in Latin America, a movement called liberation theology. It is a strong and bold assessment that many people, including those of color, women, the poor and the ill, those with other nationalities and religious traditions, have been mistreated in nearly every society and denied the basics of nutrition, clean water, education, and the right to have a say in the formation of a just social order. These are the people with whom Jesus identified and for whom he cared. Jesus gives his life in his charismatic teaching, his compassionate healing, and his radical prophetic challenge to entrenched power structures. It is from this hermeneutical starting point that we should begin to understand Jesus for our time and follow his example.

Guidelines for Interpreting the Actions and Sayings of Jesus

In these first three chapters, we have been preparing ourselves to understand, wisely interpret, and follow the teachings and actions of Jesus. As we enter into this endeavor, we discover that there are many passages in the Gospels whose meanings are elusive, and about which there have been debates for centuries. Consensus on their precise meaning has evaded scholars and devout teachers, although very thoughtful and persuasive suggestions have been presented. It would be altogether presumptuous of me to suggest that I could provide the correct interpretation of these passages. My goal is less ambitious. It is to introduce many of them and then suggest ways they have been understood and which interpretation might be the best, given our current base of knowledge and what is needed in our circumstances.

One example may be suggestive: the sayings of Jesus about destroying the temple. "When some were speaking about the Temple, how it was adorned with beautiful stones and gifts dedicated to God, he said, 'As for these things that you see, the days will come when not one stone will be left upon another, all will be thrown down'" (Luke 21:5–6). What did Jesus mean when he spoke this way about the temple? Is this a statement about how the temple represented a shallow religion that will be replaced? Is it a statement about the misuse of money in the temple, practices that must be changed? Might it be a passage written following the destruction of the temple by the Romans three decades after the suggested time of this conversation? We will explore these kinds of difficult passages. I have divided these passages that have been both hard to understand and to bring into harmony with other teachings of Jesus into the three categories:

1. The Difficult Teachings
2. The Difficult Events
3. The Difficult Decisions

On occasion, I use the term "hard" in reference to some of the teachings of Jesus. It is somewhat synonymous with difficult, although there may be times when the terms will have slightly different meanings. In order to guide us as we move to these passages, let me summarize three major aspects of biblical interpretation:

1. First, of course, we underlined that we must do the careful work of scholarship in order to arrive at the best interpretation of a passage of Scripture. We should use the best tools of the historical-critical method in that they may be helpful in our interpretation of a particular passage. We spoke briefly about literary and narrative criticism, textual criticism, source criticism, and form criticism. This may mean, for example, searching for the subtle meanings of words, translated from a different language into English. We will need to have an understanding of the history and culture surrounding the narrative we are studying. We should understand the development of the passage through its various stages and be aware of the purpose of the authors of the Gospels.

2. It is important to be sensitive to our hermeneutical starting points. This will mean that we should carefully select approaches that will help us understand the meaning of the passage in the time in which it was spoken, as well as how it might and could have application for our setting. We should be self-aware about our own preconceptions, practice

the "hermeneutics of suspicion" on the passages we are interpreting, and be sensitive to the ways that the meaning may change for us as we approach and then return to the passage; we operate within the hermeneutical circle.

3. As we search for the meaning of the passage, we should be clear about our goal for arriving at an interpretation. We may tilt the meaning in a way that helps us to accomplish our goal. Is it being used for a sermon, an academic lecture, or for a publication? Are we using it in a Christian context for understanding and nurture leaning toward the Christ of faith, or for an article in an academic journal focused on the historical detail of the Jesus of history?

With these three principles in mind, I would like to add one further frame of reference. It is the more personal one that may not be central in every study of Scripture, but one that has to do with our desire to hear the message of Scripture for the cultivation of our spiritual life. It is to say "yes" to the invitation of Jesus. I would like to stress that we prepare ourselves with an open mind and heart as we "walk on holy ground." As we approach the Bible, we may desire in some cases to hear its message in a way that will transform our lives so that we may flourish. We may want it to speak to our deepest pain, our most pressing needs, and our fondest hopes. We may want it to give us insight that empowers us to move toward becoming a more mature, responsible, and loving person.

Study Resources

Study Questions

1. Do you think the work of the Jesus Seminar helped the Christian community to understand the difficulties of accessing information about Jesus, or did its participants go too far and cause Christians to doubt the foundations of their faith?

2. How do you interact with those whose religious views and outlooks differ from yours? How might you improve the quality of these conversations?

3. How did Jesus view the expectations of the law (Torah) in the Judaism of his time? What did he teach in reference to it?

4. Do you think it is wise and helpful to use contemporary concepts and ideas in articulating the teaching of Jesus? Or do they distort his teaching?

5. Are you inclined to accept the Christian church's teaching about the life of Jesus, or are you free to reject parts of it and have you own views about the life and teaching of Jesus?

Terms and Concepts

1. Hermeneutics: the locus and principles of the interpretation of literature, especially of ancient texts. It may also include the way that the meaning of ancient texts may be brought into the present for guidance.

2. Objective study: the method of studying reality (and, in our case, history) from a point of view that is free from preconceptions that may distort its meaning.

3. History: the study of the past that includes both the discovery of what happened *and* its interpretation.

4. *Quelle*: the German word for source used in biblical studies to describe a now lost source of the teaching of Jesus.

5. Hermeneutics of Suspicion: The goal of testing various interpretations to see if there may be hidden preconceptions that shape the interpretation.

Suggestions for Reading and Reference

Funk, Robert W. *Honest to Jesus: Jesus for a New Millenium.* San Francisco: HarperSanFrancisco, 1996.

Gadamar, Hans-George. *Truth and Method.* Translated by Joel C. Weinsheimer and Donald G. Marshall. New York: Crossroads, 1965.

Grant, Robert M., and David Tracy. *A Short History of the Interpretation of the Bible.* 2nd rev. ed. Philadelphia: Fortress, 1984.

Jasper, David, *A Short Introduction to Hermeneutics*, Louisville: Westminster John Knox, 2004.

Murphy, Frederick J. *The Religious World of Jesus: An Introduction to Second Temple Palestinian Judaism.* Nashville: Abingdon, 1991.

SECTION 2

The Difficult Teachings

What Are the Components of the Invitation?

We have spoken about the difficult access to the life and teachings of Jesus and suggested ways of gaining access through careful historical scholarship. We were keenly aware that recovery of information was crucial if we are to understand the way of life that Jesus invites us to follow. We maintained as well that it had to be coupled with the wise use of hermeneutical principles as we interpret this information and bring it forward into our time. We move now to the specific teaching of Jesus that speaks to his invitation. As we do, we will keep in mind two categories about his teaching: (1) that it may be difficult to understand; and (2) that it may be hard to apply to our personal lives and to our circumstances. It is radical in the sense of challenging the cultural norms that shape the way we live. We will need to be somewhat selective for two primary reasons:

1. There is an abundance of material that fits one or both of these categories of "difficult" or "hard," and so we will have to make a judgment about which passages are in some way especially difficult for us, but crucial to our theme.

2. We will have to be aware about whether the passages are likely authentic, based on what Jesus probably said or implied in his teaching. We will select those that are generally judged to be authentic and those

judged to be in the spirit of his teaching, even if the precise words were not actually spoken by Jesus.

In chapter 4, we will work primarily with the ethical teaching of Jesus, then move on in chapter 5 to the teachings about the kingdom of God, and then in chapter 6 to the teachings and, to some extent, the actions of Jesus in reference to the differences he encountered with his contemporaries and how the conflicts were managed.

> You have heard it said, "You shall love your neighbor and hate your enemy," but I say to you, "Love your enemies and pray for those who persecute you."
>
> (MATT 5:43–44)

4

The Ethical Demands

Do They Apply to Us?

As WE MOVE TO and read the ethical teachings of Jesus, we discover that there are occasionally ethical expectations that are hard to understand as we try to translate the guidance given by Jesus into our context. The contexts, his and ours, are quite different. We also find these ethical expectations difficult as we try to apply them to our lives. The expectations are so high that it is very hard to live consistently in accord with them. Much of his ethical teaching is both difficult to fully understand and especially hard to follow.

In fact, there have been those teachers and scholars of the New Testament who have sought ways to say that these teachings were not intended to apply to the normal everyday lives of the followers of Jesus. For example, no less a person than Albert Schweitzer suggested that these ethical demands, particularly those found in the Sermon on the Mount, were for the brief period before the full realization of the kingdom of God. Schweitzer suggested that Jesus gave this guidance to his followers as a pattern for life until God directly intervened in their history and ushered in a fundamental shift in the social order, the full coming of the kingdom of God. Schweitzer maintained that Jesus believed that this would occur during his lifetime and that the ethical teachings are kingdom ethics for a special time.[1]

---

1. See the two books by Schweitzer: *Mystery of the Kingdom* and *Quest for the Historical Jesus*. Their discussion is complex, and given more than the hundred years of continuing study of the New Testament, his views seem a bit dated. However, he did point the way to the understanding of Jesus as a first-century Jew who had clear expectations of the coming of the kingdom of God. Schweitzer maintains that Jesus

Other Christian teachers have made similar suggestions. For example, there is a branch of the Christian church that understands biblical time in terms of dispensations. This point of view—dispensationalism—of a small denomination called the Plymouth Brethren maintains that God intends for there to be seven segments of history, one of which occurs when the kingdom of God arrives. This theological orientation is caught up in outlining the series of events that precede the second coming of Christ and plotting the course of the end of human history as we know it.[2] In this interpretation, the ethical teachings of Jesus are designed for the coming kingdom.

The mainstream of New Testament scholarship and church leadership has been more inclined to see the ethical teachings of Jesus as a norm for all who want to follow the will and way of God. The ethical teachings are an integral part of the invitation of Jesus. His invitation is to an ethical way of life. So, as we say yes to the invitation, we pray what Jesus taught us to pray: "Your kingdom come, your will be done, on earth as it is in heaven" (Matt 6:10). Most segments of the Christian church have accepted this challenge while acknowledging that the demands are indeed very difficult to follow. The church has generally taught that, because of this difficulty, God empowers us to live up to them. This teaching, fully developed in the thought of the apostle Paul, suggests that God is present with us and in us as the Holy Spirit, and that it is by the power of God's Spirit that we are able to live up to the ethical norms in the teaching of Jesus. The teaching of Jesus, with a comparable meaning, is that as we are open to the presence of God by endorsing the kingdom or reign of God, we are empowered to live in harmony with the ethical teaching of Jesus. The prayer to God of St. Augustine was "Ask what you will, and give what you ask."

I have often thought that Christian ethical standards should be high, out ahead of us, and motivating us to reach beyond our current state. Through the cultivation of the spiritual life, the insights of education and self-understanding, and the benefits of experience, we can continue to grow and mature, becoming more deeply ethical in our inner life and our behavior. I am grateful for this challenge and experience; it is an integral part of life's meaning. I would like us to look at the ethical challenge of Jesus in three categories:[3] (1) love and compassion; (2) justice and law; and (3)

---

understood the coming kingdom as an eschatological and apocalyptic event, and may have gone to his death disappointed that it didn't occur.

2. See Lindsay and Carlson, *Late Great Planet Earth*. First published in 1970, this book has sold over fifteen million copies. See as well the sixteen-volume fictional series by Lahaye and Jenkins, *Left Behind*, published between 1995 and 2007.

3. Of course there are many other categories from which to select, but we will allow these three to illustrate and represent other categories.

truth and integrity. There are three words to keep in front of us as we seek to understand and follow the ethical teaching of Jesus: love, justice, and truth.

The Ethics of the Kingdom Life: Love and Compassion[4]

I want to begin with the call to love and compassion because, in many ways these traits are integral to and foundational for all of the ethical teachings of Jesus and central to the way of life he invites us to live. Jesus, true to his Jewish heritage, turns to his Bible when asked by a lawyer what is the greatest commandment. He says: "You shall love the Lord your God with all your heart, and with all your soul, and with all your mind. This is the greatest commandment. And a second is like it: You shall love your neighbor as yourself. On these two commandments hang all the law and the prophets" (Matt 22:37–40).[5] *Agape* love is the foundation of the ethical teaching of Jesus, a concept that includes the meaning of at least two words in English: "love" and "compassion." Note three concerns that are implied in this exchange:

1. One is that Jesus, in speaking with a Pharisee who may also have been a scribe and an expert on Jewish law, goes to the source of authority, the Hebrew Bible made up of the law and the prophets. The lawyer (scribe) would have to say that Jesus was correct in his response.

2. A second point he makes is that the foundational statement implies that the ethical life depends upon a whole-person response to Yahweh, a total commitment of heart, soul, and mind. Such a relationship is transformational as one shifts primary loyalty from the self-centered quest for power, prestige, and possessions to the will and way of God. This is the invitation.

---

4. The word "kingdom" remains somewhat problematic in that it is clearly masculine and represents in our minds many kingdoms that have been autocratic and unjust. Substitute names have been suggested such as "the commonwealth of God" or "reign of God." Reign of God is my preference. It is interesting to note that the term is "kingdom of heaven(s)" in Matthew, likely because there was reluctance to use God's name, Yahweh, orally; it was too sacred. An alternative with a somewhat different meaning is kin-dom, suggesting that we are kin, a human family under God. I'll expand on this point in chapter 5.

5. The question arises as to whether Jesus actually said these words. My judgment call on this exchange is that the passage represents his fundamental convictions, although in the exchange there may have been other words. The pericope is not a recording, but an expression of the true intention of Jesus. There is a comparable passage in Mark 12:31, and the author of Matthew likely had it in front of him as he wrote.

3. As one makes this shift and endorsement of the reign of God in one's life, the second part of the double-love commandment comes into play.[6] As one endorses the reign of God and is filled with divine love, then one naturally loves one's neighbor. We are to love our neighbor with great intensity and wisdom just as we love ourselves and care deeply about our own health and happiness. Note that the teaching acknowledges that self-love is seen as foundational as well. We are better able to truly love others when we have self-love in the sense of feeling good about ourselves and feeling united rather than filled with needs that drive us to self-preoccupation. We need to be free to selflessly care for others.

This teaching is somewhat difficult in both of the ways that we have spoken about the hard sayings of Jesus. Often when we hear this counsel "as we love ourselves" we misunderstand it. The all too common assumption is that to speak about and practice self-love is to imply that we are selfish and want only to satisfy our own needs and desires. Jesus is saying the opposite. Selfishness is often rooted in our fears and insecurities. It is when our needs are met and we have a sense of being a mature person that we are emancipated from self-preoccupation and able to move to a more pure love for others.[7] This pure care for others includes both love and compassion. By this we mean that we love them in the sense of affirming them and including them in our circle of acceptance (love), and also that we want to relieve their suffering and to seek their well-being (compassion).

To embrace another in these ways makes this a hard teaching in the second sense as well. It is not easy to reach the point in our lives when we gain freedom from self-centeredness and then to be fully present for another person. We are often bound by cultural norms that evoke and authorize the selfish life. We fall for the norms of consumerism and a commodity-centered and predatory culture. We do need to be transformed by the grace of God and to cultivate a deep spiritual life that empowers us to be a loving person.[8] There will be days when the double-love commandment, to love God with our whole being and to love our neighbor as we love our self, is very difficult. For example, loving God may seem abstract, distant, and irrelevant, unconnected to anything in our daily lives. We may ask, who is

---

6. Jesus is following the teaching of Leviticus 19:18.

7. The book by Sharon Salzberg called *Real Love: The Art of Mindful Connection* insightfully speaks about the need for self-love in order to connect in healthy way with others. See especially the section dealing with the difficulty of self-love (Salzberg, *Real Love*, 9-99).

8. I speak about this point in my book *Mindful Spirituality*, 133–265.

God and what is God? And our daily life may be so filled with guilt, anxiety, and demands that we have nothing left to give to others. Or, as it is for so many of us, we are caught up in our commodity culture. The foundation of the ethical teaching of Jesus, to love God and neighbor, is very difficult and needs daily cultivation across our lifespan.

It becomes even more difficult when we add the additional teaching of Jesus about loving our enemies. "You have heard it was said, 'You shall love your neighbor and hate your enemy.' But I say unto you, 'Love your enemies and pray for those who persecute you, so you may be children of your Father in heaven; for God makes the sun rise on the evil and the good, and sends rain on righteous and the unrighteous'" (Matt 5:43–44). The commandment to love in the teaching of Jesus includes loving those who are enemies, people who do not like us and may want to hurt us in some way. This addition to the commandment to love can only be followed if we are truly "the children of your Father in heaven." We must be filled with the power and presence of God to love those who threaten us. I find this commandment very difficult, in part because those who reject me threaten me, and it is very hard to love those who make me afraid. This command requires that I get out of myself and identify with the needs of my enemy. As I understand my enemy's motivation and needs, I find it easier to at least take one tiny step toward identifying with them and try to show love for this person who is in need. It is a hard saying!

This point on loving our enemies directs us to an expansion of this teaching of Jesus, which is that loving our enemies leads us to the challenge of learning how to forgive. The spirit of forgiveness is implied in the Lord's Prayer, as we say: "forgive us our debts as we also have forgiven our debtors."[9] Other translations use the word "trespasses" for "debts." A more comprehensive translation is sins. In short, we pray for the capacity to forgive others. The point is made more candidly when Jesus is asked by Peter, "'Lord, if another member of the church sins against me, how often should I forgive? As many as seven times?' Jesus said to him, 'Not seven times, but, I tell you, seventy seven.'"[10]

This teaching does not imply that we should be weak and allow others to walk over us at will. It is possible to push back, both in terms of a personal affront, and also if the action represents an unjust pattern in society. If it is a norm of the culture, we need to raise our voice and take action in support of the formation of a more just social order. The notion of forgiveness does not

---

9. Matt 6:12.

10. Matt 18:21–22. There are some biblical scholars have interpreted this passage as saying seventy times seven.

mean we easily accept trespasses. We forgive the trespass or sin against us and seek to find ways to change the behavior of the one who has hurt us. We try in the right spirit to change harmful and hurtful behavior, and the reality of God's forgiveness of us is the motivating message. We are to be God-like. Even if we forgive, we won't easily forget being hurt by another; it stays with us in our memory. Our goal in the spirit of the Lord's Prayer is to move our focus from our hurt and pain and attempt to understand the offending person and why they behaved the way they did. This behavior reflects the presence of God within us. In time, our sense of being mistreated evolves into caring for the welfare of the other person.[11]

Our willingness to forgive is very often transforming for those who have trespassed against us. They understand our effort to reach out, begin to see it as a kind of nonviolent resistance and an expression of compassion, own their offense, and the break in the relationship can be healed. Of course, it doesn't always happen that easily, but we live by the guidance to forgive seventy-seven times, or however long it takes to heal the relationship. This is the nature of *agape* love, of God's love, and a hard teaching of Jesus.

I have wondered from time to time why Jesus didn't sit down, and, like Plato and Aristotle, write philosophical essays and explain the foundations and patterns of the ethical life. Had he done it, it might have been easier for those of us who have attempted to explain with clarity what Jesus said on a range of important topics, especially about love and compassion. On the other hand, the fact that he taught by example and story has invited his followers to participate in a more creative endeavor. As we teach, we do not recite a series of logical propositions hoping that they might be at least of interest to a few very dedicated and bright students. Rather, his teaching comes to us in descriptive actions, remarkable stories, and the dramas of everyday life. We become engaged as we might with a suspenseful novel or a brilliant movie. I find this way of teaching especially poignant as we try to understand the teaching of Jesus about love and compassion.

Let me illustrate by inviting us to reflect on the story of Jesus healing the leper (Mark 1:40–45). A leper comes directly to Jesus, kneels down, and asks for healing. He says, "If you choose, you can make me clean." The reference to being made clean reveals that those with contagious skin diseases were isolated from society and prevented from normal activity in a town or a village; they were unclean or impure. They suffered not just from the disease, but also from loneliness and isolation. They had no one to give them care and compassion.

---

11. Helmick and Peterson, *Forgiveness and Reconciliation*, provides an excellent description of the role of forgiveness in the process used in South Africa in the formation of the nation, a process that can move to other countries and continents.

It is a bold move on the part of the leper to approach an important person, one who had become a popular teacher, a courageous prophet, and a compassionate healer. Yet this important person welcomes the leper, reaches out to touch him at significant risk of catching the disease, and says in response, "I do choose. Be made clean." Jesus in this response illustrates the nature of love and compassion. He is not limited by the norm that people with a skin disease should remain isolated, but allows the leper to approach him. The touch of Jesus sends the message that the sick person has worth as a human being. Jesus pays attention to the person in need and distress, allowing his busy schedule to be interrupted.

This story invites the followers of Jesus to engage in difficult acts of love and compassion. It teaches us that we are to care and show love and compassion for those who are ill, in distress, and in great need. The story suggests several ethical guidelines that become part of a response to the invitation of Jesus. I'll mention four that are worth our attention and should be followed:

- Jesus is very busy, yet takes time to pay attention to an isolated person in great need. There is the suggestion in this passage that to give a person in great need care and compassion should be a higher priority than other routine activity and responsibilities.

- He does what he can do to make the person well—healing in this case. According to the Gospels, Jesus did have the gift of healing. As we read the Gospel records, he appears to be a channel for the healing power of God, and he consistently credits God for the healing. Our gifts may differ from his, yet there are many ways for us to show love and compassion for those in great need.

- He touches the leper and loves him with unconditional acceptance. Again, touch may not be altogether appropriate in every situation, although some gesture of respect and care delivers a powerful message, one that is often more healing than just words. Empathic listening and responding in love and compassion rather than reacting in frustration when we are interrupted will deliver an *agape* message.

- He counsels the sick person to follow the norms of society and be sanctioned by the priest as a well person. He needs to meet the purity expectations of Jewish law. He asks the sick person to go to the priest and request a clean bill of health. We are living in a time when any act of caring or affection might be and could be insensitive, inappropriate, and have an oppressive and hidden motivation. To make the act both more public and in line with the norms of society protects both the one who offers care and the one who receives care.

In summary, we might say that the example of Jesus in giving love and compassion to the leper demonstrated a foundational component of his ethical understanding. It is a hard teaching and a dramatic invitation and call to be a person for others.[12]

The Ethics of the Kingdom Life: Justice and Law (Torah)

Another difficult set of teachings of Jesus has to do with his understanding of a fundamental component of Judaism, the Torah. The Torah, sometimes misunderstood as exclusively a list of laws, is more than just a list. Although there are specific ethical norms in Torah, it is basically a foundation for the instruction and guidance about all of life. This counsel comes from the Hebrew Bible and is often mediated through the religious leaders, priests (Levites), and scribes (experts in the Torah teachings). At the core of Torah is the ethical principle of justice. Inevitably, Jesus would have to give attention to this foundational aspect of the Judaism of his time. It was his religion and his way of life.

It is occasionally easy to lose sight of the Jesus of history who was rooted in the beliefs and practices of the religion into which he was born and lived.[13] We often and in some cases justifiably place Jesus above his context. When we do, we tend to draw upon much that we have learned in the Church's teaching about Jesus. We need to be guided by those great minds and spirits that have gone before us. We can learn from them how his teaching speaks to us in our contemporary context. As we do, however, we run the risk of slightly altering a passage in order for it to meet our deep longings and needs. In general, the church has found good ways to move from the Jesus of history to the Christ of faith, even as the New Testament writings invite us to follow such a path. I have learned from Paul and the authors of the Gospels, and have taken this way of bringing Jesus into my world for instruction and guidance. This model of interpretation has great value, yet it must be kept in balance with the ways that Jesus drew upon his context and religion. The teaching of Jesus is best understood as we factor in

---

12. A wonderful example of this kind of love was and continues to be in the work begun in Calcutta by Mother Teresa. See a description of the work in Muggeridge, *Something Beautiful for God*.

13. See the thoughtful treatment of the view of Jesus regarding the law in Sanders, *Jesus and Judaism*, 245–69.

his life situation. If we do not understand his context, we may inadvertently introduce some distortion in our interpretation of his teaching.

On this journey of interpretation, I know I am running the risk of creating Jesus in my own image and have tried as far as possible to avoid this common mistake. I do want to be fully informed and inspired by this extraordinary human being; it is a deep longing of so many who want to accept his invitation and truly follow him. But there have been times when I have only chased his shadow (the church's teaching), changing as the sun moves across the sky (across history).[14] I do admit that it is difficult to get a clear picture of Jesus. The finest minds and spirits have tried and given us several pictures of Jesus, many of them historically grounded and profound. And the search goes on in many good ways.

One of the ways of expanding and deepening our understanding that I have appreciated is the trend in recent New Testament scholarship to carefully trace the way that Jesus did not discard his Jewish heritage but honored it and deepened it by his teaching and actions. It is so important to remember that he was a first-century Jew living in the region of Galilee and was nurtured by Second Temple Palestinian Judaism.[15] There are many characteristics of this era in Jewish life. As a deeply religious person, Jesus would have understood them, given thought to them, and endorsed many aspects of these trends and rejected others. Central to the Judaism of his time would be the way that the Law (Torah) was interpreted to ensure justice for the complex circumstances of the era in which Jesus lived. The Jewish people honored the Law, although the interpretation of the Law varied among the many segments of Jewish society.

In particular, one influential group within Jewish society, the Pharisees, was especially concerned with the way the Law should be the guide for all of life. This branch of Jewish leadership emphasized two domains in which the Law should be understood and followed. One was the belief that the Law taught a righteous and just pattern of life, both for the individual and for the social order. There was a profound sense that, to be a righteous person in the eyes of God, one should follow the ethical norms of Torah. And, as far a possible, there should be social justice built into the laws for Jewish society. There were clear ethical standards and expectations. These patterns were often spelled out in some detail, as for example what it meant to rest on the Sabbath. The details of following the Sabbath law applied to

---

14. See Nolan, *Jesus Before Christianity*, 3–9.

15. Several thoughtful scholars have reminded us of this reality, including Vermes, *Jesus in His Jewish Context*; Zeitlin, *Jesus and the Judaism of His Time*; Charlesworth, *Jesus within Judaism*; Sanders, *Historical Figure of Jesus*; and Murphy, *Religious World of Jesus*. Many others books could be listed.

both the individual and also to the way social norms were built into the laws for the Jewish community.

In addition, there was another concern in the Law that was emphasized by the Pharisees, one that required holiness and purity. Certain religious practices, especially as one moved closer to Yahweh, mandated holiness, being free from anything offensive to God. To assure that one be holy or set aside for God, there were guidelines regarding diet, customs for washing and hygiene, and practices to insure purification. Clean and unclean were categories understood by the religious people.

The Gospel records indicate that Jesus challenged some of these beliefs and practices. As he did, he threatened the prevailing practices and beliefs of the Judaism of his time. There is a sense in which many Christian interpretations of these challenges by Jesus may have gone too far by saying that Jesus exclusively taught a religion of grace and transformation whereas the Jewish tradition in his time was legalistic and placed too much emphasis on external obedience. It is true that Jesus likely did question certain practices and attitudes, but he did not reject the ethical and purity norms of Torah. His challenge had to do with the interpretation and understanding of the Torah, not that the guidance and instruction of Torah was no longer central to the religious life. His views of Torah might be summarized in the statement attributed to him in the Gospel of Mark: "The Sabbath was made for humankind, and not humankind for the Sabbath" (Mark 2:27). The hard teaching of Jesus is that the Law is the foundation of justice and the means of instituting ways that lead to the common good.

As Jesus spoke about certain teachings of the Judaism of his time, he had a way of getting to the fundamental issue and of setting clear priorities. Two events recorded in the Gospels underline the attitude of Jesus toward the Law and ensuring that people are treated fairly. The first has to do with whether it is right to make sure people are fed, even if the preparation takes place on the Sabbath. The account tells how Jesus and his disciples were walking through grain fields on a Sabbath day and took advantage of the grain for nourishment. The Pharisees challenged this behavior and called it a violation of Sabbath laws. Jesus rises to the occasion and notes that even King David did something comparable, and this precedent of David and basic human need justify taking care of hunger on the Sabbath (Matt 12:1–8).

The Gospel account records a similar situation in reference to human need and ensuring justice. Jesus enters a synagogue on a Sabbath day and encounters a person with a withered hand. Jesus immediately responds to this human need and heals the person. The Pharisees challenge Jesus and say that such an action goes against Sabbath norms (Matt 12:9–14). There is similar incident with a crippled woman (Luke 13:10–17). In both cases,

Jesus maintains that activities of meeting human need (feeding and healing) are legitimate on the Sabbath. Jesus does not object to the principle of Sabbath rest and a time set aside to honor God. What he is concerned about is the way that the fundamental principle of Sabbath is distorted in a narrow legalistic pattern rather than viewed as time to show compassion for those in need. The Law is there to increase the quality of life rather than to prohibit ways to take care of human need. The Law is for the welfare of humankind, and especially those who are poor, hungry, and ill. Jesus taught that the opposite of caring for human need was not legalistic obedience to the customs surrounding Sabbath practices, but a commitment to justice.[16]

What becomes difficult for us is to interpret these actions within the context of our own religious beliefs and practices, especially those that are integral to organized religion and the institutional church. This difficult teaching of Jesus asks us as his followers to maintain the priorities of compassion and ensuring justice as the central core of our religious institutions. If the church becomes defensive about socialization of the values we honor and overly protective of organizational practices and traditions, then people will walk away with the goal of being spiritual rather than religious. It is a phenomenon we have observed for the past several decades, especially in those cases when church leadership has been preoccupied with preserving proper regulations.

Our religious institutions must be willing to change and respond in compassion to human need and to be diligent in the pursuit of a just society. If the religious institutions are unable to make these changes, then their members will miss the benefits of a healthy and life-giving community that is designed to continue to instruct and guide them. The teaching of Jesus about Torah was difficult for the Pharisees to hear and understand. It is equally difficult for modern-day Pharisees who defend outdated traditions and fail to make compassion and justice the heartbeat of the religious community.

The Ethics of Kingdom Life: Truth and Integrity

The ethical teaching of Jesus, while rooted in his worldview of the kingdom of God, was not abstract and vague, but direct, and pointed to events, conditions, and practices he observed as he met people and carried out his mission. He spoke with individuals who struggled and needed help with life. And life was not easy to navigate in his time; there was poverty, illness, and the injustice of overlapping and foreign government structures. The

---

16. See Stevenson, *Just Mercy*, 3–18.

people who came to him wanted emancipation from suffering and longed for happiness. As we read about these encounters, we begin to discern an additional ethical norm that is foundational in the ethical teaching of Jesus. It is that we should speak the truth and live with integrity; these principles are part of his invitation. As before, we discern these foundational values in his encounters with people, the Gospel descriptions of his actions, and the stories that he tells. I want to use three accounts from the Gospels to illustrate his concern for truth: (1) his observations about money, wealth, and possessions; (2) his teaching about oaths that were integral to the informal legal system of his time; and (3) his passion to live with integrity in regard to religious beliefs and convictions.

In his time as in ours, there was and is the mistaken notion that happiness consists in the abundance of things possessed. As Jesus encountered people with this outlook, he spoke directly to it. He underlines that it is a self-deception from which one needs emancipation and enlightenment. It should be noted that, from the beginning, he did not counsel all of his followers to lead an extremely stoic life, dedicated to a life of poverty and free from possessions. In that Jesus spoke as a religious teacher and prophet, there were many who thought that he would advise living the ascetic life, one somewhat comparable to his life and that of his band of followers. Religious sages have often taught that the ascetic life is the way to enlightenment and salvation.

Once again, he surprises his listeners and suggests an alternative point of view that would have been initially difficult to grasp. Rooted in a wisdom culture, Jesus gives them wisdom, perspective, and balance in reference to wealth and possessions. He does not teach that the truly religious life is fundamentally ascetic in character, but rather a life with the clear priority of doing the will and way of God, part of which may be wisely using wealth and possessions. There is nothing wrong with having enough money to live with some comfort, nor does one need to get rid of those possessions that may make life easier.

I want to underline three primary teachings of Jesus about wealth and possessions. These teachings were difficult for his followers in that they likely expected different answers, and perhaps even more difficult for us in that we live in a consumer society of abundance and a predatory economy. Our culture has bought the lie that happiness consists of accumulating possessions, ones that promise far more than they deliver.

The first principle that Jesus stresses in reference to wealth and possessions is that wealth and possessions easily become the focus of our lives, rather than God. They are not inherently evil, but the quest for wealth and the management of our possessions can easily shift our priorities and even our deepest values. There is an insightful, even somewhat sad story in the Gospels, in which Jesus speaks with a young man who has wealth. He approaches Jesus and asks, "What good deed must I do to have eternal life?" (Matt 19:16–22). Jesus takes the question seriously and reminds him of the great commandments. The wealthy young man replies, "Which ones?" Jesus answers clearly and summarizes the commandments. The young man says, "I have kept these; what do I still lack?" Jesus goes on to say that he lacks one fundamental value and commitment, which is giving his life fully to God. Jesus says to this young man that God must be preeminent, and doing the will and way of God must be his highest priority. The sad ending is that "he went away grieving, for he had many possessions."

Jesus then explains the conversation to his disciples, who have questions about the hard answer and direct invitation given by Jesus. He tells them that it is very difficult for a rich person to enter the kingdom of God because riches tend to be all consuming. He explains that it is even easier for a camel to go through the eye of needle than it is for a rich person to give the highest priority to the reign of God. As the discussion continues with the confused disciples, who are also asking the same question, he acknowledges that he has given the rich young ruler a difficult answer. He reminds his disciples that that the rich young man will need to seek God's sustaining presence and power and, in so doing, he will get the priorities of life in order. God can enable a person to change values and motivations. Jesus explains to the disciples that a person can begin to understand what should be the aim of life, although "for mortals it is impossible, but for God all things are possible." Jesus teaches his disciples: "Yes, it is hard to love God with your whole being, but don't forget that God is able to transform us and empower us to enter the kingdom of God. God gives what God asks."

Jesus makes a similar point in the Sermon on the Mount. He says: "Do not store up for yourselves treasures on earth, where moth and rust consume and where thieves break in and steal; but store up for yourselves treasures in heaven, where neither moth nor rust consumes and where thieves do not break in and steal. For where your treasure is, there your heart will be also" (Matt 6:19–21). For Jesus, the principle is where your heart is, and the love for God should be "where your heart is." Your love for and commitment to God must be preeminent. As I reflect on the answer that Jesus gives, I begin to see more clearly how easily we are deceived about our priorities, and how in our consumer and market economy wealth and the accumulation of possessions soon become our goal in life. Often it is how we calculate our value and rank in society.

A second hard teaching of Jesus about the management of wealth and possessions is directed in a slightly different direction to those who worry that they will not have enough to take care of their families and manage life. It is not wealth, but the lack of it that is troubling. It is natural for the poor to worry about money, even as it is for the wealthy to be preoccupied with their possessions. Once again, Jesus articulates the wisdom that should guide those of us who worry about not having sufficient wealth to manage life. The principle is to seek first the kingdom of God and a righteous life, and to trust that God will supply what we need (Matt 6:33). I find this teaching quite difficult in that it appears on the surface to border on being a pious platitude that doesn't work in real life. I find myself wanting to push back and say to Jesus: "There are just too many poor people in the world who suffer, regardless of whether they trust or don't trust God. World hunger and the global distribution of food rank toward the top in terms of the world's problems." As I am writing, I identify with the young people in Florida whose classmates were killed in gun violence. One of their leaders said to Congress that the comment "my thoughts and prayers are with you" was hollow without action on gun control. It is hard to accept the answer "just pray about it" when life is in danger from hunger or guns.[17]

As we struggle with this teaching, it is important to keep in mind that the author of the Gospel of Matthew is summarizing much of the teaching of Jesus and placing it in a pattern that has come to be known as the Sermon on the Mount. It is likely that this saying, when Jesus taught it, may have been expanded and been a longer conversation. It is clear that Jesus identified with the poor and lived in solidarity with them. He himself was poor, and the majority of his early ministry in Galilee was in caring for the poor, often by feeding them.

It is my conviction that what Jesus was saying was intended to comfort his listeners, not to fully address the social problem of poverty and hunger. He is providing a profound insight about how worry can be defeating. So he urges his contemporaries not to give their exclusive attention to food and clothing. Learn how to be content with having basic needs met and give your attention to the reign of God in your lives. It is not that food and clothing are unimportant and unnecessary; they are true needs that we all have! But Jesus is concerned once again with helping people have the right attitude and getting their priorities straight. The highest priority is seeking the presence of God in our lives. Life can be managed, even in poverty, with God's guidance and empowering presence and when there is a more just social order.

I want to add one more difficult teaching of Jesus in reference to wealth and possessions. It speaks both to those who are wealthy and those who are

---

17. I also think of the current situation in Yemen, with millions of people starving.

poor. It is that one should be generous in sharing with others in need in order to rectify injustice and seek the common good. The account of Jesus finding a way to feed the five thousand who had come to hear him teach underlines this point. It may have been a miraculous feeding, although I am drawn to another interesting interpretation of the feeding of the five thousand. It is that the real miracle was not that Jesus was able to magically multiply the five loaves and two fish. It was rather that he shared what he had with them and asked that all the others who were present share what they had brought with those who were in need. It was his example of caring for those who were tired and hungry after a long day away from home.

There is also the teaching of Jesus about the giving of alms to take care of those in need. He affirms this practice and underlines the importance of the motive we have in giving. Again, we have only a short passage in the Gospel of Matthew, although it may have been the case that Jesus spoke at length on this subject. What is preserved for us, once again, has to do with priorities and how we set them. He says that we are to give to others in the spirit of love and compassion, not to be thought of as one who should be honored and praised for generosity. Jesus was very sensitive about hypocrisy in religious practices and spoke strongly against it.[18] So whether we are rich or poor—or, like most of us, who are somewhere in the middle—we are to give to others in need and do our part to sustain a more just social order. And we should do it because our motive is to love others rather than to seek praise and power for ourselves.

There is another way that I would like to illustrate the way that Jesus taught that his followers should be honest and live with integrity. It is implied in the way that he spoke about religious leaders who sought praise and adulation for giving alms. It was the custom in the culture of Jesus to swear an oath as a means of securing a transaction or exchange with another person or organization. There were some written legal documents, but in an essentially illiterate society, people used the swearing of an oath as a means of securing an arrangement. Again, the Sermon on the Mount describes the concern of Jesus that these oaths and promises can easily be broken, which amounts to dishonesty and hypocrisy. He is especially concerned when the oaths are sworn in the name of God. He is recorded as saying: "Again, you have heard that it was said to those in ancient times, 'You shall not swear falsely, but carry out the vows you have made to the Lord.' But I say to you, do not swear at all, either by heaven, for it is the throne of God, or by the earth, for it is his footstool, or by Jerusalem, for it is the city of the Great King" (Matt 5:33-35). In this passage, the author of Matthew's Gospel has

---

18. See the teaching in Matt 23:1-36.

Jesus speaking firmly about the risk of the oaths. Even if we sincerely expressed them at the time, oaths may be dishonest and hypocritical if they are often not followed. He counsels a simple form of exchange: "Let your word be 'Yes, Yes' or 'No, No'; anything more than this comes from the evil one."

Perhaps the strongest statements attributed to Jesus in regard to speaking the truth and living honestly with complete integrity is in reference to the practice of one's religion. As we read these passages, we need to remember and take into account that they come to us many decades after the life of Jesus. It was a time when there was a measure of conflict between the emerging church based on the teachings of Jesus and mainline Judaism, especially with the Pharisees. New Testament scholars have pored over this material and acknowledged that there was a genuine conflict and that there was resistance to the teaching of Jesus by religious leaders. But there has been caution as well about stereotyping the Pharisees as hypocrites, and the recognition that the material in the Gospels tells the story from one side of the conflict. As the oral tradition was passed on to later generations and was written down and recopied, the actual words and even the attitude and spirit of Jesus in these conflicted exchanges may have been altered. It is likely that Jesus did have concern about certain religious practices, and as a prophet, he spoke directly to these practices. What we are safe in saying is that Jesus had little patience with hypocritical religion. He likely did address the concern in the statement in the Gospel of Matthew: "Woe to you, scribes and Pharisees, hypocrites! For you tithe mint, dill, and cumin, and have neglected the weightier matters of the law: justice and mercy and faith. It is these you ought to have practiced without neglecting the others. You blind guides! You strain out a gnat but swallow a camel" (Matt 23:23–24). In summary, we read that we are to live with integrity and speak the truth in the way we practice our faith in the account of the life and teaching of Jesus that comes to us in the Gospels.

We turn now to a discussion of a central teaching of Jesus, the kingdom of reign of God. In many ways, it is the foundation of the teaching of Jesus.

Study Resources

Discussion Questions

1. In what ways was the intellectual, political, social, and religious context of Jesus different from ours?

2. What made and still makes the ethical teachings of Jesus so difficult?

3. What does Jesus mean when he invites us to love others as we love ourselves?
4. How would you describe the attitude of Jesus toward the commitment of the Judaism of his time to the Law (Torah)? How does it shape his invitation to live a life devoted to the will and way of God?
5. What generally upset Jesus the most about the practice of Judaism and religion in his time? Why did he invite his listeners to another way of life?

Terms and Concepts

1. *Agape*: A Greek word for a love that is unconditional and unlimited, although for Jewish people, linked to the *Shema*, the commandment in Deuteronomy 6:4–5 that says we are to love God with all of our heart, soul, and might.
2. Alms: Gifts to the needy people in the community, often managed and distributed by religious leaders.
3. Scribe: an educated Jewish person in the time of Jesus who was an expert on the interpretation of the law
4. Pharisees: a religious group of people in the time of Jesus who were dedicated to applying law to all aspects of life.
5. Second Temple Palestinian Judaism: a term that applies to the religious outlook and vision of Jewish people following the return to Palestine after the destruction of the First Temple during the Babylonian captivity (587 BCE). It was the hope for a new temple and the formation of a religious outlook that prevailed up to the time of Jesus. The temple was a unifying symbol for most of the Jewish people at the time of Jesus.

Suggestions for Reading

Charlesworth, James H. *Jesus within Judaism: New Light from Exciting Archaeological Discoveries*. New York: Doubleday, 1988.
Nolan, Albert. *Jesus Before Christianity*. Maryknoll: Orbis, 1978.
Sanders, E. P. *Jesus and Judaism*. Philadelphia: Fortress, 1985.
Vermes, Geza. *Jesus in His Jewish Context*. Minneapolis: Fortress, 2003.
Zeitlin, Irving M. *Jesus and the Judaism of His Time*. Cambridge: Polity, 1988.

5

The Nature of the Kingdom of God

IN THE LAST CHAPTER, we discussed how and why the ethical teachings of Jesus are so difficult. We noted in the first place that they are difficult because he lived in a quite different historical and cultural context than ours and that his ethical teachings, reflect his context, at least partially. We have to do some careful translation in order to understand what he did to demonstrate ethical norms and what he taught about ethics. We also underlined that his ethical teachings are difficult because it is so hard to live in accord with them. They are demanding and require a whole-person transformation and commitment. For example, the Golden Rule, doing for others what we would want them to do for us, asks selfless and unlimited love. When we add his additional teaching that we are to love our enemies, we often sense our inability to follow this guidance. We often seek the empowering presence of God in our lives so that we are able to follow his ethical teachings and to live with integrity in reference to them. The invitation of Jesus is to follow this demanding ethical way of life.

We now want to explore how we can be empowered to accept the invitation of Jesus and live in accord with his teachings. Jesus teaches that we are able to live a truly ethical way of life as we receive the power and presence of God into our lives. Jesus refers to this acceptance as saying yes to the invitation of and opening our hearts to the kingdom or reign of God. So we pray as Jesus taught us: "Your kingdom come, your will be done, on earth as it is in heaven" (Matt 6:10).

The Kingdom of God: Toward a Definition

In talking about the ethical teaching of Jesus, we encountered the concept of the kingdom of God and saw that it was central to his ethical teaching and to his total outlook on life. It was the way he spoke about his worldview or the frame of reference in which he understood the ways that God was active in individual lives, in the nation, and in the world. The kingdom of God was the good news that God's loving presence was available to us as we open our hearts and minds to the presence of God.[1] We noted in the previous chapter that the translation of the term as the "kingdom of God" has the disadvantage of being masculine (king) and references a governmental source of authority and power (kingdom) that has not always been just in its historical manifestations. Yes, there have been good kings (and queens) who ruled justly and administered their policies to serve the common good. Yet we still tend to have more confidence that justice will prevail in a more democratic social structure, one with checks and balances.

I will often use the term reign of God instead of kingdom of God and, on occasion, also speak of the realm of God. These terms may be a better rendering of what Jesus was teaching.[2] Jesus understood the term "kingdom of God" as an active and dynamic concept; it was not a passive reference to a country somewhere ruled by a king. The Gospel of Mark begins his account of Jesus by saying: "Now after John was arrested, Jesus came to Galilee, proclaiming the good news of God, and saying, 'The time is fulfilled, and the kingdom of God has come near; repent and believe the good news'" (Mark 1:14–15). This foundational passage points to the special way that God was at work in the setting of Jesus and the role Jesus had in expanding the reign of God.

Jesus likely assumed that when he used the term "kingdom of God," his listeners would understand it, or at least its general meaning: the way that God is like a king, having power to reign over the world, in their land, and in their lives and settings in particular. Jesus reinforced this idea in his teaching and said that his presence and ministry were an expression of the expansion of God's reign. The ministry of Jesus is to proclaim that the

---

1. The term "worldview" may not be precise in that it generally points to a philosophical foundation for understanding the nature of human life, human history, and the rhythms of the universe. Jesus was more focused on God's interactions with human beings on earth, and spoke about and acted in reference to this interaction within his larger outlook that we might call a worldview.

2. *Basileia*, the Greek term for "kingdom," implies both authority (reign) and the realm of the king's authority. The biblical usage focuses on the reign or the exercise of power by the king, a metaphor for God. The use of "kingdom" was an easily understood metaphor for the reign of God (of Christ, of heaven) in the time of Jesus.

kingdom of God has come near and it is good news.³ He says that his ministry is to expand the realm over which God reigns and increase the ways and settings in which the will and way of God will prevail.

Thoughtful contemporaries of Jesus would have said that they welcome this good news, but might have wondered what it really means. Might it be a reference to the prophetic and healing ministries of Jesus? Is Jesus referring to the way God's power is present in him so that he may improve the lives of others? Or is it a concept that is more directly related to a troubled people and nation under the oppression of an alien government? To ask the question in a slightly different way, we enquire whether it is a reference to the way that Jesus healed the leper or the way he spoke about the restoration of Israel, a concept central to the hope of Second Temple Judaism? In both of these settings or realms, the transformation of the individual person and the renewal of the nation, there is a need for God to reign. Jesus invites his listeners to endorse the reign of God in their lives and their social setting; these are the realms in which God's will and way should be followed.⁴

The question we face is whether Jesus primarily used the term to refer to God's way of entering into human life, caring for personal needs, and empowering individuals to lead a spiritual life; or did the term point to the more apocalyptic, even eschatological, notion of the dramatic restoration of Israel? This question has resulted in a continuing debate for years in New Testament scholarship, and indeed almost since he chose the term to speak about his mission. The goal of the debate has been to determine more precisely what Jesus meant. Persuasive arguments have been put forward for both personal transformation and for corporate change. Each of the views has been articulated with subtle differences, often within the context of a theological outlook. Others have made a strong case for the integration of both the personal and corporate definitions, affirming that Jesus understood the concept of the reign of God to be both for individuals and for the social structures in which individuals live. Central to a vast range of views has been the conviction that the kingdom of God is the way that God enters into human history for the welfare of the human family, with Jesus being the expression of this special divine entrance.

---

3. See as well Matt 4:17.

4. See Beasley-Murray, *Jesus and the Kingdom of God*, for an exploration of what Jesus meant by the kingdom of God.

Positions in the Debate: The Gospel Stories

Many of the contemporaries of Jesus, those who encountered him and listened to his teaching, would have thought that his presence with them was indeed the special entrance of God into their experience. They understood the teachings and actions of Jesus to be the manifestation of the kingdom of God, the tangible expression of the power and presence of God. The model of his life and the profound insight of his teaching demonstrated to them the way to live a deeply spiritual life. It was truly transformative for them. He called on them to repent, change the direction of their lives, and follow the will and way of God. More specifically, his invitation to his listeners was to follow the ethical and holy practices of Torah. Torah would have been understood as teaching, guidance, and instruction that went beyond a list of laws to include attitudes, social conduct, and public policy. In particular, he urges them to focus their attention on the essence of Torah, on the double-love commandment, to love God with heart, soul, and mind, and to love your neighbor as you love yourself (Matt 22:37–40). To live a life in this way was to fulfill what God expects, for "on these two commandments hang all the law and the prophets."

There is a fundamental internal logic to the double-love commandment. First, there is the call to love God with one's whole being, a process that is a conversion to a particular way of life. It is not a single act (although it may begin with one), but a profound reorientation and the beginning of a lifelong process of growth toward maturity and unity with God and obedience to God's will and way. Perhaps the most compelling definition of the spiritual life is to go through the several stages of conversion and transformation. The stages represent a development process of growth toward spiritual maturity and include repentance (purgation), gaining insight (illumination), and making change (regeneration), all leading to a beatific vision (eternal peace or bliss), a pathway that leads to oneness with the God.[5] For the majority of Christian teachers, to learn how to love God is developmental, a series of stages or a process that moves from contemplation of God to health and wholeness, and from this maturity comes empowerment to expand outward and love one's neighbor.[6]

---

5. The great teachers of the spiritual way vary in the description of the stages of transformation, but nearly all see it as a process. In my *Mindful Spirituality*, I speak about the process as Reaching Upward, Opening Inward, and Expanding Outward in the spiritual journey. I use the directional metaphors, drawing (for example) on Psalm 121:1: "I will lift up my eyes unto the hills, from whence my help comes."

6. Ken Wilber has provided thoughtful summaries and profound descriptions for the developmental models in several of his books. See his new and very detailed book: *The Religion of Tomorrow: A Vision for the Future of the Great Traditions: More*

Jesus teaches that the reign of God in our lives heals us, transforms us, and gives us life-changing insight that reorients our lives. I want to pause for a moment on that part of the transformation that is healing in character. Jesus enlightened minds and transformed souls, and he also had a way of healing bodies. Many of the people that he encountered came to him with illnesses, disabilities, and deformities. We will say more about this aspect of Jesus' ministry in chapter 8, but here I want to underline that Jesus understood the coming reign of God as restoring a person to wholeness and health. The scriptural account tells us that a large percentage of the people he met came to him with physical ailments. Those who came to Jesus, or were brought by friends to him, really had few other options. Those who were thought of as doctors at that time had little grasp of what we now understand as the practice of medicine. There were no modern hospitals filled with healing medicine, advanced equipment, and well-trained doctors. He gave attention not only to enlightening the mind and the transformation of the soul, but also to the healing of the body. The healing that took place through Jesus in the bodies, hearts, and minds of the people he met was the manifestation of the reign of God. For example, when he healed the leper and the paralytic, the people "were all amazed and glorified God, saying, 'we have never seen anything like this'" (Mark 2:12). Jesus does not take pride in these healings, as if some sleight-of-hand magic had been performed, but senses that it is God's healing power that flows through him.

As people are restored spiritually, emotionally, and physically, Jesus calls on them to endorse the second part of the double-love commandment. He gathers disciples around him and continues the ministry of the entrance and emerging spread of the kingdom of God. He invites those who hear him and are healed and transformed by God's power to join him in the extension and spreading of the kingdom of God. Those who gather around him were not necessarily from the aristocracy or the meritocracy. In fact, the majority were common people. He was inclusive, inviting all to become a part of a new community. As he gathered them into a group of followers, he gave some a special status as apostles (ones sent with authority to act on behalf of the sender) and disciples (learners or pupils attached to a teacher). There were many men, but an equally large number of women who joined the movement as well, not the least of whom was Mary, the mother of Jesus. They come from different cultures and speak different languages, yet accept the common message of the invitation to accept the reign of God and live lives of love and compassion. Later, devastated and somewhat confused by

---

Inclusive, More Comprehensive, More Complete. James Fowler provides a concise description of these stages in *Stages of Faith*. Here I am using the more traditional language of spiritual formation than the language of developmental psychology.

the tragic death of Jesus, they come together as a community that became the church (a gathering or an assembly of bonded people) to continue the ministry begun by Jesus.

This part of the story expresses the way that the kingdom of God is experienced as transformative in the present. As people say yes to the invitation, they are reoriented, healed, and sent into the world to spread the news that, through Jesus, the power and presence of God are now available in a special way. Another part of the gospel story, present in the Gospels and further developed by the apostle Paul and other New Testament documents, is that the kingdom of God is about the future. The contemporaries of Jesus have a profound need for personal healing and transformation, and at the same time, many of them also longed for a more just and peaceful society. They experienced the temporary and relative peace of the established yet alien government of Rome, but still had to deal with the harsh and unjust ways put in place by the indigenous governments arranged by Rome (e.g., Herod and the Idumeans). Those near Jerusalem were even suspect of their own government and did not fully trust the actions of the Sanhedrin. They wondered if their own leaders had been coopted by Rome. They longed for a better future and dared to hope, knowing full well that to hope is to risk frustration and disillusionment. Their vision for a better future took many forms.

One part of the vision for the future was resistance and protest, actions taken to be responsible for shaping their own future. It had a revolutionary tone.[7] For example, during the lifetime of Jesus, a group identified as Zealots advocated violence to overthrow the colonial government of Rome. Along with others, this group unsuccessfully led the revolution against the Romans in 66 CE. The resistance to alien governments (a succession of them) had been present among the Jewish people for many years prior to the Zealot movement. One source of inspiration for the rebellion was the memory of the Babylonian exile that occurred in 587 BCE, which really meant the end of the kingdom of Judah. Many of the great prophets of the Hebrew Bible, including Jeremiah, Ezekiel, and Second Isaiah, spoke of the causes of this tragedy and gave guidance and hope for a new era based on peace and justice. As the exile ended, some of the leadership of the Jew-

---

7. Henri J. M. Nouwen, in his book *The Wounded Healer*, speaks of three options for social change and the way to liberation: the mystical way, the revolutionary way, and the Christian way. He maintains that the mystical way may lead to a neglect of justice, the revolutionary may lead to violence, and the Christian way is guided by love and justice (Nouwen, Wounded Healer, 16–22). In Thomas Merton's *New Seeds of Contemplation*, he outlines a comparable formula for liberation and justice (Merton, *New Seeds*, 130–49).

ish people returned to Palestine in 538 BCE to a land ruled by Persia. This extended period of time, even with the succession of alien governments, is often spoken of as the Restoration. It was a period in which there were several attempts to build a new nation.[8]

This period of time and effort for restoration was not free from foreign control and influence. There was a period of Greek rule followed by the influence and control under the leadership of Alexander the Great. Following the demise of the reign of Alexander the Great, Judea became part of the Ptolemaic (Egyptian) Empire during the third century BCE. The Syrians continued the colonial control and were led by their king Seleucid and the dynasty that followed in his wake. Their rule was over a vast region that included Persia, Babylonia, Syria, and southern Asia Minor.

The tensions and conflicts during this foreign control were numerous. They often surfaced over cultural and religious ideas and practices. One incident, remembered and celebrated in Judaism across the centuries, was the revolt against the Maccabees (part of the Seleucid Dynasty), who ruled the region in the second and first centuries BCE. The revolt occurred during the reign of Antiochus IV Epiphanes, who decreed that sacrifice to the Greek deities be offered in every Judean city and village. An alter was built in the temple in Jerusalem in 167 BCE, and Mattathias and his five sons—with the older son, Judas, as a key figure—led a revolt, escaped, and fled into the wilderness, becoming the leader of a pocket of resistance. The name "Judas Maccabees" is remembered in connection with a bold revolt that helped to restore hope and preserve the monotheism of Judaism.[9]

As Rome expanded its empire, it claimed the land of Palestine in 63 BCE. While Rome, as was its policy, did encourage indigenous leadership and governance, there was still a clash of cultures and a resistance to the Hellenism that encroached on Jewish belief and practice. It was during the Roman occupation that the life and teachings of Jesus occurred. This continuing colonial occupation becomes part of the backdrop and context for his teaching on the subject of hope and the reign of God.

Initially, as Jesus enters his public ministry, there was perhaps less attention given to the confusing and unjust political environment in his ministry and teaching, in part because he centered his ministry in the region of Galilee, where there was less visibility and interference by the colonial government. The accounts in the Synoptic Gospels focus more on obedience to

---

8. It is a fascinating story, one that need not be told here, but which is in the Hebrew Bible. The books of Haggai, Zechariah 1–8, Isaiah 56–66, Malachi, Ezra, and Nehemiah describe the context, spirit, and dimensions of the restoration.

9. First and 2 Maccabees tell this story. The Jewish holiday, Hanukkah, is a remembrance of this event.

Torah and the ministry of healing. Mark, for example, in speaking about the early phase of the public ministry of Jesus, writes:

> Jesus departed with his disciples to the sea, and a great multitude from Galilee followed him; hearing all that he was doing, they came to him in great numbers from Judea, Jerusalem, Idumaea, beyond the Jordan, and the region around Tyre and Sidon. He told his disciples to have a boat ready for him because of the crowd, so that they would not crush him; for he had cured many, so that all who had diseases pressed upon him to touch him. (Mark 3:7–10)

It wasn't too long, however, before there was increasing resistance to his teaching and ministry by the religious leaders in Jerusalem and, to some extent, from Rome, as his gatherings caused social unrest.

Rising to the surface at this time were two fundamental concerns. The first was the issue of his identity. Many people, including religious and government leaders, wondered who this person was whose teaching and healing ministries attracted such large crowds. The common people began to wonder if he might be the expected messiah. The second and related concern had to do with the aim of his teaching and ministry beyond the nurturing and healing goals. Was Jesus, as he spoke about the kingdom or reign of God (or the heavens), suggesting that there might be a fundamental change in the social order? Was he acting and speaking about not only personal transformation, but also about the restoration of the nation of Israel? Was Jesus a messiah who would be similar to King David and restore the autonomy of the nation? And at the end of his life, did he enter Jerusalem with the thought of ushering in a new political kingdom?

Some of the more difficult passages that are attributed to Jesus in the Gospels speak of these concerns and frame the debate about what Jesus meant as he spoke about the kingdom of God.[10] I want to focus on four subjects that might suggest that Jesus really did hope for the dramatic restoration of Israel. The first has to do with the actual references to a restored kingdom. The Gospel of Matthew records an account of Jesus saying: "And the good news of the kingdom will be proclaimed throughout the world, as a testimony to all the nations; and then the end will come" (Matt 24:14). There was a profound hope by some of the followers of Jesus that he would become a king, not unlike David, and bring in a restored kingdom of Israel.

---

10. As we look at these passages, there is the continuing issue of whether he actually spoke to them in some form, or whether they are redactions to advance the point of view of the Gospel writer. I will try to be sensitive to this concern and careful about the risk of proof-texting.

Of course, Jesus would have been acquainted with this expectation. Some of the language attributed to him references this positive outlook.

Associated with this hope was the expected coming of the messiah, a complex term that had more than one meaning. In the minds of many, the messiah would be a historical figure, instrumental in the restoration of the kingdom. In the end, after conversations with both the Sanhedrin and Herod, this view became the reason for Jesus' crucifixion; he is convicted of treason. At his Roman trial, Pilate asks Jesus if he is the King of the Jews, to which Jesus simply replies, "You say so." At the end of these deliberations, Jesus is accused of seditious behavior and given the sentence of crucifixion.

The question remains whether Jesus thought of himself as a kingly messiah and envisioned the role of king in the restored nation of Israel. My view is that it is unlikely that he thought of himself in this way, although he no doubt understood the longing of the Jewish people for a restored nation and may have thought he might have a part in the restoration as an apocalyptic prophet.[11] He may have even considered whether he was the expected messiah, although he likely rejected some of the ways the term was understood. It is no accident that he was given the term of "messiah" (Christ) almost as a last name, which he has carried throughout history. But, in my judgment, there is little evidence that he had personal aspirations for kingly rule.

He more likely saw himself as both a prophet pointing to the future and a humble servant seeking to follow the will and way of Abba, an Aramaic term for father. Further, he was careful not to claim that he knew about the time of any future events. There is even a passage in Mark attributed to Jesus speaking about the future. In reference to the end times, Jesus says, "But about the day or hour no one knows, neither the angels in heaven, nor the Son, but only the Father" (Mark 13:32). He longed for a restored Israel that would be a society dedicated to peace and justice, but remained unsure of the timing and did not describe himself as a coming king. He stays true to his role as a prophet who brings hope, and always in the role of one who serves. The so-called triumphal entry into Jerusalem was on a humble donkey. This triumphal entry was perhaps concurrent and in contrast with the entry of Roman soldiers on white horses, marching to trumpets as they come into another part of the city. In the mind and heart of Jesus, if there is to be a restored kingdom, it will be one rooted in the values of peace and justice, not autocratic power and the oppression of the poor.

---

11. I have been helped by literally dozens of books that address this subject. I'll mention one here, since the author does call Jesus an apocalyptic prophet: Ehrman, *Jesus: Apocalyptic Prophet*.

There is a second group of passages that ascribe the title of "son of man" (*ben'adam*) to Jesus, referencing a passage in the book of Daniel: "I saw one like a human being [son of man] coming with the clouds of heaven. And he came to the Ancient One and was presented before him. To him was given dominion and glory and kingship, that all peoples, nations, and languages should serve him. His dominion is everlasting dominion that shall not pass away, and his kingship is one that shall never be destroyed" (Dan 7:13–14). It is the case that Jesus does reference himself on many occasions as the Son of Man (or human) although, in most cases, these sayings of Jesus are not a reference to the vision expressed in the book of Daniel. He is not claiming that he is the one whose dominion is everlasting and shall not pass away, and his kingship shall never be destroyed. However, it was likely that those surrounding Jesus may have understood him as one "coming in the clouds of heaven."

There is a passage in Matthew 13 that casts light on the notion of kingship in which Jesus explains the parable of the mustard seed to his disciples. The author of Matthew, using the phrase "kingdom of the heavens," does explain that the Son of Man sows good seeds and that the crop from these seeds is the faithful band of children of the kingdom. The weeds, however, are the children of the evil one, and their product will be collected and burned. The Son of Man is active in this parabolic picture of the future, but there is no immediate claim by Jesus that he is this son of man referenced in Daniel. Even if one reads these passages in a way that indicates that Jesus made such a claim, it may be difficult to sustain the view that it is an authentic saying of Jesus, in that the author of Matthew does have a clear point of view in his writing. In this passage and some others, as for example Matthew 24:29–31, Mark 13:24–27, and Luke 21:25–28, we read that Jesus speaks about the coming Son of Man, but does not claim to be that messianic person. Some of his followers and a second generation of Christians may have thought of him in this frame of reference, but I remain unconvinced that the description from Daniel was central to the self-understanding of Jesus. It is more likely that he may have pointed to this expectation and called upon his followers to be ready.

A third set of passages, also pointing to the future, has to do with sayings attributed to Jesus about the temple. The temple had a primary place in shaping the beliefs and practices of the Jewish people in the time of Jesus.[12] Since the reign of David, it was viewed as the place where God could be encountered and truly worshiped. When the temple was destroyed, there

---

12. Sanders, *Jesus and Judaism*, provides a good description of the place of the temple(s) in Jewish life. See, for example, his review of the sayings about the temple in the Gospels (Sanders, *Jesus and Judaism*, 71–76).

was a longing for a new temple that would be the symbol of the restoration of the nation and the central place of faith in the nation. Jesus spoke about the temple, and toward the end of his public ministry, he used the temple as a place to proclaim his message.[13] The primary incident recorded in the Gospels (Matt 21:12–17; Mark 11:15–19; Luke 19:45–48; and John 2:13–22) is referred to as the "cleansing of the temple." On this occasion, Jesus challenges the practices occurring in the temple and says, "My house shall be called a house of prayer for all the nations, but you have made it a den of robbers" (Matt 21:13). In John's Gospel, Jesus adds the comment in response to a question: "Destroy this Temple, and in three days I will raise it up" (John 2:19). The interpretation of these exchanges and the cleansing of the temple have been intense and varied. I want to note three dimensions of the attempts to explain the meaning of the "cleansing of the temple," specifically how they are germane to our subject of the way Jesus speaks about hope in the future.

1. One point of view (perhaps the dominant or at least the most popular one) is that Jesus was saying that the practices in the temple, and that of the moneychangers in particular, were unfair. The exchange rate, for example, may have favored the moneychangers. In addition, such practices, including the selling of sacrificial animals (doves), turned certain sections of the temple into a secular market and made it difficult for poor people to participate because they could not afford to buy the sacrificial animals. So Jesus says, "you have made it a den of robbers." The reservation about this point of view is that what was happening was fundamental to the practices of worship in the temple. Alms and sacrifices were expected, and the moneychangers made these practices possible within the temple. So why, then, did Jesus overturn their tables and challenge their practices? Perhaps the simple explanation of people being treated unfairly and making the temple secular partially explains the prophetic actions of Jesus. Other interpreters suggest that more than just the challenge of unfair commercial exchange in a religious setting was at stake in the prophetic action of Jesus.[14] It may be important to note this concern, but it was not likely the only reason for the action of Jesus.

---

13. The account of the interaction of Jesus in the temple occurs at a different time in the Gospel of John (2:13–25).

14. There were separate sections in the temple that allowed for normal human activity, and other inner space devoted to the worship and presence of God. In addition, there really wasn't a clear separation of sacred and secular in the thought of people at that time, although there were separate sections in the temple.

2. A second set of explanations for the incident focuses more on the comment of Jesus about destroying the temple and then restoring it in three days. It is relatively clear that Jesus is not speaking about bricks and boards, but the symbolic character of temple. In his role as a prophet, Jesus is saying that the temple no longer really meets the religious needs of the people and that he will attempt to restore the true spiritual meaning of the temple. The passage in John states that Jesus was speaking about his death and resurrection (in three days), but this comment attributed to Jesus in John's Gospel clearly reflects a much later time period. It is more likely the understanding of the new Christian community, and may not be an authentic statement of Jesus, although this is the belief of the early Christian community.

3. A third group of interpretations of this cleansing of the temple has elements of the first two, but speaks more broadly about both the identity and aim of Jesus. It affirms that Jesus is bringing in a new era in the religious life of the people. At the heart of this new perspective is reclaiming both the purity and ethical dimension of Torah. The temple, in the view of Jesus, has failed in its spiritual mission, and the practices in the temple are a mere formality, not the expression of the true spirituality inherent in Torah. Some Christian interpreters have argued that Jesus is speaking about that which became the Christian faith with some foreknowledge about his death and resurrection. I am more inclined to stick with the view that Jesus the prophet was speaking about the urgency for the Jewish people to follow the true practices of both the purity and ethical expectations of Torah and not let incidentals get in the way.

One outcome of this incident in the life of Jesus, especially if it occurred in the last week of his life, is that it was used against him in his trial before the high priest. Matthew records that two witnesses come to the trial and testify that Jesus said, "I am able to destroy this Temple of God and to build it in three days." Jesus is asked how it is possible to destroy and rebuild the temple, which misses the metaphorical use of the language. The high priest then tells Jesus, "I put you under oath before the living God, so tell us if you are the Messiah, the Son of God." The passage continues, and Jesus answers, "You have said so. But I tell you, from now on you will see the Son of Man seated at the right hand of Power and coming on the clouds of heaven." The high priest calls this answer blasphemy and says that Jesus deserves death. It is difficult to fully reconstruct this conversation and the many others that occurred during these two days. Let me suggest three points that might serve as a summary:

- Jesus did present a genuine challenge to the practices of Judaism and said there was a better way. He did not speak in opposition to the Law, but challenged the way it was being interpreted. He humanizes the Law and interprets it for the welfare of the people, not as a way to control the people and catch them as they broke the law. He especially challenges those parts of the Hebrew Bible that have become orthodox rituals, and those passages that are narrowly tribal and cultic. He spoke about the reign of God as the revolutionary invitation and alternative way of following Torah and YHWH.

- He saw himself as the prophetic representative and spokesperson of that better way. Jesus understands his mission and identity in reference to the reign of God and invites all to follow. The Gospel of Mark, as we have noted, expresses it the following way: "Now after John was arrested, Jesus came to Galilee, proclaiming the good news of God, and saying, 'The time is fulfilled, and the Kingdom of God has come near; repent, and believe the good news'" (Mark 1:14–15).

- The Jewish leaders were offended and, ultimately, in the back and forth of authority, the Romans condemned Jesus for treason under Pontius Pilate. Jesus died for his mission. Christians claim that this death was in fact the victory of love and the invitation to accept the power and presence of God.

The final set of passages having to do with the teaching of Jesus about the kingdom of God and giving hope to a despairing people has to do with what has become a major Christian teaching: the second coming of Christ. Following the crucifixion of Jesus and the new faith of the Christian community that Jesus rose from the dead, defeating sin and death, there was a developing belief in some parts of the new church that Jesus would return or come again. The belief is expressed in the Gospel of Matthew and linked to both the title "son of man" and the image drawn from the passage in Daniel 7.[15] In a symbolic way, the author of Matthew says: "Immediately after the suffering of those days the sun will be darkened, and the moon will not give light; the stars will fall from heaven, and the powers of heaven will be shaken. Then the sign of the Son of Man will appear in heaven, and then all the tribes of the earth will mourn, and they will see 'the Son of Man coming on the clouds of heaven' with power and great glory" (Matt 24:29–30). This passage, using apocalyptic language, does identify Jesus as the Son of Man and asserts that he will return in power and glory.

---

15. The view is also found in Mark 13:14–23 and Luke 17:23–24, 37, and 21:25–28.

From these passages in the Synoptic Gospels and other literature, parts of the early church did begin to think that Jesus would come again and alter and perhaps change and complete the purposeful course of history. Other parts of the new Christian community were content to say that what Jesus had accomplished in his death and resurrection was a firm basis for hope. It is well beyond the scope of this volume to address the complex issue of the belief in the second coming of Jesus.[16] There is little doubt that Jesus was aware of literature that spoke about God's dramatic entrance into human history, but the accounts we have of what Jesus said and did do not give us a clear and complete picture of his view of the future. With lingering questions, I have learned to be content with what we can know about what he said and did and allow faith in a loving and sovereign God to give us hope and carry us the rest of the way.

Positions in the Debate:
Historical Views of the Kingdom of God.

In Christian theology, the kingdom of God and the second coming of Jesus have tended to be discussed separately with some commentary on how they are related. As a general rule, the kingdom of God has been understood as a more comprehensive term describing the reign of God in human history, tracing the coming, presence, and reign of God in the Hebrew Bible and the writings of early Judaism, and then profoundly present in Jesus.[17] The second coming, or parousia, has been understood as part of the culmination of the reign of God, a period that alters the course of history described in various ways and in different patterns, using apocalyptic and eschatological language pointing to the end times. As with nearly all issues related to the future, especially the future of humankind (and indeed, even the cosmos), there have been a variety of views. I want to briefly sketch them in three patterns and then suggest a spirit that should prevail as these issues are discussed. It is important that these conversations take place among those who feel called to reflect on this aspect of the teaching of Jesus, expanded by Paul, and reflected upon by other authors, including the author of the book of Revelation. But as they do, there will be differences of opinion, and a measure of grace and humility will make them more informative and nurturing.

---

16. A scholarly and clear account of how this belief developed and its place in understanding Jesus is in Allison, *Constructing Jesus*. See esp. chapter 2, "The Eschatology of Jesus" (Allison, *Constructing Jesus*, 31–164).

17. See, for example, Beasley-Murray, *Jesus and the Kingdom of God*, 3-68.

One of these patterns has been the conviction that what occurred in the life, teachings, death, and resurrection of Jesus was fully adequate as God's loving approach and engagement with the human family. These events were conclusive, and were all that was necessary for the full understanding and wellbeing of humankind in reference to their relationship with God. This view is often referred to as realized eschatology. A fine British New Testament scholar, C. H. Dodd, writing in the mid-twentieth century, is often associated with this position.[18] Dodd does acknowledge that there are other biblical passages and points of view within the early Christian community that speak about the a second coming of Christ, but after a careful reading, Dodd suggests that these points of view were present in the hope of Second Temple Palestinian Judaism and the apocalyptic literature of this era.[19] They are honest expressions of hope, but may be interpreted as being fulfilled by the life and events of Jesus. Respectful of this literature and that within the New Testament itself, he nevertheless maintains that the life and these redemptive events of Jesus are sufficient. With the author of John's Gospel, it is not only enough, but a wonderful blessing that another, the Advocate, the Holy Spirit, will come to comfort and empower the Christian community to survive and thrive.[20] The Word has come and spoken with clarity and deed; the human family has the message and action of God. In many ways, the majority of the Christian church has generally lived by this outlook, although it occasionally acknowledges that a more dramatic entrance of God into human history is yet to come.

Perhaps a more prevalent view for the early Christian community, continuing into the present in both thoughtful and in some cases quite ideological fashion, is that we should live with expectation of the return of Christ at any moment. We must be ready! In some ways, the crucifixion and resurrection, while redemptive and transforming, did not bring history to a just and final form. There is more to come. The apostle Paul speaks about this time in what is the earliest document in the New Testament, 1 Thessalonians. He writes: "But we do not want you to be uniformed, brothers and sisters, about those who have died, so that you may not grieve as others do who have no hope . . . Now concerning the times and the seasons . . . You know that the day of the Lord will come like a thief in the night . . . But you beloved, are not in darkness for that day to surprise life a thief."[21] This

---

18. In Dodd, *Founder of Christianity*, Jesus is described as having completed his vocation of expressing the will and way of God to the human family.

19. Dodd's other books include *The Epistle of Paul to the Romans*, *The Meaning of Paul for Today*, and *The Parables of the Kingdom*.

20. John 16.

21. 1 Thess 4:13; 5:1–2, 4a.

point of view, anticipating the return of Christ at any moment, is expressed in many evangelical churches, and remains in a hopeful form in the documents of most of the mainline churches. In times of crisis (and we seem to continually live in them), the message does bring an apocalyptic hope rather than one that is present in the more progressive churches which, in one form or another, believe that it is possible with God's empowerment to create a more just and humane society and world. The point of view that we should live with the expectation that Christ will return at any moment is often articulated around accompanying events such as the millennium, the tribulation, and the rapture, with debates about the order of events at the end of time. The debates are honest, and the belief in these coming events is very sincere, although I confess to finding it hard to view the future in this way.

A third view, in some ways drawing the best from both of the previous positions mentioned, is what has often referred to as "the already-not yet" belief. In many ways, this point of view is the living reality in the majority of Christian churches around the world, although not always expressed in the language of "already not yet."[22] This position affirms that Jesus came with the clear message of the kingdom of God and spoke about how his ministry was the expression and realization of the reign of God. The reign of God is already present, and profoundly so in the life and ministry of Jesus, although the ministry of Jesus and our continuation of this ministry as followers of Jesus have not brought the reign of God to its full culmination. As Christians, we do follow the way of Jesus, attempting to show compassion to all those in need. We work diligently for a more just and peaceful social order. We engage in ministry to expand the realm of God by working toward creating a society and a world in which the deepest values of the biblical faith, and indeed the values of nearly all the great religious traditions of the world, will be a reality. But taught by such wise and respected scholars as Reinhold Niebuhr, I (we) know that our work will never end. Indeed, as we observe our world, we are drawn to the conclusion that, while there are committed and moral people who labor in and for love, the condition of society and the world will not ever become fully just and peaceful.[23]

---

22. There are numerable books that articulate this point of view. I have been helped by the position of George E. Ladd, whose writing was published in a previous generation. His book *The Blessed Hope*, published in 1956, is a clear statement of the "already not yet" perspective.

23. For example, see Niebuhr, *Moral Man and Immoral Society*, for a commentary on how an individual may have a compassionate and sensitive conscience, but collectives such as the state do not have a conscience.

As I have reflected on these views, continued my study of the biblical literature, and read widely about the hope and the future, I have found some peace of mind in the following insights and affirmations:[24]

1. The first is that, as a Christian person, I must take the Bible seriously, but need not accept it as free from error and interpret it in a literal fashion. I affirm the fundamental hermeneutical principle that those who wrote this literature were inspired by God to express their faith in the best possible way and guide others in their writing. Yet they drew upon the worldview of their time and used the descriptive categories that were available to them in their culture and language. We too must do the same, taking great care as we proceed. In doing so, I do not need to use apocalyptic language, nor should I even reflect in an absolute way about the future of humankind and of the cosmos. My concern, as it was the concern of those who wrote in the literature of the Bible, is to speak about the central theme of hope and to attempt to express this positive outlook in ways that encourage those who live with fear and despair. I sincerely believe that is what Jesus did and said, although accessing it in the exact and precise language of Jesus is not possible. I believe as well that Paul and the author of the book of Revelation were trying to give hope to despairing people, although with language and concepts that are not as meaningful and persuasive to us as they were to their contemporaries. We are able to speak about hope within our frame of reference.

2. The second insight and affirmation that comes from this topic and the biblical literature is that I should live with a deep commitment to use my life and limited talents to work toward the expansion of the reign of God in all aspects of my immediate environment. In addition, I should lend a hand in creating a more just and peaceful world. I join with others from other cultures and religious traditions to shape public policy and social structures that are just and compassionate. I give myself to the reign of God as I seek to find ways to incarnate the common good. I need to find new and creative avenues to show compassion and give hope to those living with despair.

3. The third insight and affirmation is that the assurance of hope need not be expressed in the culture and language of a previous era, but resides in the foundational belief of our faith that our hope is dependent on the unlimited love of God. I affirm that the God who is love chose to express this love in many ways, and obviously so in the first-century

---

24. I had been informed by Moltmann, *Theology of Hope*.

Jewish prophet Jesus of Nazareth. I follow his example, live with the harsh realities of life, and approach them not so much with the optimism that all will be well because of human effort, but in the hope that the God of love is present and gives healing, comfort, vision, and meaning to all of life.

Study Resources

Discussion Questions

1. Do you think that when Jesus spoke about the kingdom of God he was describing something that was occurring in the present or was he pointing to what God might do in the future? Or was the reference to both the present and the future?
2. What do you think was the role of Jesus in bringing in and expanding the reign of God?
3. Are there ways that we might help expand the reign of God? If so, what are they?
4. Do you think that the use of violence is ever an option for expanding the reign of God? Do the means of violence justify the ends of a more just and peaceful society?
5. As you speak about Jesus, what terms do you use to describe him? Do you think that the term "messiah" is a good way to identify Jesus?

Terms and Concepts

1. Kingdom of God: The reign of God in the sense of creating a realm in which the will and way of God will prevail.
2. Hope: The belief that there are new conditions that are in the future that will make life better, usually associated with the way the power and presence of God will change our situation.
3. Apocalyptic: terms and language that describe the dramatic entrance of God into human history, in some cases associated with the end times.
4. Eschatology: The study of the end of the world as we know it, associated in Christian thought with the second coming of Christ.

5. Parousia: a Greek term that references the second coming of Christ, often associated with hope.

Suggested Reading

Allison, Dale C., Jr. *Constructing Jesus: Memory, Imagination, and History.* Grand Rapids: Baker Academic, 2010.
Beasley-Murray. G. R. *Jesus and the Kingdom of God.* Grand Rapids: Eerdmans, 1986.
Ehrman, Bart D. *Jesus: Apocalyptic Prophet of the New Millennium.* New York: Oxford University Press, 1999.
Fredriksen, Paula. *Jesus of Nazareth: King of the Jews.* New York: Vintage, 1999.
Ladd, George E. *The Blessed Hope.* Grand Rapids: Eerdmans, 1956.

6

Dealing with the Realities of Conflict

WE ARE EXPLORING WAYS to understand the gracious invitation of Jesus to all people to endorse a way of life that is God-centered. We have maintained that this way of life will enable us to flourish in many ways. We should also note that it is a radical invitation in that it asks us to fundamentally change the direction of our lives. If we say yes, a full commitment will be necessary. There will be a *metanoia*, a total conversion involving repentance and a new dedication to follow the will and way of God. It means that we must learn how to carefully manage our evolutionary needs and give up persuasive cultural values and norms. It means that we will have to say no to our tendencies to want power over others, to pursue possessions, and to long for attention and praise.[1] It is the affirmation of a new way of life. It is to be open to the reign of God and to ask the kingdom to come as we pray in the Lord's Prayer. Jesus is quite pointed in his offer in reference to the renunciation of negative and harmful tendencies. He then underlines that we must give ourselves to a new way of life.

As part of the Sermon on the Mount, the author of Matthew's Gospel quotes Jesus as saying: "But strive first for the kingdom of God and his righteousness, and all these things will be given to you as well" (Matt 6:33). Jesus is quite clear that, as we say yes to the invitation of Jesus and receive the power and presence of God into our lives (the kingdom or reign of God), our lives will be transformed and our basic needs will be met. The passage

---

1. Jesus said, "Those who find their life will lose it, and those who lose their life for my sake will find it" (Matt 10:39). The self-centered life is a life lost, but the God-centered life is to find the true meaning of life.

continues: "So do not worry about tomorrow, for tomorrow will bring worries of its own. Today's trouble is enough for today" (Matt 6:34). Note the two major points made by Jesus about mindfulness from the larger section of Scripture from which these verses are taken:[2]

1. We need not yield to excessive fear and anxiety, or worry about food, clothing, and other basic needs in life. After all, the birds of the air neither sow nor reap and are taken care of by God, and the lilies of the field are effortlessly more beautifully attired than Solomon in all of his glory.

2. Instead of fear, worry, and self-destructive habits, we should seek the God-centered life in which the power and presence of God reigns. It is liberating and fulfilling. The implication is that we will find a good measure of peace and purpose and not be tyrannized by worry and anxiety. We can trust that God will provide for our basic needs. Being reassured, we will then begin to flourish as increasingly mature persons, give the highest priority to loving others, and use our God-given talents to serve the common good. We learn to give rather than to receive.

This invitation of Jesus is a radical one in that it goes against our natural tendencies to be excessively worried about our own welfare. We are offered an alternative narrative. The commitment to the reign of God in our lives will set us free from being exclusively self-centered and liberate us from the tendency to endorse the norms of our culture that invite us to seek power over others, wealth and possessions, and ego-gratification. We underlined in chapter 4 that this new life asks us to live an ethical life, one in which we internalize and practice the values of integrity, compassion, and justice. We maintained in chapter 5 that God gives what God asks, and that as we endorse the reign God in our lives, we will be empowered to love, to be a person for others, and to pattern our life based on the model of Jesus.

The Challenge of Dealing with Conflicts

One of the most difficult challenges of leading the God-centered life is related to the way we deal with conflicts. And there will be conflicts within as we commit to the God-centered life and yet feel the tug of the self-centered life. There will be conflicts with others whose values, goals, and priorities are different from ours. We will face conflicts within as we endeavor to follow

---

2. Matt 6:25–34.

the Golden Rule, yet often fail. There are conflicts as we seek to extend the reign of God by working toward a more just and peaceful society, yet encounter seemingly insurmountable problems. And there are conflicts as we encounter the threats to our welfare, sense criticism of our decisions and actions, and feel defeated and struggle with a poor self-image. We are not able to speak about all of the conflicts we may encounter in life in that it would require another book (or two), but we can be selective and address those areas of inner tension, threat, and conflict that were present in and spoken about in the life and teachings of Jesus and where his guidance is quite specific. An integral part of the invitation of Jesus is that, as we receive the reign of God by faith into our lives, we are led and taught how to deal with conflict with integrity, fairness, forgiveness, and compassion.[3]

The Domain of Power and Authority

One of the areas of conflict that we observe in the life of Jesus and about which he teaches often occurs within the domain of power and authority. In this domain, the basic question is who has power and authority, and how are they administered in the settings in which we live? I write during the Trump presidency, in which these concerns about power and authority are central to the thinking of a large part of the country's population. In a vast nation like the United States, these issues are very complex and engage both Houses of Congress, state governments, and a range of national, regional, and local committees. As we attempt to resolve the issues, it usually requires extensive interviews, evidence, and documentation. Depending on the importance of the issue, we can anticipate a steady stream of news from the press. We ask, "Does the President have too much power, and does he exercise this power within the guidelines of the Constitution and the accepted norms of the office of the President?" As we face these questions that are so much in our consciousness, it affects our behavior and impacts our relationships. For example, we may even have to be careful what we say in conversations, fearing that we might offend a close friend with different views.

As we look inward, we ask if and how our faith might guide us. Is it possible to receive some guidance and answers to these questions as we study the ways that Jesus dealt with the issues of power and authority? Jesus taught about these concerns with wise guidance and healing insight. The people who heard his teaching and met him in person expressed gratitude

---

3. Golemen, *Emotional Intelligence*, has several sections on how to deal with conflict in a healthy and constructive way. See, for example, pages 264–67, the section entitled "A Point of Contention."

and affirmation. He was a truly charismatic teacher whose words were liberating and transforming. One fundamental component of his ministry in which the issues of power and authority emerged was his healing ministry. He was a compassionate healer who cared deeply about the suffering of others. He became a channel for the healing power of God. People were healed of their emotional and physical illnesses. Again and again, questions were raised about power and authority regarding when and how he healed.

In addition, he was a forceful and articulate prophet who boldly spoke truth to power and established authority. He questioned some of the practices of the religious establishment and asked if the spiritual needs of the people were being met. In part because there was no real separation of religion and the state, he called into question whether the governments were pursuing the common good, maintaining justice, and meeting the basic needs of the people. The questions he asked created conflict.

It was inevitable as Jesus carried out these ministries that there would be questions about what he said and did. These questions came primarily from those in positions of power and authority. He was remarkably free to question the established patterns of power if the basic needs of people were not being met. As he did, he was often asked the fundamental questions about power and authority. We read that,

> One day while he was teaching, Pharisees and teachers of the law were sitting near by (they had come from every village of Galilee and Judea and from Jerusalem); and the power of the Lord was with him to heal. Just then some men came, carrying a paralyzed man on a bed. They were trying to bring him in and lay him before Jesus; but finding no way to bring him in because of the crowd, they went up on the roof and let him down with his bed through the tiles into the middle of the crowd in front of Jesus. When he saw their faith, he said, "Friend, your sins are forgiven you." Then the scribes and Pharisees began to question, "Who is this who is speaking blasphemy?" When Jesus perceived their questionings, he answered them, "Why do you raise such questions in your hearts? Which is easier, to say, 'Your sins are forgiven you,' or to say, 'Stand up and walk?' But so that you may know that the Son of Man has authority on earth to forgive sins," he said to the one who was paralyzed, "I say to you, stand up and take your bed and go to your home." The man did go home, glorifying God, and the people were amazed. The comment at the end of this day was, "We have seen strange things today." (Luke 5:17–24, 26b)

The issues of power and authority are clearly present in this exchange, although the passage concludes with an emphasis on the issue of authority. Does Jesus need to have the sanction of the religious leaders to say that he forgives sins? Or is Jesus saying that God forgives sins and the healed paralytic may go in peace? The conflict has begun with those in authority as Jesus reassures the paralytic that his sins are forgiven. They ask, "Who can forgive sins but God alone?"

There is another passage that underlines the issues of both power and authority as well. The author of Luke's Gospel writes,

> One day when he was teaching the people in the Temple and telling them the good news, the chief priests and the scribes came with the elders and said to him, "Tell us by what authority are you doing these things? Who is it that gave you this authority?" He answered them, "I will ask you a question, and you tell me: Did the baptism of John come from heaven, or was it of human origin?" They discussed it with one another, saying, "If we say from heaven he will say, 'Why did you not believe him?' But if we say, 'Of human origin, all of the people will stone us, for they are convinced that John was a prophet.'" So they answered that they did not know where it came from. Then Jesus said to them, "Neither will I tell you by what authority I am doing these things." (Luke 20:1–8)

Jesus, of course, believed that the baptism offered by John was from God.

What wisdom might be gleaned from these two incidents in the ministry of Jesus? As we read the stories, we get few simple answers, but there is great wisdom and usually a few more questions to ponder.[4] Let me suggest of list of attitudes and actions of Jesus that appear to be present in these stories, which might guide us:[5]

- Again and again, Jesus assumes that he was guided and being used by God. It is from God that he receives power and gains authority to heal. He is especially sensitive in discerning the will and way of God, and has an openness and receptivity to the Spirit of God. It is this deep spirituality that we observe in Jesus that we must cultivate and sustain if we are to discern the will of God in conflicted situations. It is especially important in those cases that are ambiguous and may be argued

---

4. Kirkpatrick, *Communication in the Church*, is especially helpful in finding healthy ways to deal with issues of power and authority in the church setting (Kirkpatrick, *Communication in the Church*, 117–58).

5. Margaret Benefiel has an expanded treatment of leadership in reference to conflict in her book *The Soul of the Leader* (110–16).

wisely and logically either way. I fully acknowledge that there is great risk in saying that what one is doing, especially over against the views of others, is because of being led by the Spirit of God. It is all too easy to call your own inclinations and needs in decision-making a message from God, when in fact you are just trying to get your own way and meet your own needs. There may be no divine guidance. Careful discernment is essential. Consulting with other people who have integrity and whom you trust is one way to check your own inclinations. Jesus was confident he was following the will of God. Never do his actions reflect even a trace of self-serving.

- The fundamental values guiding the actions of Jesus in these situations are unlimited love and compassion. He genuinely cares about the ill person and wants to relieve suffering. Jesus appears to be saying that healing the sick and relieving suffering are the primary values that must be honored in these situations, even if there is some conflict over power and authority. Jesus believes that God comes down on the side of love and compassion rather than choosing sides and spending time in debates about power and authority.

- Jesus is concerned about the body and the soul of the person whom he encounters. He wants the ill people to be healed, but in the case in which the sick person is passed down to him from the roof, it is recorded that Jesus initially says to the sick person that his sins are forgiven. Jesus heals the soul, and then he heals the body. This passage teaches us that Jesus is interested in whole-person healing; that the soul needs to be close to God and the body needs to function well. Jesus uses both his pastoral skills and his healing gifts.[6]

- In these two cases recorded in the Gospel of Luke, Jesus is not openly antagonistic toward the priests and scribes (lawyers and experts in the Law). Neither is he fearful of authority nor intimidated by their power. There is no defensiveness in his behavior. He does what he believes is the primary task of his ministry; he loves and heals the paralytics. He has complete authenticity and integrity in his actions, and does not get sidetracked by excessive debate and self-doubt.[7]

---

6. I have been informed by the way the Myers-Briggs Inventory may be used to help us understand the gifts we way have in resolving conflicts in constructive ways. See Meyers and Meyers, *Gifts Differing*. Understanding one's own personal style and those of others in conflict situations enables us to make less conflicted decisions.

7. Jesus has what Daniel Goleman calls social intelligence. The Gospel accounts, although very brief, point to the ability of Jesus to manage very complex social environments in which a number of different styles and points of view are present. See

- There is a remaining question of whether Jesus' action was taken in part for the sake of countering the established authority, in that he believes that those in authority are failing in their responsibilities. Was he in fact engaging in an act of civil disobedience? Or was he simply caring in a compassionate way for suffering people? I am inclined to say that this issue cannot fully be resolved with these two cases. There needs to be a review of the several other accounts in which he has conflict with officials over power and authority. I suspect there may be some justification for Jesus to push back against the laws and norms of the culture and use a form of civil disobedience. He cared about individuals, and also about the social structures that impacted the lives of individuals. But, for the most part, we observe Jesus being fair to all the people involved in these stories, although he may have been treated unfairly. His behavior as he encounters those in need is always respectful, caring, helpful, and appropriate. In general, as he interacts with those in authority, we see no evidence that he primarily wants to antagonize those in authority; the conflict arises when they challenge Jesus, who is healing and helping those who are in need.[8]

- There may be no one single, simple answer about resolving conflicts on issues of power and authority for all situations. We are wise to use the criteria of love and compassion as we encounter the kinds of situations with which Jesus was dealing as he faced conflicts over power and authority. Some conflict will often be present, and even when it is not obviously present, the issues of power may be just below the surface. We will be close to the right approach when we act with integrity, respect, and unlimited love.

- There are times when we might like a simple and straightforward answer from the biblical accounts. The risk, however, is that if such an answer were given, it might not take into account the complexity of the situations that are described. What we often have in the Gospels are stories that have only limited details, and we do not always find it easy to draw from the stories a universal principle. But what these stories do for us is to invite reflection and stimulate our imagination. It is often the story or the parable in the teaching of Jesus that is so thought-provoking; it engages us in a deep and profound way. We often learn

---

Goleman, *Social Intelligence*, 223–310.

8. As we read these stories, we do need to take into account that the Gospel authors may have an agenda which surfaces as the story describes what Jesus does and says. For example, Jesus likely had more respect for the scribes and Pharisees than is evident in the account in Matthew 23.

more as we are taught by parable and story rather than when we are taught by propositions. We receive wisdom rather than a detailed list of dos and don'ts.

The Domain of Values

We now turn to another dimension of our study of how Jesus deals with conflicts. It is implicit in the one we have already studied, but needs to surface as another primary cause of tension needing conflict resolution. It is the issue of whose values should prevail. As I interact with family, work on church committees seeking to make wise decisions, observe governmental agencies make policy, and watch our nation at election time, I observe a conflicted discussion about values. For nearly five years, our family lived in Alaska and watched the conflict between those who wanted to expand the petroleum industry and those who wanted to preserve and protect the patterns of native Alaskan culture, the beautiful forests, and the remarkable wildlife of the region. It was a conflict between those who favored economic development and those who wanted to preserve the natural order and the beauty of the environment. Politicians weighed in on the question of which values should prevail, and as one might expect, large corporations encouraged further development, and Alaska natives and many other citizens argued for the preservation of the natural environment.

As we read the stories about Jesus in the Gospels, we often observe a conflict of values. In many cases, the conflict was with the established authority over the interpretation of Torah.[9] It is sometimes maintained that Jesus moved beyond the Law and taught a religion of grace. There was certainly the presence of grace in the ministry of Jesus. It is profoundly present in the teaching of Paul. However, neither Jesus nor Paul fundamentally discounted the value of the Law, but called for alternative ways of understanding and interpreting it. In particular, Jesus remained faithful to his Jewish faith, and often humanized the Law and interpreted it in a way that nurtures the spiritual and ethical life. He opposed a view of the Law that had become institutional legalism, a series of rules and regulations that lead to guilt or self-righteousness, and protected the established social order. Jesus understood that the Law is the gift of grace, guides people, and leads them into healthy patterns of life. He viewed the Law as more charismatic than institutional. John's Gospel summarizes this point of view by giving credence to the Law and interpreting the way in which Jesus supplements and completes

---

9. Or the Tanakh (sometimes spelled Takhan) meaning the Hebrew Scriptures.

the value of the Law: "The law indeed was given through Moses; grace and truth came through Jesus Christ" (1:17).

One of the most important dimensions of the Law was the Sabbath, a day of rest and restoration for the people. As time went along in the history of the Jewish people, this part of the Law received amplification and development, perhaps with the best of intentions to guide the people. But the regulations about what one could do and shouldn't do on the Sabbath became numerous and detailed. The Gospels record the way Jesus challenged the regulations because on occasion they overwhelmed people, made them feel guilty if all of them were not followed, and did not improve their lives, but burdened them. As Jesus was teaching in one of the synagogues on the Sabbath, he met a handicapped woman. "She was bent over and was quite unable to stand up straight. When Jesus saw her, he called her over and said, 'Woman, you are set free from your ailment.' When he laid his hands on her, immediately she stood up straight and began praising God." There was a strong reaction. "But the leader of the synagogue, indignant because Jesus cured on the Sabbath, kept saying to the crowd, 'There are six days on which work ought to be done; come on those days and be cured, and not on Sabbath day.'"[10] But Jesus answered him and noted that people lead their livestock to water on the Sabbath. Isn't this woman as important as the donkey? The people in the synagogue supported Jesus and rejoiced in the healing of the woman. With careful reflection, we learn from this story at least three primary points.

1. We learn that the fundamental value of Jesus is the health and well-being of the woman he meets in the synagogue. The leader of the synagogue, somewhat ironically, is so caught up in the rules and regulations imposed by the Sabbath observance that he forgets that the Law was made for the welfare of the people. The Sabbath is for the good of the people and should not lock them into a prison of detailed legalism. The very meeting in which this event occurred was designed to improve the lives of the people. The value conflict is between those who understand the Law as a means to nurture and guide the people, and those for whom the Law is the detailed control of the lives of the people. Jesus is clear that his value is compassion for the handicapped woman. The leader of the synagogue fails to see that loving-kindness is integral to the law and designed to improve the life of the faithful.

2. Jesus has the courage to challenge the understanding of the Law that prevents the expression of compassion and the pursuit of justice by

---

10. Luke 13:10–17.

a controlling legalism. He is taking on the established order and will face resistance. He values the welfare of this woman, and indeed all of those in need of healing and health, over a tightly controlled religious observance. He becomes prophetic in challenging a preferred cultic practice and tribal self-certitude and was likely aware that such a challenge might later be used against him. He has the courage to express and practice his deepest values of love, compassion, and justice.

3. What is not said in so many words is that Jesus was also inviting the gathered community in the synagogue to begin developing a moral code that is rooted in the identity and character of their lives. He is nurturing a mature outlook that chooses the good and just from within a fully developed moral compass rather an orientation that merely follows external rules. He is saying that the deep teachings of compassion and justice in the Law must be internalized and become a part of one's character. One must be on the developmental path that leads them to become a person who loves deeply and acts justly, not just one who obeys a tribal norm. Jesus invites and encourages maturity.

There are many other stories in the Gospels that reflect a conflict about values. One in particular that might be helpful to us, given the commodity culture in which we live, sets up a values conflict between the spiritual life and the pursuit of wealth. The version of this story in Mark's Gospel (Mark 10:17–27)[11] begins:

> As he was setting out on a journey, a man ran up and knelt before him, and asked, "Good Teacher, what must I do to inherit eternal life?" Jesus said to him, "Why do you call me good? No one is good but God alone. You know the commandments: You shall not murder; You shall not commit adultery; You shall not steal; You shall not bear false witness; You shall not defraud; Honor your father and mother." He said to him, "Teacher, I have kept all these since my youth." Jesus, looking at him, loved him, and said, "You lack one thing; go, sell what you own, and give the money to the poor, and you will have treasure in heaven; then come follow me." When he heard this, he was shocked and went away grieving, for he had many possessions.

The disciples observed this conversation and wondered what Jesus meant as he spoke with this wealthy individual. Jesus explained to them how hard it is for a rich person to enter the kingdom of God. He said to them: "It

---

11. The story is also told in Matthew 19:16–30 and Luke 18:18–30. The authors of these Gospels are likely following the account in Mark.

is easier for a camel to go through the eye of a needle than for someone who is rich to enter the kingdom of God" (Matt 19:24). As we unpack this story, there are many lessons; I want to emphasize two of them:

1. The first is that the value conflict in this account is between giving one's life to the will and way of God (the kingdom of God) or accumulating and holding on to one's possessions as the fundamental value in life. Jesus does love the person with whom he is speaking, and he takes the question about inheriting eternal life seriously. The rich person is asking a basic question about the meaning of life. Jesus does not give a trivial answer; he says you won't get there if having possessions is your deepest value. There is a value decision to be made between following God or seeking wealth and possessions. It is the same conflict for so many in our present-day commodity culture.

2. Jesus and his followers did live an uncluttered life free of possessions. But the emphasis was not on extreme poverty and sacrifice as the way to be spiritual. It was a way of life that enabled them to carry out their ministry. In fact, the record indicates that there were times when Jesus enjoyed others and shared meals and a glass of wine with good friends. There were sacrifices and suffering, but he did not say that the ascetic life of suffering was the heart of spirituality. What he did say was that the essence of spirituality is to be one with God, to accept the reign of God in one's life, and to follow the will and way of God.

The "rich young ruler," as he is often called, faced a conflict of values and Jesus was direct in his answer. It was not a harsh answer, full of judgment, but one filled with understanding and love. Yet he spoke directly, knowing that the life full of peace and joy does not consist of the abundance of things possessed, but the receiving of the abundance of God's love into one's life.

One of the greatest challenges that Jesus faced in his own life was about value choices. One very obvious illustration of his value choices occurred in the story of the temptations in the wilderness as he prepared himself for his vocation. The description of the choices he faced as he began his ministry may be in part a reflection on what might have occurred in the life of Jesus; it is more of a thoughtful reconstruction in the form of a story than an actual recording of what occurred. The story nevertheless captures the spirit of the choices he made as he began his life's work. While preparing himself for his calling in the wilderness of Judea, he is faced with three possibilities that would have led him away from his vocation. The deepest values of Jesus become clear in this story as he faces the evil one personified. The evil one, *diabolis*, is translated in the New Revised Standard Bible as the devil. This

Greek word, *diabolis*, means "accuser" or "slanderer." It is clear that Jesus is facing one who seeks to take him off course and follow the values inherent in the self-centered life.[12] The story begins,

> Then Jesus was led up by the Spirit into the wilderness to be tempted by the devil. He fasted forty days and forty nights, and afterwards was famished.[13] The tempter came and said to him, "If you are the Son of God, command these stones to become loaves of bread." But he answered, "It is written, 'One does not live by bread alone, but by every word that comes from the mouth of God.'"

Jesus is facing the first temptation designed to turn away from his life's calling. He is essentially invited to arrogantly assume that he can take the place of God and make miracles happen. Instead of following the will and way of God, he is tempted to act like God and perform a miracle that will meet his need for sustenance. He is tempted to pretend that he is God, and because he is famished, he can use his power to make bread out of stones. The devil tells a good lie, but Jesus, given his deep spirituality, does not yield to the abuse of power or to his physical needs. He draws upon his deepest value, his devotion to the will and way of God, and says, "One does not live by bread alone, but by every word that comes from the mouth of God." Tempted by the conflicting value of following a self-centered way, he rejects the values of arrogance and yielding to physical needs and chooses to follow the will and way of God.

The second temptation was also designed to keep Jesus from following his God-given vocation.

> Then the devil took him to the holy city and placed him on the pinnacle of the temple, saying to him, "If you are the Son of God, throw yourself down; for it is written, 'He will command his angels concerning you,' and 'On their hands they bear you up, so that you will not dash your foot against the stone.'" Jesus said to him, "Again it is written, 'Do not put the Lord your God to the test.'"

---

12. I will use the account in Matt 4:1–11. Luke also records this exchange (Luke 4:1–13), and Mark has a brief account (Mark 1:12–13). Many interpreters have interpreted this passage as a reflection on the internal workings within the mind and heart of Jesus, and the account of the story was likely preserved in the oral tradition.

13. The forty-days period of time may not be precise, and this number was used often in the Hebrew Bible for an extended period of time. See Genesis 7:17 in regard to the flood.

Jesus, spiritually discerning as always, resists the temptation that he can tell God what to do. He knows that such an act would be inappropriate. It is not that God "works for us" but that we "work for God." He does not resort to a miraculous action in order to demonstrate that he has divine powers, and he realizes that his deepest value is to yield to the reign of God in his life. Preachers occasionally offend me when they claim to have the power of God. Often when they do, they say that they will ask God for a miraculous intervention and inappropriately promise that it will happen. Jesus knows that he is the servant of God and follows God's guidance, not one who believes he can control what God does or does not do. Jesus is a dedicated follower of God.

The third temptation also invites Jesus to turn away from God's will and choose the values of power and wealth.

> Again the devil took him to a very high mountain and showed him all the kingdoms of the world and their splendor; and he said to him, "All these I will give you, if you fall down and worship me." Jesus said to him, "Away with you, Satan! For it is written, 'Worship the Lord your God, and serve him only.'" Then the devil left him, and suddenly angels came and waited on him.

The third temptation is direct and gets to the heart of the matter. It is the invitation to worship the evil one and to follow a way of life that ignores God and goes the way of the world.[14] Jesus demonstrates that he has clearly made his choice of values. He will worship God and give his life in the service of God's purposes in the world.

According to the Biblical account, we might briefly summarize the values that guide Jesus in the decisions he makes about the meaning of his life.

1. He remains a humble servant of God and refuses to place himself in a divine role. It is not for him to turn stones into bread, even though he is hungry after fasting for forty days and forty nights. His priority was to go into the wilderness to prepare for his divine calling, and fasting was one of the ways he was developing his capacity, his discipline, and his conditioning to deal with the challenges he will face as he takes up

---

14. I admit to have some trouble believing in a personal devil, but I have no trouble identifying with Jesus as he faces these temptations. There is a clear and dangerous pattern of life that leads us away from the will and way of God as we make value choices. This way is occasionally called "worldly" or "of the world" in the Bible. For example, 1 John 2:15–17 says, "Do not love the world or the things in the world. The love of the Father is not in those who love the world; for all that is in the world—the desires of the flesh, the desire of the eyes, the pride in riches—comes not from the Father but from the world. And the world and its desires are passing away, but those who do the will of God live forever."

his vocation. He will not turn away from his life's work at the end of this period of preparation.

2. As he assumes his role to be God's chosen servant, he remains humble and sensitive to the leading of God in his life work. He may be doing the work of God, but he does so as a humble servant empowered by the reign of God in his life. He always shifts the focus from himself to God. As he is led by God to carry out his ministry, he is never self-seeking. He does not want the attention and credit that sometimes comes to those who have spiritual gifts such as great wisdom and healing powers. "To God Be the Glory" is his life song.

3. Worldly values such as the desires of the flesh, extraordinary beauty, and riches and the possessions that go with wealth do not turn him away from the will of God. Jesus lives by the value of worshiping God and serving his will. On occasion, as we attempt to follow the example of Jesus, we fail to live up to his standards. Often our rationalization is to say, "Jesus did it because he was the divine Son of God. We are not like him in that regard." It is important to stress, as these thoughts enter our minds, that Jesus was a first-century Jewish man whose exemplary life was so because he yielded to the reign of God. He was a human being who committed his life to the will and way of God. It is altogether appropriate to follow his example and to understand that our quest to follow him is a way to the truly spiritual life.

The Domain of Human Relationships

There are many other dimensions in our lives in which there are conflicts. Space does not allow us to deal with all of them. However, I do want us to explore one additional area in which conflicts arise. It may be the one that is most important to us. So in addition to those conflicts that are present in the domain of power and authority and in the choice of values, we need to explore the domain of personal relationships. I imagine that we face conflict in this aspect of life as much and perhaps more than any other.

By using the category of personal relationships, I am speaking about the differences between people in style and background more than their differences of opinion about the use of power, the claims of authority, and the values they hold dear. Of course, there is conflict in many cases because all these differences and their combinations are present. The categories may overlap, and it may be a bit arbitrary and difficult to distinguish between them. However, I have found that I may be with persons with whom I share similar views on the use and abuse of power and authority and have common values, but I still find them difficult because of cultural differences and personal styles. They may say that power should be shared, authority should be sanctioned by a neutral agency, and love should be the primary value, but I nevertheless feel tension and discomfort in their presence. For example, they may talk too much, need too much air time, and be poor listeners. They may judge others harshly and have a cultural perspective that discriminates against women or people of color. Or I might have an insecurity or psychological need that is not being met when I am in their presence. I am continually learning how to love those who rub me the wrong way. Gratefully, there are few of these people in my life and, over time, I have learned and continue to learn how to be accepting of those who are different from me.

Again, we will look at the life and teachings of Jesus for guidance on how to handle these conflicts. As we read the Gospel stories about Jesus and his interaction with others, we need to be very careful not to read too much into these brief accounts. It is all too easy for us to suggest that Jesus has certain feelings and attitudes that match those we admire, love, and want in our own lives. Unfortunately, we have little specific information about the inner life of Jesus, although his actions and speech do give us hints about his attitude and spirit. There is an interesting account in Luke's Gospel that describes a time when Jesus was invited for dinner at the home of a Pharisee, a person from a religious and political party. Just the term "Pharisee" suggests that there will be some difference in background and orientation among those at the dinner table, with Jesus coming from Galilee as working-class person and the Pharisee (and other such guests) from a different social class with particular views about the Torah and how it should be followed. As Jesus is waiting for dinner, a sinful peasant woman wants to express her respect and love for Jesus. The setting is a sociologist's dream for a case study, a nightmare for the host, and a challenge for the guests.

The account begins: "One of the Pharisees asked Jesus to eat with him, and he went to the Pharisee's house and took his place at the table. And a woman in the city, who was a sinner, having learned that he was eating in the Pharisee's house, brought an alabaster jar of ointment."[15] As the story continues, we read that she was moved with tears to be in his presence and then bathes the feet of Jesus and dries them with her hair. She continues to show her deep love and appreciation for Jesus by kissing his feet. Jesus senses that the Pharisee, Simon, is offended as Jesus allows the woman to care for him, although it was an occasional practice. In that culture, people often wore sandals, and the streets and paths on which they walked were

---

15. The full story is in Luke 7:36–50.

very dusty. It was a kind gesture on the part of the woman, and Jesus honored her deep need to show her gratitude. Jesus speaks with Simon and gives him a brief story, as he so often did to illustrate why he allowed the woman to wash his feet. Jesus then compares her love for him to that of Simon to make his point. He says to Simon that because of her love, her sins are forgiven. The Pharisees jump in at this point and begin to ask the question about who has the authority to forgive sins. There is both a social and religious conflict brought on by a kind action in a setting where there were people with different styles and backgrounds. As I read the story, I am made aware of the following dimensions of the event:

1. I note that Simon is the host and has a sense of what he wants the evening to be like; he wants the dinner to go well. He is a Pharisee, and has guests who are Pharisees. This group of people had a certain unspoken protocol and expectations.

2. Jesus is a special guest, and perhaps he had the hope that he might be able to explain his ministry to these religious leaders. He wants them to understand and be less resistant to his teaching and healing.

3. A lower-class woman who has a shady reputation breaks into the pre-dinner conversation and expresses her love for Jesus in a very tangible way. She does violate the cultural norms and protocol of the Pharisees.

4. Jesus honors the woman, even at the risk of offending the expectations of the host and the other guests. Jesus makes an honest effort to explain to Simon why he allowed the woman to express her act of love. He goes on to say to the woman that her faith has saved her and that she can go in peace.

5. Again, as before, the Pharisees ask whether Jesus has the power to forgive sins, although Jesus may be reassuring the woman that God has forgiven her sins. He says, "Your faith has saved you; go in peace."

In this case, Jesus has honored a disenfranchised and poverty-stricken woman. He treated her with respect and reassured her that she is loved and accepted by the God of love. His priority is the healing acceptance of the women, and he tries to help Simon understand what he has done. There are times in our lives when we must make similar decisions complicated by different styles and backgrounds. In this case, Jesus chose to show love and compassion, and attempted to explain his choice to those with different styles and backgrounds. There are times when our choices may be difficult, as they were for Jesus that day. But Jesus once again demonstrates that love and compassion are always the values that guide his behavior.

A somewhat similar situation occurred when Jesus was going through the region of Samaria. The group of people living there had nearly the same beliefs and practices as the Jewish majority, but there was sufficient difference in cultural norms and details of belief that made them a distinct minority in Palestine. As Jesus passes through the region on his way from Judea back to Galilee, he stops at historic Jacob's Well about noon. John's Gospel (4:1–42) recounts the story. "A Samaritan woman came to draw water, and Jesus said to her 'give me a drink.' The Samaritan woman said to him, 'How is it that you, a Jew, ask a drink of me, a woman of Samaria? (Jews do not share things in common with Samaritans.)" The story continues between Jesus and the woman. Jesus speaks with her about living water, a metaphor for faith and how it can change her life. Her life was difficult and troubled, having had five husbands and working on a possible sixth. Jesus shows great empathy for her and explains that to follow and worship God in spirit and truth is to find a new way of life that will bring her peace and hope. She responds positively to the invitation of Jesus and is transformed. She returns to her village and speaks to the people about what has happened to her in meeting Jesus. Nearly the whole village rushes to meet Jesus. Many people respond to his invitation to accept the reign of God.

As the disciples who had left the well for a few hours return, they are quiet, but they wonder why Jesus was speaking to a minority woman who was so troubled. But they soon discover that this woman has been transformed, and people from the region believe her story and follow Jesus as well. "Many Samaritans from that city believed in him because of the woman's testimony" (John 4:39a). From this story, we learn more about how Jesus deals with those whose style and background are quite different than his own and that of his disciples. We note that

1. Jesus accepts the woman at the well, takes time to speak with her, shows great empathy for her, and guides her into a new way of life. He invites her to accept the "water of life."
2. He reaches across boundaries of cultural difference and shows no partiality. He rejects the norms of racism, tribalism, nativism, and class interest, and invites her into the family of God.
3. By this action, he says that everyone is welcome into the family of God.

I want to turn to one more story as an illustration of the way that Jesus handles conflict between those with different styles and personalities. It is the well-known story about two women who are hosting Jesus in their home. Their names are Mary and Martha. The story is recorded in the Gospel of Luke (10:35–42), and it begins:

> Now as they went on their way, he entered a certain village, where a woman named Martha welcomed him into their home. She had a sister named Mary, who sat at the Lord's feet and listened to what he was saying. But Martha was distracted by her many tasks; so she came to him and asked, "Lord, do you not care that my sister has left me to do all the work by myself? Tell her then to help me." But the Lord answered her, "Martha, Martha, you are worried and distracted by many things; there is need for only one thing. Mary has chosen the better part, which will not be taken away from her."

This short account has been commented upon extensively, with defenders of both Mary and Martha and a measure of curiosity about why Jesus said what he is recorded as saying. There are, of course, questions about what really was said and how much the story may have been shortened and changed over the period of the oral tradition.

We will simply take the story at face value and attempt to understand the behavior of Jesus in reference to the minor conflict between Mary and Martha. The first observation is that Jesus feels welcomed by the two women, is grateful for their hospitality, and enjoys their company. I can imagine as he travels by foot from place to place and is received as a guest that he does not really want a "fuss" made over him. He is also a person who speaks kindly to the people he meets and honors their questions, many of which may be about very important topics. He may have engaged in one of those conversations with Mary, and he felt it was important to have that conversation. He therefore underlines this point when Martha raises the concern about Mary not doing her share of the work. His response to Martha might be a gentle reminder, as may be seen in the affectionate repeat of her name: "Martha, Martha, you are distracted and worried, but my conversation with Mary has been very important and she needed the time."

Martha, on the other hand, was concerned about getting the house in order and preparing the meal—legitimate concerns. In addition, she may have wanted Jesus to give her more attention. However, in a difficult and sensitive call, Jesus gently reminds Martha that Mary's need was very important, "the better part, which will not be taken away from her." I suspect that we all have some of Mary and Martha in us, and that to cultivate good hospitality and deep conversation are both important. As Jesus mediates in the conflict of styles between Mary and Martha, he was most likely kind and gentle, but chose Mary's need because he judged that she needed his attention and care regarding what she considered to be an important concern.

Navigating requests for attention because of need and yet being grateful for the welcoming hospitality was not easy, because both women thought their concern was important. One chose hospitality for an honored guest, and another asked an important question about life to the wise and kind teacher. I can imagine that, before the evening was over, Jesus had responded with gentleness and understanding to both women.

In summary, accepting the invitation of Jesus is to accept the reign of God, to engage in the process of being transformed by the Spirit of God, and to follow the example of Jesus and become a person for others, treating all with compassion and sensitive care.

Study Resources

Discussion Questions

1. How would you describe your personal style of dealing with conflict? Is it something you manage well, or is it difficult for you?
2. How would you describe the ways that Jesus dealt with conflict?
3. What sorts of manifestations of power and authority did Jesus encounter in his public ministry?
4. How would you describe the way that Jesus managed the issues of power and authority? Is it a pattern from which you might learn?
5. What were the values of Jesus, and how did these values impact his relationships with those whom he encountered?

Terms and Concepts

1. *Metanoia*: A Greek word for conversion implying a total transformation of one's way of life.
2. Authority: a founding document, or a body of people, or a person sanctioned to exercise power and make decisions that are binding.
3. Torah: A name for the Jewish law that is found in the Hebrew Bible, and especially in the first five books of the Hebrew Bible, called the Pentateuch. It is often capitalized as a reference to a specific law.
4. Civil Disobedience: The action of a person or a group that chooses to challenge what is considered an unjust law or a binding decision and precedent by a court of law.

5. Worldly: A way of life that is self-centered and follows the quest for sensual gratification, personal glory, wealth and possessions, and power over others.

Suggested Reading

Benefiel, Margaret. *The Soul of a Leader: Finding Your Path to Fulfillment and Success.* New York: Crossword, 2008.

Goleman, Daniel. *Emotional Intelligence: Why It Can Matter More than IQ.* New York: Bantam, 1995.

———. *Social Intelligence: The New Science of Human Relationships.* New York: Bantam, 2006.

Kirkpatrick, Thomas G. *Communication in the Church.* Lanham: Rowman & Littlefield, 2016.

Meyers, Isabel Briggs, and Peter B. Meyers. *Gifts Differing.* Palo Alto: Consulting Psychologists, 1980.

SECTION 3

The Difficult Events

What Are the Implications of Accepting the Invitation of Jesus?

We have maintained that the invitation of Jesus goes out to all people regardless of location, language, and culture. However, in its original form, the invitation comes in the language and cultural norms of a particular time and place in history, first-century Palestine. Therefore, for us to clearly hear the invitation requires that we do rigorous historical study of the life and teachings of Jesus and look carefully at his context. It is from this context that the invitation comes. There is also a need to take into account the range of interpretations of the life and teachings of Jesus since his time. As we do this work, we find these interpretations a wonderful gift, and also a challenge, in that they too must be studied with care and require that we keep an eye on the assumptions and preconceptions they contain. We are asking four basic questions as we do this work.

Our first question is this: How do we access the invitation? Our thesis is that we access the invitation by studying the literature of the New Testament and the history of the times in which he lived.

Our second question is as follows: What are the components of the invitation? We are attempting to answer this question by looking at the way he spoke about living the ethical life, focusing primarily on his teachings about love, compassion, and justice. We underlined that we are able to live in accord with these ethical guidelines as we accept the presence and power of God (the kingdom of God) into our lives. We then turned our attention to the challenges of living the spiritual life, especially as we face the conflicts that surface in committing ourselves to a life of love.

We now turn to the third question: What are the implications of accepting the invitation? We will explore answers to this question by carefully examining the major events in the life of Jesus in the hope of discerning from this extraordinary life how we cultivate a deep spirituality in our time and place in history. How do we follow the model of Jesus in our extraordinarily complex, difficult, and challenging times? We will look at his early life and calling, his ministry of proclamation and healing, and his last week in which all of the life and teaching of Jesus reach their conclusion and culmination. Our final question will be this: How do we respond to his invitation?

> I appeal to you therefore, brothers and sisters, by the mercies of God, to present your bodies as a living sacrifice, holy and acceptable to God, which is your spiritual worship. Do not be conformed to this world, but be transformed by the renewing of your minds, so that you may discern what is the will of God—what is good and acceptable and perfect.
>
> (Rom 12:1–2)

7

The Birth Stories and the Calling

JESUS WAS A MARVELOUS teacher, charismatic and profound, empowering his listeners to gain knowledge, insight, and wise guidance for the day-to-day demands in first-century Palestine. His words healed, inspired, and guided people to a better life, one that was God-centered, although not necessarily easy and carefree. People accepted his invitation to a new way of living, and learned how to manage and even flourish in demanding circumstances.

The invitation of Jesus to his listeners was to endorse and accept the reign of God. They learned what this meant as they listened to him teach, experienced his empathy, and had conversations with him. But like most of us, they also observed the life of their teacher and saw with great amazement that he lived what he taught. He became a model for them regarding how to live a life that is God-centered rather than self-centered. He taught by his actions and demonstrated the meaning of love, compassion, and justice by being loving to all who came his way, by showing compassion to all those whom he met that were suffering, and by prophetically challenging injustice.

We will be somewhat selective in our choice of stories from the Gospels about the way Jesus lived in accord with his commitment to a life of love, compassion, and justice, in part because there are many stories and space is limited. Additionally, some stories may be more accurate than others in portraying what occurred. We know that they were written many years after he lived, and were modified by an oral tradition that carried them forward to edify the new community of people that followed the way of Jesus. As the stories were told and retold in many settings, there was likely some redaction in order to meet the needs of this new community, the church. We will also be careful in our interpretation of the stories in that the categories that were often used by those responsible for the stories were unique to their culture and contained a premodern understanding of reality as they described the actions of Jesus. They used the categories of miraculous and divine intervention for all that they could not explain in the simple and natural patterns of cause and effect. To be sure, what Jesus accomplished was a miracle in one sense, but to explain a great deal of his work by saying that God directly intervened in a miraculous way to make things happen may not be easily accepted by our modern consciousness. Those who told the stories did not have the categories of modern science and critical history to use in their accounts, although they certainly understood unconditional love when they saw it and experienced it.

The Birth Stories

I want to begin at the beginning because, according to the accounts that we have, those who were present at the birth of Jesus and his infancy were filled with the hope that this child would be the chosen one that was promised, the messiah. They longed for the loving and compassionate action of God that would bring some relief from their suffering and the injustice they experienced from alien governments. They saw in this child the fulfillment of what they understood as the promise from God, that a messiah would come and that there would be the restoration of their country. They wanted to live in a setting that was free from conflict and war, was safe and secure, and had just laws. They looked back with a trace of naïve nostalgia about their country ruled by King David. They even dared to hope that the promised one, the messiah, might be a descendant of David and, like David, a royal figure with strength and power.

The birth and infancy stories are in two of the Gospels, Matthew and Luke.[1] They have slightly different viewpoints that need to be taken into account. The authors of these two Gospels saw the world from their own vantage point, and so they came to their writing with a slightly different purpose in telling these stories. The author of Matthew's Gospel writes out of and to the Jewish Christian community, whereas Luke, not unaware of the Jewish connection, spoke as well to those outside of the Jewish milieu.

We turn first to the birth story in Matthew. It is not easy to identify the author of the Gospel of Matthew, although there were efforts to do so in the

---

1. I have been informed about the birth narratives in the book by Raymond E. Brown, *The Birth of the Messiah: A Commentary on the Infancy Narratives in Matthew and Luke.*

THE BIRTH STORIES AND THE CALLING

early life of the Christian church. There was a desire to attribute the Gospel to one who was close to Jesus, perhaps one from his inner circle. Modern scholarship has generally maintained that the author of the Gospel was not writing from firsthand experience with Jesus, but one who had unusual gifts and was able to tell the story of Jesus from the oral tradition about him and the several written sources such as the Gospel of Mark and the Q document. The Gospel was written in Greek, and it is likely that the author was at least bilingual and perhaps a Jewish scribe intimately familiar with the Hebrew Scriptures and Jewish values and customs.[2] Most New Testament scholars place the approximate date of the writing of the Gospel of Matthew to be from 80–90 CE, a judgment based on references in Matthew to events that occurred after 70 CE. The author has designed the book with great care, and it is easy to follow the outline of the book. The birth story comes first and has the following components:

1. The genealogy of Jesus (Matt 1:1–17): The author is careful to describe the several generations that trace the plan of God leading up to the birth of Jesus. It begins: "An account of the genealogy of Jesus the Messiah, the son of David, the son of Abraham" (Matt 1:1). Jesus arrives fourteen generations later as a continuation of God's plan.

2. The next paragraph (1:18–25) explains that Jesus was born of Mary in an unusual way. There is the explanation to Joseph that the Holy Spirit caused Mary to be pregnant, and that he need not feel betrayed or be embarrassed by the pregnancy in that they were not yet married. It is noted that Mary and Joseph had no sexual relations prior to the birth of Jesus and their marriage.

3. Chapter 2 begins with the visit of the wise men (magi) from the East, guided by a star to Bethlehem, where Jesus was born. The placing of the birth in Bethlehem fulfills a passage of Scripture that says that a new ruler will be born in Bethlehem. This passage also has the account that the magi informed Herod about the birth of a possible king. Herod, of course, was threatened by the news that a prospective king was born. The magi then visit Mary with the newborn child, Jesus, pay homage, and give the gifts of gold, frankincense, and myrrh. The magi leave the region when they learn that Herod may take action against the newborn king and those who honor him.

---

2. Some have suggested that Matthew 13:52 may be a reference to the author, and the renaming of the tax collector, Levi, in Matthew 9:9 may be a significant clue as well.

4. The next paragraph describes the escape from Herod by Joseph, Mary, and Jesus to Egypt, also a fulfillment of a scriptural prophecy in Matthew.

5. There is the massacre by Herod of the infants in the area of Bethlehem.

6. In time, following the death of King Herod, the holy family returns to Nazareth in Galilee, also fulfilling a prophecy that Jesus, the Messiah, might be called a Nazorean.

It is a fascinating story, one that is told with great drama and educational content year after year, often mixed with additional detail from the story in the Gospel of Luke. For our purposes, I want to underline that one primary purpose of the story is to situate Jesus in the appropriate context to fulfill his mission, a mission that we are calling an invitation to the human family to commit to and embrace the God-centered life. This is done in Matthew's account. The birth of Jesus is viewed as an act of God entering into human history. This point is demonstrated by the genealogy beginning with Abraham, continuing with David, and leading up to the birth in Bethlehem. The author of the Gospel of Matthew connects the birth of Jesus to the way God entered human history in a special way with Abraham and the genealogical linkage with King David. Implicit in the detailed accounts in the narrative of the Hebrew people is this divine purpose. It is one that has been largely accepted by the Christian church, although with the finest scholarship examining every detail and raising some fundamental questions.

Among the questions raised is whether the historical account is accurate in its description and detail about the birth of Jesus. Reputable historians have asked a number of questions, such as whether Jesus was born in Bethlehem or Nazareth, whether Mary was a virgin, whether there was a star for the magi to follow and where they were from, whether there was a slaughter of the innocents by Herod, and whether Joseph and Mary took Jesus to Egypt. Even with these difficult questions, the Christian community has maintained that the Bible stories can be fundamentally true without every detail being literally true. God has entered into human history, and significantly so in the coming of Jesus.

This foundational belief of the Christian church that God entered into human history in Jesus is one that has been understood in different ways. There is the majority view within the larger Christian church that affirms that there was a unique act of God in the coming of Jesus. The church largely accepts the perspective of Matthew's Gospel and affirms that the events described and given meaning by Matthew are true. The birth of Jesus is generally theologically understood as the incarnation; in some sense, Jesus was the expression of God.

Others, a minority within the Christian church, also maintain that God's influence was in the event. However, Jesus was essentially human, was born as a Jewish boy, grew up in Galilee, and became a remarkable teacher and prophet. We learn about the divine will and way from Jesus without the need to describe him as divine. He sensed that God had called him to proclaim the kingdom of God and invite people to accept this good news. Jesus was filled with the divine presence, followed the will and way of God, and sacrificed his life for love and truth. But he was human, demonstrating what it means to be truly human and live as God intended. But there is some caution in this progressive outlook about saying that Jesus is divine. What is said more frequently is that Jesus was God-like in the way he lived his life. In that our purpose is more historical than theological, we will focus on what we can learn about Jesus from careful historical scholarship.

Those with a more secular outlook have maintained that the belief in what has been called the Incarnation was a way for people with a premodern consciousness to explain and make sense out of certain dramatic events that were not daily occurrences. The followers of Jesus needed to find a way to describe his divine qualities. They used the categories available to them in their language and worldview. They drew upon the Jewish heritage and placed Jesus in the categories of prophet, priest, and king. They also drew upon the Greek perspective that was prevalent in their culture as well.[3] Jesus may have been an extraordinary teacher and prophet, but was certainly not divine, nor were the events described necessarily facilitated by the divine hand. He was gifted and remarkable in so many ways and a model for humankind, but not God incarnate.

For Christians, the issue is how to understand the way God was behind and integral to these events. Christians affirm this great truth, although a minority of Christians would be cautious about using the category of incarnation, a once-and-for-all event that is not part of the cause and effect sequence of other historical events. To do so is to move beyond historical and scientific explanation and venture into the domain of faith. At the heart of the question is whether there is some hermeneutical legitimacy, even in the Christian context, to interpret the story as a premodern account of a person who was truly spiritual, gifted, and a good human being whose life

---

3. For example, there was the belief, rooted in the thought of Plato, that objects in the world have a distinctive substance. A chair is a chair because it has the substance of "chairness." Jesus had both human and divine substance, and therefore could be called God. The Christian church worked across a couple of centuries to clarify the meaning of the belief that Jesus was both human and divine.

and teachings have great relevance for the people today. There are many Christians who follow Jesus but have essentially moved beyond the supernatural accounts; they understand Jesus as one who was sensitive to the will and way of God and followed it with remarkable integrity, courage, and wisdom. They can affirm the mission of Jesus without saying that Jesus was God. They are also able to endorse and commit to the invitation of Jesus to live a God-centered life and to follow his teaching and the example of his life.[4]

These questions carry over to our reading of the birth story in the Gospel of Luke. The author of Luke's Gospel, perhaps the gentile doctor who traveled with the apostle Paul, provides additional material to the account in Matthew. Each of the two accounts has a slightly different perspective about the birth of Jesus. A careful reading of the Gospel of Luke may suggest that the author may not have been Luke, the doctor and colleague of the apostle Paul. It could have been a later Jewish writer who had a mastery of Greek but also Hebrew, and a clear understanding of Jewish customs and culture. He diligently connects the birth of Jesus with the history of God's people in Israel. Yet he is also aware of the larger world, the Roman Empire, and his writing reflects the way a scholarly history would be written at that time. The sophistication of the writing suggests that the author was well educated and had access to a wide range of resources. The Gospel of Luke was written near the time of Matthew's Gospel, between 75 and 90 CE, although an earlier date is possible if we hold to the view that Luke was the author. As with Matthew, there is obvious dependence upon the Gospel of Mark, but also, as with Matthew, there is material in Luke that is not contained in the Gospel of Mark. The birth story is one of those units.

The author, perhaps Dr. Luke, tells his story of the birth of Jesus in the following way:

1. He dedicates his account to Theophilus, a Greek acquaintance, so that Theophilus may "know the truth concerning the things about which you have been instructed" (1:1–4).

---

4. I admit to having considered these points of view with an open heart and mind. I received my theological education largely in a neoorthodox frame of reference that had a high regard for the views of Karl Barth. But I was also vitally interested in the hermeneutical views of Rudolf Bultmann, with his desire to stay in the Christian family and yet demythologize the premodern views present in the New Testament that explain the life and teachings of Jesus. I have also been interested in those who speak about finding true transcendence behind or beyond religion, moving away from an anthropocentric understanding of God. More recently I have been interested in those who take a more developmental view of Christian belief and practice. The writings of Pierre Teilhard de Chardin, James Fowler, and Ken Wilber have been very helpful in this regard.

THE BIRTH STORIES AND THE CALLING

2. He provides important background prior to the birth of Jesus and speaks about the birth of John the Baptist, a cousin of Jesus and one who influenced Jesus as he began his public ministry. It contains the account of John's parents as well. John's father was a priest named Zechariah, and his wife, the mother of John, is named Elizabeth. Zechariah is informed by the angel Gabriel that Elizabeth is pregnant and will have a son whose name will be John. Zechariah is quite old, and so has doubts when he hears the news; consequently, he loses his ability to speak.

3. Gabriel continues the work of God, visiting Mary in Nazareth, and tells her that she will have a son. Mary is overwhelmed because she is quite young and embarrassed about being pregnant before she is married (1:5–38).

4. Mary visits Elizabeth, is comforted, and together they praise God for what has happened to them (1:39–56).

5. John the Baptist is born, his father Zechariah's voice has returned, and he is able is able to praise God. John "grew and became strong in spirit, and he was in the wilderness until the day he appeared publicly to Israel" (1:57–80).

6. Chapter 2 begins the account of the birth of Jesus. The Roman Emperor Augustus issues a decree that there will be a census, and that all of the people living in the region of Palestine need to register in their own family towns. Joseph takes his pregnant wife Mary to Bethlehem, the appropriate place for the as a descendent of David. It is there that Jesus is born in a manger because "there is no room for them in the inn" (2:1–7).

7. The shepherds and the angels visit Mary and Joseph and celebrate the birth of Jesus, "a Savior, who is the Messiah, the Lord" (2:8–20).

8. Jesus is named and presented in the Temple. A devout man named Simon is present and takes Jesus in his arms, praising God and blessing the child, and Anna, an elderly female prophet, praises God as well (2:21–38).

9. Mary, Joseph, and Jesus return to Nazareth. "The child grew and became strong, filled with wisdom; and the favor of God was upon him" (2:39–40).

10. A few years later, when Jesus is twelve, the family goes back to Jerusalem for the festival of Passover. In the rush of crowds, Jesus disappears, and they get worried about him. "After three days, they found

him in the temple, sitting among the teachers, listening to him and asking him questions. And all who heard him were amazed at his understanding and his answers." The family, relieved to find him, then returns to Nazareth, where "Jesus increased in wisdom and in years, and in divine and human favor" (2:41–52).

I want to underline several key points that emerge from Luke's account. The author of the Gospel of Luke begins with the understanding that God was present and guiding the events of the birth of Jesus. The birth of Jesus is the culmination of a historical process and central to the plan of God. Those present at the birth give praise to God that the messiah has been born. Further, the identity of Jesus is spoken of as well. The identity is proclaimed by a messenger of God, an angel, who speaks directly to the shepherds who are terrified by what they see. "But the angel said to them, 'Do not be afraid; for see—I am bringing you good news of great joy for all the people; to you is born this day in the city of David a Savior, who is the Messiah, the Lord'" (2:10–11). Jesus will be good news of great joy for all people. He will give all who come to him an invitation to the God-centered life.

As mentioned, Luke's account has the same assumption as the Gospel of Matthew, which is that God has been active in and guided the birth of Jesus. Yet there are some differences in Luke's Gospel. One difference is that the Gospel of Luke introduces different characters into the story. For example, John the Baptist plays an important role in the unfolding of God's plan. He is seen as a forerunner of Jesus, and later as one who baptizes Jesus. His parents, Zechariah and Elizabeth, are key observers of the birth. Elizabeth, also pregnant with John, is described as an older and a kindly aunt who is able to comfort Mary. In addition, there are beautiful songs of praise for the birth of Jesus, one by Mary and another by Zechariah. Mary rejoices that she has been chosen as the mother of Jesus, and she sings: "My soul magnifies the Lord, and my spirit rejoices in God my Savior, for he has looked with favor on the lowliness of his servant. Surely, from now on all generations will be blessed" (1:47–48). Zechariah prophesies that "by the tender mercy of our God, the dawn from on high will break upon us, to give light to those in darkness and in the shadow of death, to guide our feet into the way of peace" (1:78–79).

Luke is slightly different than Matthew in another way as well. The author of Luke introduces not only the shepherds who are near Bethlehem, but also the magi "from the East." Common people such as shepherds and distinguished wise people from another culture and background come to pay homage. The birth of Jesus is not an exclusive blessing for the Jewish people, but will become a blessing for all people. Even angels play a role in guiding the activities. The author of Luke, though perhaps a gentile, nevertheless speaks about the Jewish custom of taking a child to the temple in Jerusalem for circumcision and "the purification according to the law of Moses." It is important to note that the devout observer, Simon, speaks of the child being "a light for Gentiles and for glory to your people Israel" (2:32).

How are we to interpret what we read? As I try to answer this question, I find myself reflecting on the following observations and descriptions by Luke:

1. I notice the same foundational assumption in the account of the birth of Jesus in the Gospel of Luke, as is present in the Gospel of Matthew. There is divine intervention and divine guidance present all through the description of this extraordinary event. God acts in the womb of Mary, she hears the voice of God that she has been chosen, magi are guided by a star, Zechariah was "filled with the Holy Spirit," angels speak to shepherds and sing, and Simon understands that the Holy Spirit would not allow him to die before the messiah is born.

2. As the author of Luke writes the account, he is likely informed by an oral tradition that has been passed on across months and years. He may have some written materials as well. He speaks at the beginning of the Gospel that others "have undertaken to set down an orderly account of the events that have been fulfilled among us, just as they were handed onto us by those who from the beginning were eyewitnesses and servants of the word" (1:1–2). The Gospel of Luke is written with these resources many years after the events.

3. I am deeply moved by the beauty of the description of the birth of Jesus in both Matthew and Luke. The story carries the profound theological affirmation that God was present in the birth, teachings, actions, and life of Jesus. Yet I do find it somewhat difficult to accept a literal reading of every detail in the account. I view it as the account of sincere and dedicated people who draw upon the premodern understanding of their religion to describe the birth. They use the beautiful language of story, filled as stories are with traces of magic and myth. The story has great value as it describes a profound truth, yet it is clear that the author is not using the historical-critical method of the modern historian as a means of discerning what really happened.

4. Yet the story is true in a metaphorical sense, not unlike other ancient stories that contain theological and moral truth that is integral to a beautiful story. I find myself drawing upon the hermeneutical principle

that deep truth can be contained in story form, not unlike the parables that Jesus used to make his message known. In the parables, the content of the story need not be describing actual events and people, yet the story carries a profound message. One great truth of what we read in Gospel stories is that Jesus came with the invitation to humankind to lead the God-centered life. As we accept the invitation and endorse the way of life entailed in this acceptance, we are truly "saved" from self-destructive patterns of life and can lead a life of goodness, truth, and beauty.

The Calling

The concluding sections of the account of the birth of Jesus give us an indication of how Jesus developed and became the charismatic teacher, the compassionate healer, and the courageous prophet that we see in his public ministry. There is little detail, and such a lack has stimulated the imagination of many writers, who have suggested that Jesus had some unusual experiences in his youth. I am reluctant to go far beyond what we have in the Gospels. It is enough to study what it may have been like to grow up in a small village in Galilee in the first century of the Common Era. We will look first at the two passages from the Gospel of Luke that reference the early life of Jesus. Then we will turn to a brief description of the setting in which Jesus lived prior to his public ministry.

The first passage about Jesus as a young boy is found in Luke 2:39–40: "When they had finished everything required by the law of the Lord, they returned to Galilee, to their own town of Nazareth. The child grew and became strong, filled with wisdom; and the favor of God was upon him." The passage is quite brief, yet we are given a broad outline about the early life of Jesus. The common explanation for brevity is that the Gospel of Luke is not a biography, but a gospel or extended sermon, which is a distinctive literary genre. The purpose of a gospel is to share good news, and the Gospels of Matthew, Mark, Luke, and John all say in their own ways that Jesus has come, full of grace and truth, to improve our lives.

We are not sure where that author of Luke gained this information about the early life of Jesus. There may have been an oral tradition that was carefully passed on through the newly developing church, or perhaps there was a written logion that referenced the development of Jesus. What we do have is the description that he grew and became strong. The sentence gives us little detail, and it may have been all the information that was available to the author of Luke. Yet it is enough to suggest that Jesus developed like a normal child. Perhaps because his father, Joseph, was a carpenter, Jesus as the eldest child in the family may have assisted his father in the hard outdoor work of building and became physically strong. The word "strong" more likely suggests that his strength was emotional as well, and that he was a strong person in the sense of emotional maturity. The Jerusalem Bible translates the phrase as "grew to maturity." The next phrase, "filled with wisdom," adds to the notion of emotional maturity, and also suggests that he developed into a person who was able to manage the challenges of life in a healthy way. It was clear to those around him that God had touched his life.

The next passage describes the visit of the immediate and extended family of Mary and Joseph to Jerusalem for the festival of Passover. While we have no record of it, they may have visited Jerusalem for this festival, or for another holiday previously, trips not uncommon for faithful Jewish believers. The city would have been crowded. It is likely that many of the visitors would have had to camp rather than find housing in the city. Jesus and his family were part of a larger group ("relatives and friends"), and children of twelve years of age would have had some freedom within the contingent of people. At the close of the festival, the family left the city with many others from the region of Galilee. They had even traveled for a while, but then discovered that Jesus was not with them. Worried, they returned to Jerusalem, and after an extensive search, they found him in the temple,

> sitting among the teachers, listening to them and asking them questions. And all who heard him were amazed at his understanding and his answers. Mary, still anxious, says to Jesus, "Child, why have you treated us like this? Look, your father and I have been searching for you in great anxiety." Jesus responds, "Why were you searching for me? Did you not know that I must be in my Father's house?"

After this conversation, Jesus joined his parents and returned home and "was obedient to them. His mother treasured all these things in her heart. And Jesus increased in wisdom and in years (or stature) and in divine and human favor" (2:47–52).

Again we are unsure just how the author of the Gospel of Luke knows about this occurrence and the conversation. Perhaps, as before, the author did have access to both the oral traditions and a possible written fragment about the event. As we have it, the passages suggest ways that Jesus was developing. We see:

1. That the family was devout and loyal to the practices of their religious faith. They go to Jerusalem, the center of the their religion, and participate in the festival of Passover. The early life of Jesus would have placed him within the beliefs and practices of a devout family.

2. That there was a group of family and friends, and within this group, people would take care of all of the children. Parents would feel the safety of this care and allow children of twelve years of age some freedom, especially if they were emotionally mature.

3. Jesus had the freedom to move away from the campsite and visit the city, and he chose to go to the Temple and join in the conversation. This action suggests his interest and the level of his education and understanding. "They were amazed at his understanding and his answers."

4. Mary, the good mother that she was, did feel anxious when she discovered that Jesus was not with them as they began their trip back to Galilee. The passage about the exchange between Mary and Jesus, inserted by the author of the Gospel of Luke, reflects her anxiety, and the answer of Jesus seems a bit abrupt. More may have been said, but the passage does have the ring of authenticity.

5. The passage in Luke underlines that Jesus was an obedient boy. It is noted that he possessed an interest in understanding his religious heritage and that he matured. There is the additional observation that people noticed these developments. It was evident as well that the divine hand was on this child.

With this background in mind, I want to now turn to two other major events in the life of Jesus that are recorded in the Gospels of Matthew and Luke as he prepares for his life calling as a teacher, healer, and prophet. They are his trip south to the wilderness east of Jerusalem to visit John the Baptist and the several days of retreat and fasting to prepare for his vocation. We turn first to the visit to John the Baptist. John had already begun his ministry as a prophet. It was "in the fifteenth year of the reign of Emperor Tiberius, when Pontius Pilate was the governor of Judea, and Herod was the ruler of Galilee . . . during the high priesthood of Annas and Caiaphas, the word of God came to John son of Zechariah in the wilderness" (Luke 3:1–2). John "went into the region around the Jordan, proclaiming a baptism of repentance for the forgiveness of sins" (3:3). Crowds of people from the region and in the city of Jerusalem came to John, and after their baptism, they asked him what they should do. John tells them to share their food and clothing with the poor. He tells the tax collectors to "collect no more than the amount prescribed," and the soldiers not to extort money from anyone with threats or false accusations. John tells them to act in a moral and loving way. They then ask him if he is the messiah, and John answers them: "I baptized you with water; but one more powerful than I is coming; I am not worthy to untie the thong of his sandals. He will baptize you with the Holy Spirit and fire" (3:16).

I pick up the story now from the Gospel of Matthew: "Then Jesus came from Galilee to John at the Jordan, to be baptized by him. John would have prevented him, saying, 'I need to be baptized by you, and do you come to me?' But Jesus answered him: 'Let it be so now; for it is proper for us in this way to fulfill all righteousness.' Then he consented." Jesus is baptized by John and "suddenly the heavens were opened to him and he saw the Spirit of God descending like a dove and alighting on him. And a voice from heaven said, 'This is my Son, the Beloved, with whom I am well pleased'" (Matt 3:13–17).

As I review this story, and even place myself in the setting drawing upon my several visits to the region, I find myself quite humbled and inspired by it. So much is packed into a few short verses. I am especially moved by the following insights inherent in the story:

1. It is probable that the authors of Matthew and Luke have Mark's briefer account in front of them. In addition, they may have been informed by an oral tradition that had been carefully passed down from those present at the baptism. It may be that they had other written material in front of them. Both authors are quite careful to place the event in a particular time and place. Luke adds the information about who was in authority in the region in which the events take place. There is sufficient detail in the accounts to give them authenticity; it took place, and was not just the product of the imagination of a good storyteller. Of course, there are some interpretive elements in the story, such as Jesus hearing the voice of God, but this is a metaphorical reference to the divine affirmation Jesus felt following his baptism. We also have the conversation between John and Jesus about the baptism, and again the account projects what was likely said given the occasion and the meaning of the event. But these elements in the story do not take away the likelihood that the event occurred and that the meaning of the event was a description of how Jesus prepared himself for his public ministry.

2. John the Baptist is often depicted as a wild prophet, given the way he dressed, his location in the wilderness, and the way he pronounced judgment on all those who came to hear him. There is some truth to this depiction, but I want to underline that John's message was to invite his listeners to ask for forgiveness and be baptized as a sign of being

cleansed, and he then challenged them to "do good" by helping the poor and calling on government officials and officers to be helpful and honest in their work. To follow the will of God requires a moral and ethical life. The caricature of John as a religious fanatic may distort his contribution to the spiritual life of the people whom he served. It is clear that Jesus had great respect for John and feels profound grief when he hears about his death at the hand of Herod Antipas. John had told Herod that it was wrong for him to take his brother's wife, and in the middle of a complex family conversation, Herod had John decapitated.[5]

3. In addition, I am quite taken by John's humility as he encounters and speaks with his cousin from Nazareth. There is a small thread in New Testament scholarship about the relationship between John and Jesus that suggests there may have been some competition between them. It is a point worth considering, but the larger truth is that John likely did understand his role as a forerunner for Jesus, and that he carried out this role with humility and wisdom. The actual wording in the account may be a product of the story being told many times by several people in different locations, but the meaning of the conversation comes through to us as an accurate description of what occurred. John's ministry had its own integrity, and was not simply or exclusively a preliminary ministry in anticipation of the ministry of Jesus. But when Jesus arrived in the wilderness near the Jordan River, John was reluctant to baptize Jesus, feeling like he was not even worthy to lace the sandals of Jesus. He says that Jesus should baptize him. It is probable that John did say that there was one coming with a divine calling and empowered by the Holy Spirit to proclaim a profound message.

4. Jesus did not take over the ministry of John, but submitted to it with humility and integrity. He learned about the appropriate role of the prophet from John, and asks John if he too can be baptized. Little is said about the meaning of the baptism for Jesus, except that he did it "to fulfill all righteousness." Jesus, the very human carpenter from Nazareth, is eager to do all that he understands to be the will and way of God. He was also demonstrating solidarity with the people who had come to be forgiven and restored to a God-centered life. He does not set himself apart from the common people who are seeking to live their lives in harmony with God's will. He becomes one of them, lives with them, and cares for them.

---

5. See Matthew 14:1–12 for the dreadful story of John's death.

THE BIRTH STORIES AND THE CALLING 129

5. And deep inside, Jesus senses the affirmation of God at his baptism. He senses the presence of God's approval, expressed in the account in Matthew as "like a dove alighting on him" and then he hears "a voice from heaven" saying "This is my Son, the Beloved, with whom I am well pleased." Jesus is beginning to sense that he is nearly ready for his life's work. He has learned from John and hears within himself that God is pleased with his progress and is deeply loved.

We are tracing the ways that Jesus prepared himself for his vocation. He has left his immediate family, his location in Galilee and the village of Nazareth, and traveled south to the wilderness east of Jerusalem near the Jordan River. There he meets his cousin, called John the Baptist. John's title as "Baptist" was given to him because he was engaged in a ministry of revival, calling on the people to ask God for forgiveness and to be baptized as an expression of being cleansed from sin. He calls on them to live a life in keeping with the will and way of God, such as giving food and clothing to the poor. Jesus learns from John, is baptized "to fulfill all righteousness," and takes one further step of preparation for his calling. It would later be understood in terms of the expected coming of the "anointed one" or messiah.[6] Jesus goes into the wilderness for a retreat to fast and to prepare himself spiritually for his life's work.

The landscape of the region may have looked somewhat different than it does now, although the climate was likely the same as it is now: hot and dry. The reference to the region as a wilderness might suggest a forest with streams and views of mountains, with trails around a beautiful mountain lake. The region in which Jesus went for his preparation, however, was on the edge of a desert, with some hills, little foliage, and assorted caves for protection.[7] It was dry and hot, and he was alone to contemplate the meaning of his call to a messianic ministry. Matthew gives the preliminary description, saying, "Then Jesus was led up by the Spirit into the wilderness to be tempted by the devil. He fasted forty days and forty nights, and afterwards, he was famished" (4:1–2).

We have made reference to the "temptations" of Jesus earlier, but I want to return to them and place them more directly in the context of his preparation for his life work. While we do not have full access to the inner life of Jesus apart from what others have said about him, we can imagine what he might have thought and felt from the description of what he did. It

---

6. Many of the immediate followers of Jesus and later the church understood him as the anointed one, the messiah, with the Greek title of *Christos*. There is the lingering question of whether Jesus saw himself as the messiah.

7. It is the region in which the Dead Sea Scrolls were discovered.

is a risk, however, to go too far in our imagination and inadvertently create Jesus in our own image. It is a common practice. However, we do have the accounts of the temptations in the wilderness prior to his public ministry that invite us to ponder what Jesus may have thought and felt. Matthew and Luke provide more information about the temptations than Mark.[8] All three agree that he was "led by the Spirit" in order to prepare himself for the great challenges he would face in following the will and way of God. There continues to be some debate about the process of how the descriptions were developed. Many think that the account of the temptations came directly from Jesus, were preserved in an oral form, and later put in written form. Others suggest that Jesus did go into the wilderness on a retreat to prepare himself for his life work, but the descriptions are more of a metaphor of what probably occurred in the mind and heart of Jesus, and should not be taken literally. There is a great truth inherent in the accounts either way.[9]

The "great temptations" of Jesus are often associated with the title of messiah, and one of the ways Jesus prepared himself for his messianic vocation. It was a term associated with one who has been anointed, often with symbolic ointment, to carry out a great task. It was certainly part of the inauguration of one who was to serve as a king. The Jewish people longed for God to send a great leader who would be anointed (a messiah) as a king. They looked back on their history to the time of King David when the nation was strong and a worthy equal to the existing nations. This concept would have been in the mind of Jesus. Many believe that he did understand his mission in life as messianic, as one anointed to help the people. Traditionally this anointed person was understood, not unlike David, in terms of power, strength, and conquest. Some have suggested that the temptation of Jesus was to become like a traditional king with great political power and the grandeur of royalty. The Romans feared that Jesus might have thought of himself in terms of becoming such a king.

Jesus did not choose this frame of reference for his calling. The alternative for Jesus was to be the servant of God, living a simple life of identification with the people, relieving their suffering, and calling on the governments to create a social order based on justice and peace. It was this calling that Jesus

---

8. Mark writes, "And the Spirit immediately drove him out into the wilderness. He was in the wilderness forty days, tempted by Satan; and he was with wild beasts; and the angels waited on him" (1:12–13).

9. I find it difficult to believe that Jesus had a direct conversation with a personal devil. It is easier for me to understand why he would prepare himself to withstand the temptations he would face in his calling. To put them in story form makes them more vivid.

THE BIRTH STORIES AND THE CALLING

followed. We now understand and think of him as such a messiah, anointed for a special vocation that he understood as one called to love and serve.

I often think of the forty days and nights in the wilderness, not unlike the way one prepares to run a marathon.[10] Having done that once, I remember the many days that I did not feel like running to prepare myself, especially when I knew that I needed to run about three twenty-mile distances in order to reassure myself that I was fully prepared. I wanted to know that I could finish and not drop out at the ten- or fifteen-mile marks because of fatigue and pain. I also knew that, at the twenty-mile mark, I might think about water, about a good meal, and whether it was worth it to run a marathon. Jesus had to run several marathons, and he trained in the wilderness.

The first temptation had to do with his physical needs. He had been fasting, and there was limited food and water in the desert terrain. The temptation to forsake his calling comes in the form of meeting his need for food; "he was famished." The devil, appealing to his possible need for power, invites him to turn stones into loaves of bread. The tempter says, "If you are the Son of God, command these stones to become loaves of bread" (Matt 4:3). There is nothing evil about bread, but the temptation is to act like God and turn stones into bread. It is the appeal of power (if you are the Son of God) and to turn stones into bread (if you are hungry). It is to stop running and to cease following his vocation. Jesus replies, "One does not live by bread alone, but by every word that comes from the mouth of God" (4:4).

The story of the temptations continues and shifts from physical need to forsaking one's trust in the wisdom of God and cease being faithful to one's vocation. The account begins, "Then the devil took him to the holy city and placed him on the pinnacle of the Temple, saying to him, 'If you are the Son of God, throw yourself down; for it is written, 'He will command his angels concerning you, and on their hands they will bear you up, so that you will not dash your foot against a stone.'" The temptation for Jesus is to think that he knows better than God what is good and right, and then to pretend that he won't be injured if he jumps from the pinnacle. Jesus says that he will follow the will and way of God, that God gives guidance, and I will not test God. If I stop my practice runs, I will not finish the marathon.

The second and third temptations are often placed in a high lookout outside the city of Jericho. It is possible to hike there and to imagine Jesus looking across the fields, the hills, and the towns in the region. The temptations were more likely located in the heart and mind of Jesus rather than in geographical settings, but visiting that cave on a high hill does make the

---

10. The number forty may not have been meant literally, but because many other events described in the Bible lasted for forty days, this number may have been chosen and meant by the authors as an extended period of time.

story come to life. The story continues, "Again the devil took him to a very high mountain and showed him all the kingdoms of the world and their splendor; and he said to him, 'All these will I give you, if you will fall down and worship me.' Jesus said to him, 'Away with you Satan! For it is written, "Worship the Lord your God, and serve only him." Then the devil left him and suddenly angels came and waited on him" (8–11). Jesus did not crave power, nor did he long for possessions. He did not buy the lie that happiness consists in the abundance of things possessed or unlimited power and wealth. He stayed in the wilderness until he was sure that he could overcome any temptation that might lead him away from his God-given vocation. He would become a charismatic teacher, a compassionate healer, and a radical prophet. He would give his life for the truth he spoke and for the love and compassion of his actions. His messianic calling was to serve others and model what it means to be a person for others.

Jesus began his public ministry with the foundation of a devout family, access to the Torah in his early years, trips to Jerusalem to be exposed to the center of Judaism, exposure to a diverse population in Galilee, and two very important transitional events: the time with and baptism by John the Baptist and an extended retreat for fasting and spiritual preparation. He was ready to proclaim a message that included the invitation to his listeners to accept the reign of God in their lives. Luke describes this transition in the following way: "Then Jesus, filled with the power of the Spirit, returned to Galilee, and a report about him spread all through the surrounding country. He began to teach in the synagogues and was praised by everyone" (Luke 4:14–15). Matthew adds a few details, including the information about John the Baptist. "Now when Jesus heard that John had been arrested, he withdrew to Galilee . . . From that time Jesus began to proclaim, 'Repent, for the kingdom of heaven has come near'" (Matt 4:12, 17). We turn now to discern how this active ministry of Jesus might expand and deepen our understanding of the radical invitation he extended to who came his way.

Study Resources

Discussion Questions

1. How do you understand and interpret the birth of Jesus? Should the accounts be taken literally, or is it acceptable to understand the supernatural elements as the way people at that time interpreted dramatic and unusual events?

2. How do you think the Christmas stories were preserved and then reached written form several years later? How important and trustworthy was the oral tradition?
3. How do you think Jesus understood his life calling or vocation? Do you think he thought of himself as the messiah?
4. How did he overcome the temptations to turn away from his calling?
5. Do you think you have a calling in life, and if so, how would you describe it?

People, Terms, and Concepts

1. Messiah: the anointed one, spoken about in the Hebrew Bible, translated in Greek as *Christos*, and applied to Jesus by his followers, hence, the name Jesus Christ.
2. Vocation: The sense of being called to one's life work, often used by clergy, but not exclusively a term for a religious vocation.
3. Satan: often a translation as the evil one and used as the name for the devil.
4. Elizabeth: in the family of Mary and Joseph, an older mentor for Mary in that both were pregnant at the same time, and wife of Zechariah.
5. John the Baptist: son of Elizabeth and Zechariah, a cousin of Jesus, a prophet calling for repentance in the wilderness region east of Jerusalem near the Jordan River, sought out by Jesus and baptized by him, forerunner of Jesus.

Suggested Reading

Brown, Raymond F. *The Birth of the Messiah: A Commentary on the Infancy Narratives in Matthew and Luke*. Garden City: Doubleday, 1977.
Bultmann, Rudolf. *Kerygma and Myth*. New York: Harper & Row, 1961.
Edersheim, Alfred. *The Life and Times of Jesus the Messiah*. 2 vols. Grand Rapids: Eerdmans, 1950. (This is an older book, first published in 1883, although it is a kind of classic.)
Meier, John P. *A Marginal Jew: Rethinking the Historical Jesus*. Vol. 1, *The Roots of the Problem and the Person*. New York: Doubleday, 1991.
Ratzinger, Joseph (Pope Benedict XVI). *Jesus of Nazareth: The Infancy Narratives*. New York: Image, 2012.

8

The Teaching, Healing, and Prophetic Challenge

IN MY EARLIER BOOK about Jesus entitled *The Radical Teaching of Jesus*, I spoke about the ministry and identity of Jesus as a radical teacher and prophet, using the term "radical" as challenging the religious and cultural status quo of his setting. He spoke boldly against the passive acceptance of empty and routine religious practices and the omnipresence of injustice. He described an alternative way of understanding one's purpose in life in reference to these conditions.[1] It was a challenge to the cultural norms and religious life of the time and place in which he lived. Jesus used the language of the kingdom of God as a way of speaking about how the grace of God empowers one to fundamentally change the direction of one's life. The Gospel describes the start of his ministry: "From that time Jesus began to proclaim, 'Repent, for the kingdom of heaven has come near'" (Matt 4:17). Mark, perhaps Matthew's source, has a similar description of the beginning of the public ministry of Jesus.

Jesus has come from his time with John the Baptist in the wilderness east of Jerusalem and has prepared himself by being baptized by John. Following this experience, Jesus sensed the affirmation of God that he was on the right path. He stays in the wilderness "for forty days and nights" in order to continue to prepare himself for his life's work and face the challenges he will confront in doing God's will in his public ministry. It was in the

1. There may be some repetition between this account and the earlier one. My goals in the two books differ somewhat with the current account more focused on invitation of Jesus to all people and the earlier book more focused on the content of his teaching. Inevitably there is some overlap.

wilderness that he sought to be one with God. While there is no clear record of it, he may have engaged in a form of "centering prayer." Through meditation, he may have had a profound mystical experience of the presence of God, one that expanded his inner awakening and his commitment to his life's vocation.[2] Luke's account of the devotional life of Jesus is summarized in one verse: "But he would withdraw to deserted places, and pray" (Luke 5:16). He is now ready to undertake his messianic ministry. I use the term messianic ministry with the recognition that there was more than one understanding of the hope for and the identity of the messiah to come. Jesus appears to be aware of this ambiguity, and perhaps purposely, he seldom (if ever) uses the term to describe his identity and mission. It was, however, as time went along, a title he may have accepted, and one that history has accepted as an appropriate description of Jesus. Then and now, he was called Jesus (the) Christ (messiah).

Some hoped that the messiah would come as a great king, much like David, and exercise military power, victory over enemies, and conquest. Jesus understood his mission quite differently, and came as a loving servant, charismatic teacher, compassionate healer, and radical prophet. He came as a person for others.

He begins his ministry, aware of the tragic death of John, with the simple message of repent. By this term, he means that one must change the direction of one's life and fully accept the reign of God in one's life. His invitation to his listeners is to move away from the self-centered life (repent) and to begin the God-centered life (the kingdom of heaven is at hand). He serves as an example of the God-centered life and, through his teaching and ministry, provides directions for the pathway of that life.

The Public Ministry: The Context of His Mission

Jesus returned to Galilee for the beginning of his public ministry. It is likely that this phase of his public ministry lasted approximately one year, give or take a month or two on either side. The Synoptic Gospels differ with the Gospel of John in the precise timing and location of this phase of his mission. John describes this first phase of the mission of Jesus as shorter, and a time in which he went back and forth between Galilee and Judea.[3] I am inclined to side with the Synoptic Gospels in this timing, sensing that the description of the public ministry of Jesus in John is shaped more by

2. See the thoughtful description of such an experience in Bourgeault, *Centering Prayer and Inner Awakening*.

3. John 1–6.

substantive subjects (spiritual formation and theological understanding) than by timing. I am also inclined to accept the more traditional understanding that the overall public ministry of Jesus was approximately three years, although some have maintained that it was closer to eighteen months, with only about a year in Galilee, and six months of trips to Judea leading up to the final week of his life.[4]

All of the Gospels record that Jesus went to Galilee for the beginning of his public ministry. Matthew says that he went home to Nazareth initially, and then made his base in Capernaum (Matt 4:12). Luke expands this shift from Nazareth to Capernaum, and suggests that it might have been a result of being rejected in Nazareth after he preached his first sermon in the synagogue there. Jesus is quoted as saying, "no prophet is accepted in the prophet's hometown" (4:24).

The Gospels agree that Jesus began his public ministry in Galilee. There are good reasons why this strategy was both a natural and a strategic choice. It was a setting in which Jesus was very familiar. His family was there, and it was a setting in which he knew many people and understood their needs. He also may have had a range of contacts, perhaps people he had met in the daily rounds of his early life and those who he may have met in his work as a carpenter. Further, as he chose disciples and then traveled in the region of Galilee, he and his disciples were accepted because they were from the same region. Jesus was one of them. It was a ministry that he shared with his disciples, who he had carefully chosen.[5] He and his disciples were able to interact with the people because they were familiar with the customs and culture of the region, and even may have had a similar accent in the language that they used.[6] Jesus was especially sensitive to the profound needs and concerns of the people such as poverty, illness, and the sense of injustice related to the alien governmental structure.[7]

---

4. The Gospel of Mark is quite topical, and only partially helpful in determining the sequence of events. What Mark describes could have taken place in eighteen months. Matthew and Luke have a clear purpose to describe who Jesus is and what he does, and therefore put less emphasis on specific timelines, although they do contain a sequence of events. What they describe may have occurred in a time period ranging from eighteen months to three years, with the extended period of three years being a more likely time period. While quite topical as well, John suggests a timeline for the public ministry of Jesus that lasts at least three years. For example, in John, there are three Passovers mentioned (2:13; 6:4; 12:1).

5. The Synoptic Gospels record the selection by Jesus of his disciples (Matt 4:18–22; Mark 1:6–20; Luke 5:1–11).

6. See Matthew 26:73, in which Peter is recognized as a disciple of Jesus because of his accent.

7. The direct government authority resided with the son of Herod, known as Herod

It was a region in which there was some diversity in the population. It had been ruled by Herod, who was from Samaria, a region in the middle of Palestine, although somewhat separated by culture and religious orientation from the rest of Israel. He was selected by the Romans to be the head of the regional government, even though he was from a minority population not fully accepted by the Jewish population. In addition, there were other non-Jewish Palestinians who easily traveled in the area without regard for any clearly defined county or country lines of demarcation. This diversity enabled Jesus to proclaim his message and care for people in a way that would be accepted by the people, even if it differed a bit from the thought and practices of the Judaism practiced in Jerusalem. Later, Jesus was challenged and even opposed in his ministry by those from Jerusalem, rooted as they were in their traditional practices and beliefs.

In his first year of public ministry, he became quite well-known, and large crowds sought him out for guidance and healing. Matthew describes this time, saying, "Jesus went throughout Galilee, teaching in their synagogues and proclaiming the good news of the kingdom and curing disease and every sickness among the people. So his fame spread throughout all Syria, and they brought those who were afflicted with various diseases and pains, demoniacs, epileptics, and paralytics, and he cured them. And great crowds followed him from Galilee, the Decapolis, Jerusalem, Judea, and from beyond the Jordan" (Matt 4:23–25). It is very interesting to note the distances in which he traveled during this phase of his ministry. He went to several regions in the general area of Galilee, and the author of Matthew observes that he occasionally went south to Jerusalem and Judea. Luke's account is a bit briefer in its description of the period of time: "Then Jesus, filled with the power of the Spirit, returned to Galilee, and a report about him spread through all the surrounding country. He began to teach in their synagogues and was praised by everyone" (Luke 4:14–15). It is also important to note that his ministry was primarily to the Jewish population, although the Gospel records indicate that he ministered to others as well. He used the synagogues of the region as a starting point, and then often met with people in both towns and rural settings.

Antipas, with the title of Tetrarch. Herod the Great, a Hasmonean, had distributed the power of government to his sons following his death. There was also a newly restored and fairly large city not far from Nazareth, Sepphoris, a setting that the Romans used as a base for oversight of the region.

The Purpose and Nature of His Public Ministry

As we have already noted, the primary purpose was to proclaim the good news of the kingdom of God. Jesus said that the kingdom was near, and that God's reign was available to all who wanted to change their life and make it better. Jesus spoke of the availability of the power of God, sometimes called the Holy Spirit, which one could claim and accept by an act of faith. One makes this claim by giving oneself to God and yielding to his will and way. Jesus proclaimed and demonstrated this message by his teaching, his healing, and his courage in calling for a more just and peaceful social order.

The message he demonstrated and proclaimed was articulated in the metaphor of a kingdom. There are times when this metaphor is less compelling for those of us who have learned that the power of a king is not always used in positive ways that serve the common good.[8] But it did communicate that God's power is available and will be given to all in love. Our lives, full of anxiety, poverty, and disease, can be managed and improved as we yield our lives to God in faith. We do not have a day-to-day account of his ministry in Galilee, although the Gospel accounts give us some guidance. Drawing upon the resource of the Gospels and the range of interpretations of these accounts across the centuries, we will look at this ministry of Jesus in four categories: Jesus as pastor and priest, Jesus as teacher and educator, Jesus as healer and reliever of suffering, and Jesus as prophet and leader.[9]

Jesus as Pastor and Priest

While it is not always crystal clear in the Gospels or in the Christian church's organization and practices, there is nevertheless a detectable and noticeable difference between the roles of pastor and priest. In general, the pastor is one who has been called to care for the people of God in taking the needs of the people to God, counseling them, and urging them to place their faith in God. The pastor cares for the people and directs them upward toward God's love and guidance.[10] The priest also guides the people to "reach upward," but the focus in the priest's ministry is more on taking the message and guidance of God to the people. The priest informs and guides the people to

---

8. Every metaphor both illumines and veils its subject.

9. In my earlier book, *The Radical Teaching of Jesus*, I did emphasize his role as a great teacher, and as I implied, he was more than a teacher, but also a compassionate healer and radical prophet. Here, I want to underline the several ways he carried out his ministry.

10. In my book *Mindful Spirituality*, I use directional metaphors to speak about the intentional spiritual life, reaching upward, opening inward, and expanding outward.

hear, understand, and to practice the will and way of God. In practice in the Christian community, it is the priest who invites the people to receive the presence of God in the sacraments, and especially in the Eucharist.[11] The priest has the ministry in which the arrow points down from God to the people.

The ministry of Jesus was filled with both pastoral and priestly ministry. We will look at examples of the ministry of Jesus as pastor first. I want to look at two events recorded in the Gospels: the wedding at Cana of Galilee and the ministry to the woman caught in adultery, both of which describe Jesus in his pastoral role.[12] Cana was a small village not far from Nazareth. Jesus, his mother, and his disciples were invited to a wedding in Cana (John 2:1–12). Weddings in this part of the world, then and now, were quite festive and lasted at least a full day. People were served an elaborate meal, and fine wine (the safe drink) flowed freely.[13] As the evening wore on, the hosts of the party were short of wine, and Mary notices this awkward situation. She turns to Jesus for help, and Jesus first asks his mother why he should be concerned, especially if it might give away his identity. Jesus is portrayed as not wanting to be noticed as a person with special gifts; it is enough to just be one of the guests. He says to his mother, "What concern is that to you and to me? My hour has not yet come" (John 2:4). Still having some influence with Jesus, Mary asks him to help and says to those in charge of the festive meal, "Do whatever he tells you." Jesus then points to the "water jars for the Jewish rites of purification, each holding twenty or thirty gallons." The jars typically hold water used by the household, and so when Jesus tells them to fill them to the brim, the servants oblige. He then asks them to draw some water out and take it to the steward. They again follow his guidance, and when the steward tastes what is given to him, he discovers that it is very good wine. Even the bridegroom is congratulated for serving the best wine later in the evening when usually the best wine is served first. The disciples of Jesus begin to notice that this kind of help to others is part of the ministry of Jesus. "Jesus did this, the first of his signs, in Cana of Galilee, and revealed his glory; and the disciples believed in him" (John 2:11).

---

11. This sacrament is understood differently across the Christian church, although all Christians agree that it is a way to be grateful for and empowered by the presence of God. It is to sense the presence of God in one's life.

12. Both of these passages, and particularly the one about the woman caught in adultery, have been questioned regarding their historical accuracy. Yet they do illustrate the larger point of the way that Jesus was a pastor to people. They capture a great truth.

13. Water was not always sterilized, and could cause illness.

In what sense does this event teach us about the pastoral ministry of Jesus, one that takes the form of an invitation to a better life? In many ways, but let me stress three:

- He genuinely cares about the wellbeing and happiness of those who surround him, and especially those who come into his circle of nearness. According to the short dialogue that appears in the Gospel record, Jesus is reluctant to become the center of attention and to reveal his God-given identity and mission. Both the situation and timing are slightly off, but he is nevertheless responsive to his mother's request and the potential embarrassment to those in charge of the wedding. In the end, he sides with the needs of the people, and he does what he can to make the event a truly joyous and happy occasion.

- His ministry is very contextual, and he ministers to people in the middle of their busy and anxious days. He doesn't just speak about the contours of love in a speech, although he does when it is appropriate, but responds in love and caring in the day-to-day needs of the people whom he encounters. Nor does he give advice and say to the steward that he should have planned better. Rather, he helps the steward and the wedding family in the immediate context of their lives.

- His response, quite early in his public ministry, helps the disciples to begin to see the true nature of his ministry. He is not commanding soldiers to attack a neighboring group of people and claim more land, as David might have done (and did). Rather, he responds to a deep human need to make others happy and joyful. He understands that this goal of enabling others to relax and enjoy one another on a most important event in the lives of the newly married couple and their families is also part of his ministry. It is the mark of a good pastor and part of his messianic ministry.[14]

I want to note again that the lines between a pastor and priest are somewhat blurred and overlap. This is the case as we look at another event that describes a priestly ministry, one that may be pastoral as well. As a faithful priest, Jesus brings the forgiveness of God to a person in need. The story is told in the Gospel of John (8:1–11), and it takes place in Jerusalem in the temple. Because of the location in the temple in Jerusalem, it may have occurred a bit later in the public ministry of Jesus, although the precise time in

---

14. This story raises once again the question of the ability of Jesus to perform miracles. Some would interpret this story as a time when Jesus asks the host to find the good wine for the party and serve it, not a time when Jesus turned water into wine. For those present, it was a "miracle."

the public ministry of Jesus is hard to determine. In just a few short verses, the life-changing ministry of Jesus is described. The following components are present:

- It takes place in Jerusalem, the center of the religious, social, and political life of Israel-Palestine in the time of Jesus.
- It is also in the temple, the sort of center of Jerusalem, a place with great historical, social, and religious meaning for the Jewish people.
- Representatives from the governmental and religious establishment have come to question the validity of the ministry of Jesus.
- There is a person in great need that is in the clutches of the authorities for her behavior and suffering from guilt, embarrassment, and shame.
- Jesus must navigate the interaction with the authorities while honoring his commitment to compassion for the woman. He must deal with the effort of the scribes and Pharisees to get a charge against him. "Now the law of Moses commanded us to stone such women. What do you say?"
- It is a woman caught in adultery who is brought before Jesus. There is clear discrimination against the woman. She may have been a victim of sexual assault. Where is the man involved? The #MeToo movement had not yet reached Jerusalem.

Jesus was up for the challenge, and the story captures the essence of his priestly ministry. After listening carefully to the questions from the scribes and Pharisees and with calm poise, he tells them: "Let anyone among you who is without sin be the first to throw a stone at her." He looks down, writes on the ground, and keeps an eye on them as they leave, "one by one, beginning with the elders." Jesus, left alone with the woman, says to her, "Woman, where are they? Has no one condemned you? She said, 'No one sir.' And Jesus said, 'Neither do I condemn you. Go your way, and from now on, do not sin again.'" Note the following about this incident:

1. In his priestly ministry, Jesus brings the forgiveness, compassion, and the peace-giving presence of God to a troubled person. He reassures her and does not condemn her. He then gently says to her, "As you are able, I urge you to avoid these harmful relationships in the future."
2. Jesus clearly honors the woman by taking sides with a person who has been abused and victimized. He challenges the deep prejudice in the social system that allows women to be mistreated and oppressed.

3. He clearly challenges those who have created and sustained the unjust social system to face their hypocritical and harmful ways.

Jesus shows great courage and deep compassion, the heartbeat of priestly ministry. Jesus models for us the ministry of the priest and pastor.

His ministry also included wise and charismatic teaching. He had the remarkable ability to provide life-changing insight to those who came to learn from him. He was an extraordinary educator. In my book *The Radical Teaching of Jesus*, I mention several modes of teaching by Jesus, but for our purposes I want to highlight two of them that demonstrate that he is a gifted teacher.[15] It is through his teaching that he offers the gracious invitation to change directions in life and, by doing so, to flourish and find meaning and purpose in life. By word and deed, he invites them to become a person who is God-centered and filled with love and compassion. His use of parables (telling stories) and his use of aphorisms vividly display his transformational mode of teaching.

We will first look at one of his parables and demonstrate how it illustrates and contains his invitation to a new way of life. The parable is one that is quite familiar, and it is often called the Parable of the Good Samaritan. It is located in the Gospel of Luke 10:25–37.[16] The story begins with a conversation between a lawyer (likely a scribe) and Jesus. The lawyer asks Jesus, "What must I do to inherit eternal life?" Jesus responds with a question: "What is written in the law? What do you read there?" The lawyer says, "You shall love the Lord your God with all your heart, with all your soul, and with all your strength, and with all your mind; and your neighbor as yourself." Jesus said to him: "You have given the right answer; do this, and you will live." Then, in part to justify himself and in part to test Jesus, the lawyer says, "And who is my neighbor?"

Jesus does not reply with an extended theological or sociological explanation. Rather, he uses a story that he hopes will engage the lawyer's imagination and deeply move him. Jesus begins by saying that there was a man who was taking the fairly dangerous and steep road down from Jerusalem to Jericho. It was dusty and dangerous. He was attacked by robbers who took away all that he had, beat him, and put him in a ditch, leaving him injured and alone. The lawyer could identify with this story because he knew that it was a treacherous road with no formal security measures. He also knew that people traveled the road frequently because the two cities were centers of population and activity.

---

15. See Section Two, "The Teaching: Ways of Understanding," 81-153.
16. In can also be found in Matthew 22:34-40 and Mark 12:28-34.

THE TEACHING, HEALING, AND PROPHETIC CHALLENGE 143

Jesus continues the story. He says that a priest went by, saw the injured man on the side of the road, and kept walking. No doubt the priest was busy, wanted to be on time for his meeting to arrange for the weekend worship, and perhaps thought that it was inappropriate for a priest to have dealings with one who may not have been Jewish. The person by the side of the road may have had a different ethnic background, the status of a second-class citizen, and today might be one we might call a Palestinian. He was likely a marginalized Canaanite.

Jesus continues the story. Another religious leader, a Levite, a member of a tribe of people who were especially religious and often became priests, also went by and crossed to the other side of the road. The Levite also had reasons to pass by on the other side of the road, perhaps because he knew how hard it would be to take care of the injured man, and he, like the priest, had other priorities. In addition, he may have been conscious of the social guideline that Levites only serve faithful Jews.

As Jesus wraps up the story, he says that an outsider, a Samaritan, came by and saw the injured man and was moved with pity and compassion. He knelt beside him, poured healing oil and wine on his wounds, and bandaged him. He then picked him up, placed him on his donkey, took him to an inn, and cared for him. He paid for the injured man's stay at the inn, asked the innkeeper to take care of the man, and said that he would be back after his meeting and would then pay for any additional expenses. Jesus turns to the lawyer and asks, "Which of these three do you think was the neighbor to the man who fell into the hands of the robbers?" The lawyer responds, "The one who showed him mercy." Jesus responds by saying, "Go and do likewise."

The meaning of the story is relatively clear, although it may be wise to underline the following points:

1. The story gives the lawyer an invitation to a life of care and service. He does so by answering his question in story form, a method that would engage the feelings and imagination of the listener. He invites him (and us) to receive the love and compassion of God, be transformed, and begin to show love and compassion in our lives. It is an invitation to receive the power and presence of God, become God-centered, and to decide to be a person for others. Jesus teaches that eternal life begins now. He does not understand eternal life as it is often understood today as "when we die and go to heaven." The lawyer felt like he had already covered these bases and demonstrated his understanding of the double-love commandment: to love God with heart, soul, might, and mind, and to love one's neighbor in all the ways that we love ourselves. But having this knowledge was not enough, and so he asks, "who is my

neighbor?" The lawyer's questions about eternal life and identifying one's neighbor may either be interpreted as sincere or as a test of the validity of the ministry of Jesus. Jesus decides to take the questions seriously, and uses the occasion to help the lawyer and to challenge the interpretations of mercy that had accumulated around Torah. Torah teaches that we provide mercy to all in need. It is not exclusive, commanding that we show mercy and love only those within our own circle and tribe.

2. Jesus treats the lawyer with great respect, although he may have felt that the lawyer's questions were somewhat disingenuous. But Jesus does not call him on his hypocrisy, inviting him to consider how he might change his direction and truly love all people in quite tangible ways. He shows love for the scribe in not condemning him, giving him an opportunity to endorse the full presence and power of God in his life. Jesus, ever the charismatic teacher, tells an insightful story, and the smart lawyer knew that his self-justification would not hold up.

3. Perhaps the lawyer left the conversation with new insight and a desire to change directions. He may have learned that loving God and his neighbor meant to pay attention to the people who are robbed and beaten daily and left in the ditch. There are many of them in the world, and we meet them everyday. The invitation of Jesus was to join with God and the beloved community of faith to help build a more just and humane world. This can be done daily as we travel our roads, learn how to show compassion, and help shape policies as we reflect on our troubled world. Hatred and prejudice are present; by love alone, those wounds are healed. We can advocate for ways that:

- create an earth community with ecological integrity;
- create an earth community of care and respect;
- create a global culture of social and economic justice; and
- create a global context of participatory governance, nonviolence, and peace.

The stories of Jesus had (and continue to have) a way of getting to the heart of his listeners, stirring their conscience and changing their beliefs and values. So too do the several aphoristic sayings of Jesus, which have a way of capturing our attention, causing us to reflect, and giving us a new outlook on life. There are many from which to choose, and I have selected three that cause us to ponder how to understand and find God, how we are to live, and how to frame our goals in life.

THE TEACHING, HEALING, AND PROPHETIC CHALLENGE 145

I turn first to the beatitudes in Matthew's version of the Sermon on the Mount, a section of Scripture that contains many concise statements of principles for life and terse formations of a deep truth. They have a kind of zen quality about them. I want to initially reflect on the beatitude found in Matthew 5:8: "Blessed are the pure in heart, for they shall see God." This axiom invites us to initially reflect on the meaning of the words as they have been translated. "Blessed" has the connotation of being deeply and profoundly happy or content. It is not a passing sort of enjoyment that comes from receiving a present or even the stimulation of meeting someone and enjoying warm feelings of connection with another. It is a reference to a longer lasting and deep inner peace that comes from God's presence. "Pure," which might also be translated literally as "clean," means that we have integrity; that what we think, say, and do is genuine and always truthful. A pure heart is a way of speaking about an authentic person. "Heart" is a reference to our center, what we are as a person, and our true self rather than a person with a false consciousness and alienated self, one that is controlled by ego needs. We are therefore one who can be trusted; we are clean with nothing false or hidden. And the verb "see" means that our integrity helps us to see clearly, to understand fully, and not to be influenced and swayed by hidden needs and motivations. We grasp and experience the heart of God.

The verse teaches that those with a pure heart can establish a genuine and loving relationship with God. It will be one that seeks to link with God with no hidden and calculating motives. It is to be in harmony with God and to seek to do the will and way of God. It is to become God-centered, and by having a pure motivation, we find a deep and abiding peace. We are motivated and empowered to engage in loving and compassionate behavior, and through our service to seek a more just and peaceful world for all people.

I have been nudged by this verse to find other related Scripture that can expand and deepen my understanding. For example, I seek to follow the exhortation in Psalm 46:10 to "be still and know that I am God." It is when I am still and silent that I hear the voice of God. I am motivated to be led to "still waters" (Psalm 23:2b) and, in the beauty and quiet of nature, experience the presence of God. I can even imagine myself with Jesus and the disciples on the Sea of Galilee in the midst of a storm and hear the divine voice say "Peace! Be still!" In my quiet moments of prayer, contemplation, and meditation, I begin to experience the teaching of Jesus: "Blessed are the pure in heart, for they will see God."

I want to turn to another one of the aphoristic sayings of Jesus, one that can be quoted by nearly everyone in that it is a proverb that is almost universally taught by all the great religious teachers of the human family. It is called the Golden Rule within the Jewish-Christian tradition. I quote it from Matthew 7:12: "In everything do to others as you would have them do to you; for this is the law and the prophets." The setting and context of this aphorism of Jesus is found within the verse itself, that is, the behavior described is the essence of what is taught in the Hebrew Bible, the law (Torah) and the prophets. It describes a mode of deepening our motivation to follow the will and way of God. It is a way of capturing in one short sentence the essence of the ethical responsibilities we have as those dedicated to God and to service in God's name. It has three clear components:

1. First, the passage underlines that the principle of the Golden Rule applies to all dimensions of our relationships with others. We are to be caring and compassionate and seek justice and peace in all circumstances and with all people. It is not just applicable in some circumstances and with a few people who we know and in whose presence we are comfortable. We treat every person whom we encounter in just the same way we want to be treated. We give them acceptance and respect even if they are ethnically different from us, have different customs, have different skin color, a different sexual orientation, speak a different language, and come from a different social class. Our feelings of fear and insecurity in the company of those who are different from us might cause us to turn away. Yet if we were in their culture, we would value their acceptance of us, and their willingness to help us as we try to find our way in an unfamiliar setting. So we do for others what we would want them to do for us.

2. The passage allows or at least does not prohibit feelings of hurt or anger in reference to others. In fact, we might learn from these experiences. For example, when we fail and cause harm in our relationship and responsibility with another person, we are often called into account. The moment may be painful to us and cause regret and guilt. But if we are open to learning and not defensive, we might discover new insights about our style and needs. This new information may help us in our desire to do to others what they might do to us. In time, when our intense feelings subside, we may be able to be grateful for the correction. There will be times when we fail to live up to our ideals of love and integrity. A careful and sensitive word from the one we have offended may be one to which we can express gratitude rather than feel threatened. It can be a gift. We need to be willing to accept the correction from others. In addition, we want our feelings of offense when we encounter behavior that is harmful and dishonest to be expressed in a way that might be helpful to others. We need to cultivate a sincere

desire to help others when there is conflict and pain in a way that does not just mean getting even or acting in harsh anger to hurt them.

3. In these ways, we seek to follow the will and way of God and honor our deep and profound religious heritage of the "law and the prophets." We do the will of God by intelligent and intentional loving.

I want to look at one other saying of Jesus that contains extraordinary wisdom in a short sentence. The setting for this aphorism is found in the description of the betrayal and arrest of Jesus in the last days of his life.[17] Jesus is in or near the garden of Gethsemane. While he is speaking with the disciples, Judas arrives with soldiers who have "swords and clubs" to arrest Jesus. Judas tells the armed group that he will kiss the man who they are seeking to arrest. Judas approaches Jesus, saying, "Greetings, Rabbi," and proceeds to kiss him. Jesus tells him to do what he is there to do. Then the soldiers arrest Jesus. One of the disciples (Peter is named in the Gospel of John) is very afraid but wants to protect Jesus, and so he pulls out his sword and cuts off the ear of the high priest's servant. Jesus turns to Peter, tells him to put his sword away, and says, "all who take the sword will perish by the sword" (Matt 26:52).

This comment, while spoken in a specific context, has been heard clearly across the centuries, especially in the context of violence and war. The comment is often translated as "those who use the sword will perish by the sword." One might interpret the passage as a comment meant just for the incident in the garden of Gethsemane, but it is more often understood as a universal principle in the ethical teaching of Jesus. I understand it as a deep conviction applied to a specific context in which the case of one disciple using his sword as he is surrounded by fully armed soldiers would have led to harm for many. I also see the saying of Jesus as foundational to the ethics of Jesus. Jesus is saying in the aphorism that war and violence do not generally solve problems and conflicts. Rather, they encourage more warfare and violence that harms not only the ones using the weapons, but innocent people as well. Jesus is not only wise to tell Peter to put his sword away because they are outnumbered; he is also wise to teach that his way and the way of God is to find nonviolent ways of dealing with conflict.

There are places in the Bible that do not affirm this universal principle of nonviolence. There are, for example, curses and plagues that seem to be accepted as judgment and deliverance. There is even a suggestion that God may be vengeful. Both in the Hebrew Bible and occasionally in the New Testament, especially in the book of Revelation, we see the use of violent

---

17. Matt 26:47–56.

means to resist the enemy and achieve justice.[18] There are persuasive arguments for protecting oneself from aggressive and devastating violence and perhaps a moral right to protect other innocents by resorting to arms. I have read the well-reasoned arguments for a just war. But I am more drawn to the multitude of ways to end war and resolve conflicts in a nonviolent way. I side with Jesus in the garden that we may need to find good ways to be safe and secure and explore nonviolent ways to resolve our conflicts.[19] I understand the saying of Jesus, spoken in the garden of Gethsemane, as a universal ethical norm, one that we seek to apply with great care and wisdom in our conflicted and violent world.

Jesus models the roles of pastor and priest as he carries out his ministry in Palestine, both in the region of Galilee and in Judea. As part of this ministry, he demonstrates that he is a master teacher and gifted educator, inviting those who meet him and hear his message to change directions, give up their self-centered lives, and choose a God-centered life. In my book *The Radical Teaching of Jesus*, I underlined that his ministry also included healing and finding good ways to relieve suffering. His ministry was a ministry to the whole person. As we look at the healing ministry of Jesus, I want us to note that his ministry was primarily to the Jewish population. Yet he also healed those who lived within the bounds of the larger region of Palestine and were not considered Jewish by heritage. As he healed these outsiders, he was expressing compassion and demonstrating that compassion has no ethnic or political boundaries.

There is an account in both Mark 7:24–30 and Matthew 15:21–28 of Jesus healing a Syrophoenician woman, also identified as a Canaanite and a Gentile. From time to time, Jesus crossed the artificial boundaries of the region. On one occasion, he traveled to the district of Tyre and Sidon, a coastal region in the north of Upper Galilee. There he encountered a desperate woman who was worried about her child. She tells Jesus that her daughter is tormented by a demon. Initially, Jesus was a bit reluctant to enter into her suffering and respond to her plea. The disciples discouraged her from bothering Jesus, saying that "she keeps shouting after us." Jesus gently tells her that his primary mission is to "lost sheep of the house of Israel." With a phrase somewhat difficult for us to grasp, Jesus says to her, "It is not fair

---

18. See the excellent treatment of this subject in Crossan, *How to Read the Bible*. It raises the question of whether God is violent and vengeful, with an exploration of this concern from Genesis to Revelation.

19. There are innumerable books on the ways to prevent war. I have been helped by the book written by Robert Pickus and Robert Woito from the World Without War Council entitled *To End War: An Introduction: Ideas, Books, Organizations, Work that Can Help*.

THE TEACHING, HEALING, AND PROPHETIC CHALLENGE 149

to take the children's food and throw it to the dogs." These may not be the actual words of Jesus (or at least, I hope not), but a later redaction by a Jewish insider. It may have been a common saying in the culture. The woman replies to the metaphor and tells Jesus that "even the dogs eat the crumbs from the Master's table." Jesus' reluctance fades and compassion takes over. He says to her, "Great is your faith! Let it be done for you as you wish." And the daughter was healed instantly. I select this story because it contains several important issues.

- The first is that one part of the ministry of Jesus took him to regions in the north, closer to Syria. There was a mixed population in this region, and it was likely that the Jewish people were a minority. Jesus would have been comfortable in those settings because he was born and grew up in Galilee, where there was a more diverse population. The woman he met was a Canaanite, very similar in meaning to the term "Palestinian" that we now use for the indigenous people of the region.

- The original authors who put this story in its final form in Mark, and then in Matthew from Mark, continue to understand the ministry of Jesus as not starting a new religion, but as the renewal and revival of the spirituality of Judaism. Hence, there is the analogy that dogs are able to eat crumbs that fall from the table. By the time the story was put into written form, there was tension between traditional Judaism based in Jerusalem and the Jesus movement. The tension is in the background of the story, with reference to the primary ministry of Jesus to the Jewish people. It brings some drama to the tale. As it appears in Matthew late in the first century, there would be the sense of a new community forming around the life and teachings of Jesus that made the mainline Jewish leaders uneasy.

- Those who preserve the story and put it in written form, aware of the tension, nevertheless affirm that Jesus had compassion for all who suffer, not just those within the Jewish population. This story is only one of many references to Jesus showing compassion to all the people who came to him for healing. Jesus understands the universal call for healing and relief from suffering to be a human concern, and is not limited by the borderline tribalism in traditional Judaism.

- The healing itself is not only attributed to the gift of Jesus for healing. It is also and more directly linked to the faith of the Canaanite woman. While we need to be careful not to read too much into this story, we can say that the healing gift of Jesus was in the majority of cases linked to faith in the healing power of God. Those needing healing have faith that God can heal through the ministry of Jesus. This faith in God is integral to the healing process.

- This story lends itself to an understanding of healing that has a strong psychological component. As we read several stories of Jesus' healing power, he appears to be able to heal those who are described as being possessed by a demon. These descriptions may be read literally, that there are evil demons that possess people. But I prefer to think of them as therapeutic and spiritual healings, not unlike those we might experience or observe today, but without reference to a personal evil or a demon being the cause.

I want to look at one other account of the healing ministry of Jesus that raises similar issues and questions: the account of the healing of the Gerasene demoniac, as he is called (Mark 5:1–2; Matt 8:28–29; Luke 8:26–39). The setting is on what is the Sea of Galilee, essentially a large lake that was an important source of food for the people of the region. Many of the stories of Jesus take place in this region. It is a story of Jesus crossing the Sea of Galilee, stepping out of the boat, and being met immediately by a man "with an unclean spirit." This man had lived in isolation and was often in shackles and chains because he could not control his behavior. In fact, he may have had inordinate strength and could break out of his bindings, which made the people very afraid of him. When he was not chained, he wandered through the tombs in cemeteries and hiked the mountains, "howling and bruising himself with stone." When he saw Jesus, "he ran to him, bowed down before him; and shouted at the top of his voice, 'what have you to do with me, Jesus, Son of the Most High God? I adjure you by God, do not torment me.'" Jesus speaks to him, and indirectly to the demon, saying, "Come out of the man, you unclean spirit." Jesus speaks of the unclean spirit as Legion, implying that there was more than one evil spirit in the man. Seeing a herd of swine near, the unclean spirits ask that they be sent into the swine, which all panic and rush down the bank into the sea and are drowned. People in the region hear the story, see that the man is healed (in his right mind), and then ask Jesus to leave because they are afraid of his power. The healed man asks if he can join Jesus, but Jesus encourages him to stay in the region and tell his friends how he has been healed.

This is not an easy story to interpret given the differences in understanding between the people in the time and region of Gerasene and our contemporary understanding of what we might call mental illness. It raises several important issues:

1. One issue is whether we should read the story in a literal way and assume that there was a "legion" of demons in the troubled man; or whether the story is told within a prescientific (premodern) frame of reference and contains the categories of reality that they used to explain the behavior of the troubled man. I prefer to explain the story using the modern categories of mental illness.

2. Making this choice, I am also suggesting a hermeneutical principle in the interpretation of Scripture that suggests that we look at this healing and others like it in a contemporary frame of reference, yet do so with wisdom and care. Across the centuries the church, honoring the Bible as a valuable source of information and authoritative norm for faith, has had to find ways of interpreting the Bible that are credible for their time and place in history. For example, we may interpret these kinds of healings and even the six-day creation story in Genesis in a contemporary frame of reference. We understand the creation story in a metaphorical way, stressing the foundational truth that God is Creator. And then we integrate this foundational truth into our scientific understanding of the formation of the cosmos, nature, and evolution.

3. We focus our attention in the story on the compassionate healing ministry of Jesus and his gracious invitation to the desperate man that his life could be changed and that he could return to normal life in the community.

4. We understand that Jesus was fully open to the presence of God and was able to channel the healing power of God into this desperately sick man.

5. We do not ignore the details of the story, such as the shift of the demons to the swine and their rush into the sea. Again, we have choices in our interpretation, the first being that there was an actual transfer of evil spirits into the swine that caused them to panic. Or, we could again suggest that this description drew upon categories of understanding of those living with a premodern outlook, and that there was sufficient disruption in the environment that caused the swine to panic. I prefer this option and do so within the hermeneutical principle outlined above, knowing that it does suggest an understanding of the Bible as containing the truth, but not always literally.

I would like to turn now to one other category of the ministry of Jesus, which is that he may also be understood as a radical prophet and leader. Again, by using the term radical, I am describing Jesus as one who dared to challenge the traditional formulations of religious faith and the inequity that existed in the social, economic, and political structures of his time. He advocated alternative norms of understanding, behavior, and social structures. There is a section in the Gospel of Matthew that illustrates the radical character of the life and teaching of Jesus. The author of Matthew has a general order of time in the public ministry of Jesus, although frequently the material is bunched around certain themes. It is an effective design, making the Gospel of Matthew an informed and persuasive account. One of the subjects that the Gospel places in a topical way, as well as a sequential way, has to do with the interaction of Jesus with the scribes and Pharisees. This topical unit is found in Matthew 23, and it is quite radical in the criticism of these influential people who have shaped the religious and social norms of Israel. The scribes are educated in the teachings of the Law and act like lawyers in many cases. The Pharisees are deeply committed to applying Torah to personal behavior and social norms.

Initially, Matthew's Gospel gives credit where credit is due. Matthew 23 begins with the following statement: "Then Jesus said to the crowds and to the disciples, 'The scribes and the Pharisees sit on Moses' seat; therefore do whatever they teach you and follow it.'" The passage continues with the caveat "but do not do as they do, for they do not practice what they teach. They tie up heavy burdens, hard to bear, and lay them on the shoulders of others; but they themselves are unwilling to lift a finger to move them. They do all their deeds to be seen by others" (23:1–5a). As we explore this prophetic account, we need to be sensitive that there was no audio recording of what Jesus has said, only memory and oral tradition. The author of Matthew is writing many years after the words and actions of Jesus occurred. Further, we sense that this material was written at a time when there was tension between the mainline Judaism of Jerusalem and the new movement based on the way of Jesus. What we have is a collection of sayings on the subject of the conflict, not a single speech. There is likely some modification of the sources available. Nevertheless, we sense that there was a sufficient basis to describe the leadership and prophetic character of the life and teaching of Jesus within this prophetic frame of reference. There are very critical descriptions of the hypocrisy and lack of enlightened spiritual guidance within the religious establishment. Jesus names it and calls for change.

As a summary, I want to quote one descriptive verse in Matthew 23. Verse 23 say: "Woe to you scribes and Pharisees, hypocrites! For you tithe mint, dill, and cumin, and have neglected the weightier matters of the law: justice and mercy and faith. It is these you ought to have practiced without neglecting others. You blind guides! Your strain out a gnat but swallow a camel." Again, without a definitive interpretation of the entire chapter, I

THE TEACHING, HEALING, AND PROPHETIC CHALLENGE   153

want to call attention to the implications of the kind of prophetic leadership that Jesus is giving.

1. First, this section (interpreting it with care, as I have suggested) is part of the invitation of Jesus to call his followers (and questioning listeners) to a way of life that is God-centered rather than self-centered. He is saying that we should endorse the will and way of God for ourselves and for the faithful community we lead. There is no room for hypocrisy, a characteristic in leadership that is the most damaging to the community of faith. All people, and especially leaders, must live under the reign of God.

2. It is not enough to go through the motions of the customary religious practices, such as tithing mint, dill, and cumin, as if this practice of symbolic giving is pleasing to God. It is not enough to go through the motions of religious worship and practice, and it is especially harmful to the community of faith when its leaders tell you what to do and do not follow it themselves. In my experience, there are few behaviors that hurt the community of faith more than leaders who have little integrity.

3. Jesus does have integrity, however. He practices and models what he teaches. I suspect that this is why he was so popular in the early part of his ministry, and yet opposed by the religious authorities when he prophetically and boldly spoke truth to power. He demonstrated great courage and was a extraordinary example of a leader and prophet.

4. He makes clear what the "weightier matters of the law" are! They are to seek justice, act with mercy, and to have a deep faith in and relationship with God. Note that Jesus, at least in this verse, gives a very high priority to justice. It is in many ways the heart of Torah. Jesus is concerned for the welfare of the people who live under the rule of an alien government and with a religious community that also had responsibility for the structures of society. The culture was predatory in nature and led to inequity before the law and backbreaking poverty. He also addresses the concern for mercy, to care for those who suffer and are mistreated by the unjust social systems, those who live in fear and are without hope. The people needed to be heard regarding their condition—helped, healed, forgiven, and given a hopeful future. They were short on love and compassion, the essence of the ministry and teaching of Jesus. Note that Jesus also speaks to the issue of faith. The religious leaders were not fully assisting the people in the community of faith to deepen and broaden their understanding of the

covenant love of God and the ways that a deep spirituality can make them blessed. Jesus taught about being blessed: "Blessed are the poor in spirit, for theirs is the kingdom of heaven. Blessed are those who mourn, for they shall find comfort. Blessed are the meek for they shall inherit the earth. Blessed are those who hunger and thirst for righteousness, for they will be filled. Blessed are the merciful, for they will receive mercy."[20]

The invitation of Jesus is to a way of life that is God-centered. It comes to us in many forms, and it is certainly present in a gracious and bold way through his courageous prophetic leadership. He is fond of saying "follow me."[21] We turn now to how he exemplifies his mission and invitation in the last week of his life.

Study Resources

Discussion Questions

1. In what ways do the roles of pastor and priest differ, and how did Jesus engage in both of these ministries?
2. Do you think that Jesus actually healed people such as those with a serious disease or those suffering from a disability such as a deformity or blindness? How do you understand the healing of Jesus of those described as being demon-possessed?
3. How would you describe the method of Jesus as a teacher (rabbi) and educator? What made his teaching so effective and transformational?
4. In what ways was Jesus both a prophet and a leader? What is the role of the prophet? Of the teacher?
5. How did Jesus invite people to a new way of life in his various roles as pastor and priest; teacher and educator; healer and reliever of suffering; prophet and leader?

---

20. Matt 5:3–7.
21. Matt 4:19; 10:38.

Terms and Concepts

1. Pastor: one who ministers to people in the community of faith, guiding and teaching them and helping them take their concerns and burdens to God.

2. Priest (Levite in the Jewish community in the time of Jesus): one who speaks to the people about God's expectations for them and helps them to experience the presence of God through worship and ceremony (e.g., the Eucharist).

3. Aphorism: a concise statement of a principle or a terse formulation of a truth or sentiment.

4. Prophet: one who looks to the future and calls those in positions of leadership to govern with mercy and justice, a moral and ethical leader.

5. Demon: In biblical times, it was a reference to evil spirit, often abiding in a person, causing them to be emotionally ill and act in a harmful way.

Suggested Reading

Chilton, Bruce. *Rabbi Jesus: An Intimate Biography.* New York: Doubleday, 2000.
Johnson, Elizabeth A. *Consider Jesus: Waves of Renewal in Christology.* New York: Crossroad, 1990.
Keck, Leander E. *Who Is Jesus? History in Perfect Tense.* Minneapolis: Fortress, 2000.
Lohfink, Gerhard. *Jesus of Nazareth: What He Wanted, Who He Was.* Translated by Linda M. Maloney. Collegeville: Liturgical, 2012.
Meyers, Robin R. *Saving Jesus from the Church: How to Stop Worshiping Christ and Start Following Jesus.* New York: HarperOne, 2009.

9

The Last Week

We are reflecting on what I have called "The Radical Invitation of Jesus" and have maintained that Jesus invites all people to a way of life that is God-centered rather than self-centered. In American society, it appears that the vast majority of people are driven by the self-centered quest for wealth, power, and prestige. Further, we live in a world of constant distractions, and are continually pushed by our commodity and predatory economy to a selfish way of life, believing that happiness comes with collecting the abundance of things that are attractive to us. In addition, the world in which we live is filled with suffering and violence, and the world's infrastructure problems are overwhelming. We are affected by them, often suffer, and we notice in very vivid ways the suffering of others. These conditions make the invitation of Jesus radical in the sense that he offers a profound alternative, one that goes against the norms of our society and offers a new perspective on the overwhelming problems of contemporary life. He invites his listeners to make a fundamental change in outlook and their lifestyle. His words echo the call for a comparable change in our time. His invitation and promise are that we can be redeemed, set free from harmful patterns of life, and find a better way.

In word and deed, Jesus says that such a spiritual pathway has the foundational belief that God is love, and that love should now become our deepest value and the motivating force in our lives. As we accept the invitation, we will be transformed and grow toward a life of deep inner contentment, meaning, and purpose. Jesus modeled this spiritual pathway. We see in him and through his teaching that such a life is undergirded by a commitment to truth and integrity that is centered on the practice of love and compassion, and dedicated to creating a more just and humane world. In our own way and unique life situation, as we accept the invitation, each of us will be empowered to become a whole person who lives for the welfare of others. Our deep inner self will no longer be clothed in our ego needs. We will be emancipated to become all that God wants us to be. God is Love and we are to live "in Love."[1]

In this section, we have explored the way that this invitation unfolds in the life and teaching of Jesus. It was visible in his young mother and all those present at his birth. They asked, "Is this child the promised one, the messiah?" This was profoundly evident as he dedicated himself in his baptism by John and in his time of retreat in the wilderness. The contours of the invitation became clearer as Jesus began his public ministry of charismatic teaching, compassionate healing, and prophetic challenge to the social and religious norms of his culture. His public ministry came to its dramatic conclusion in Jerusalem. In this final week, he continued his insightful teaching, had several conversations with his disciples and those in power, and engaged in prophetic action in the temple. He was arrested and sentenced to death because he would not compromise his commitment to truth, love, and justice. His disciples believed that he triumphed over death, and they sensed his presence as they continued his mission.[2]

His Entry Into Jerusalem

The Gospels, while differing some in the details, agree that Jesus did go to Jerusalem to bring his life and teaching to Israel's center of religious and political power. As his teaching and healing ministries developed in the early part of his ministry in Galilee and the occasional trip into Judea, he began to experience more resistance. There were issues to face and problems to solve. The Gospel of Luke gives careful attention to his trip with his disciples down from Galilee to Jerusalem (9:51—19:28). This account provides a good orientation to his last week. So does the Gospel of Matthew in a brief way: "From that time on, Jesus began to show his disciples that he must go to Jerusalem and undergo great suffering at the hands of the elders, and chief priests and scribes, and be killed, and on the third day be raised" (Matt 16:21).[3] Matthew records a pivotal conversation between Jesus and

---

1. Merton, Thomas, *Love and Living*, 18–22.

2. Marcus Borg and John Dominic Crossan have given us a good summary of the last week of the life of Jesus in their book, *The Last Week: A Day-by-Day Account of the Jesus's Final Week in Jerusalem*. I am following their description.

3. It is important to note that this verse reflects the point of view of the author of

his disciples regarding the trip. There is a quite direct exchange between Jesus and Peter as he informs Peter and the disciples about his true identity and that his messianic ministry will mean going to Jerusalem and facing death (16:13–23). It is the turning point in the ministry of Jesus.

He arrives in Jerusalem in a somewhat dramatic way, though slightly understated because he rode into the city by himself on the back of a borrowed colt. He did not arrive on a white stallion in a military uniform with trumpets announcing his coming. It was not the kingdom of Caesar arriving, but the kingdom of God. Those who knew of his coming did gather to greet him. Mark describes the scene by saying:

> Those who went ahead and those who followed were shouting, "Hosanna![4] Blessed is the one who comes in the name of the Lord! Blessed is the coming kingdom of our ancestor David! Hosanna in the highest heaven!" Then he entered Jerusalem and went to the temple, and when he had looked around at everything, as it was already late, he went out to Bethany with the twelve." (Mark 11:9–11)

As we reflect on his entry into Jerusalem and his visit to the temple, we should note several basic themes:

1. We are able to see the clear intention of Jesus to bring his mission to its definitive conclusion. He knows that it will be dangerous because of the opposition he has had, and yet he believes that his mission would not be complete without the visit. As a way of demonstrating this clear goal, he arranges for a triumphal entry with his followers greeting him with palm branches and other ways of honoring him. Others from the city would hear about his arrival, as would many visitors to Jerusalem. The population of the city would have nearly doubled because it was the time of a religious holiday. Christians now call this day Palm Sunday.

2. Though it is late in the day, Jesus goes to the temple, knowing that it will be at this site, the center of the social and religious life of the people, where he will make his bold statement. Their late visit enabled Jesus and his followers to plan for how he might undertake his mission. The strategy and plan lock into place.

---

the Gospel of Matthew, written several years after the life of Jesus, when there was some conflict between the new Christian movement and Judaism.

4. Hosanna is a Hebrew word meaning "save" and is used in reference to the coming messiah.

3. He makes his base in a village just outside of Jerusalem in Bethany, where he has friends and supporters and where he returns during the week to rest. Jesus is not alone, although there will be times during this complex and demanding week that he will feel isolated. He prepares himself for the week within a community of support.

Monday: Dramatic Actions

The following day, Monday, Jesus returns to Jerusalem. His disciples accompany him, and he speaks with them about how their lives and the context around them will dramatically change. As they walk into the city from Bethany, he comes to a fig tree that has no fruit and uses it as a symbol to illustrate this change. He will boldly speak about the emptiness of the religious life of the people, that no growth (fruit) can come from the current patterns of belief and practice. In the account in Mark, this teaching is the beginning of his prophetic statements and actions. He will underline his message again as they come to the temple.

Monday is a full day. The sequence of events is recorded in Mark's Gospel (11:12–19).[5] As they enter Jerusalem, Jesus and his disciples go directly to the temple and begin the bold prophetic proclamations and actions:

- Jesus goes to where they are selling and buying in the temple, and takes aim at the moneychangers. In a bold action, he overturns the tables of the moneychangers and the seats of those who sold doves.
- In addition, he blocks the pathway and prevents people from carrying their purchases through.
- As he performs these acts, he explains the reason. He draws upon the Hebrew Bible and says: "Is it not written, 'My house shall be called a house of prayer for all nations'? But you have made it a den of robbers."
- As the chief priests and the scribes hear about this protest, they look for a way to arrest and even kill him. They were threatened and afraid because Jesus was becoming too popular. Mark says that "the whole crowd was spellbound by his teaching."
- As the day unfolded and moved toward the evening, Jesus and his disciples left the city.

This account where Jesus overturns the tables of the moneychangers and the seats of those who sold doves has been variously interpreted. Earlier we did

---

5. See as well Matt 21:12–19; Luke 19:45–48; and John 2:13–22.

speak of this action,[6] but I want to return to the discussion of how it may be best understood. As we do, we need to keep in mind the larger purpose of Jesus coming to Jerusalem. His purpose is to boldly proclaim the coming of the reign of God. The incident should be understood within this larger frame of reference, and not simply as a one-time spontaneous action, a single incident that caused his irritation and offended his sensitivities about religious practice. However, we can say that one fairly obvious meaning of the incident was that the commercial character of the moneychangers and those selling doves offended Jesus. In addition, there may have been a poor exchange rate, making it difficult for those living in poverty to come to the temple with their alms and sacrifices in order to fulfill their religious obligations. They would need to get the appropriate kind and amount of money and then purchase doves. Jesus is saying that the temple is not the place to take advantage of those who have come to worship. It is a place of prayer.

The day of actions and teaching of Jesus was about the whole system. It was about the fig tree that did not produce fruit. In the view of Jesus, the religious system had lost its meaning, and was not meeting the spiritual needs of the people. Neither was it guiding the nation to pursue the welfare of the people. The current system did not give them the security of a setting in which there was peace and justice. In addition, it may have been the case that Jesus was also taking aim at the value of offering a blood sacrifice, although the people who came to worship needed some of these services in order to fulfill their religious obligations. He was more likely questioning the character of the entire system of religious life, which included making atonement through the blood of animals. His target was the emptiness of routinely going through rituals and making sacrifices without understanding that the essence of Torah is about loving God with one's whole being, living ethically in accord with Torah teaching, and seeking peace and justice for the Jewish people.

It is important to note as well that the outer section of the temple was a place "of prayer for all nations." The proclamation of Jesus is that the reign of God is universal. It is likely that undergirding this proclamation of Jesus may be the way that the author of Mark's Gospel maintains that Jesus is challenging another reign: that of the reign of Roman power. The time of the writing of the Gospel of Mark does match the time of the rebellion of Jewish people over against Rome (66–74), and while we do not have an exact date of the writing of the Gospel of Mark, the author of Mark would have the

---

6. See chapter 6, in which we discuss how Jesus managed conflict.

challenge of Roman rule in mind. There was a clear conflict between the reign of God and the reign of Caesar.[7]

Tuesday: Teaching the Disciples and Exchanges with the Temple Authorities

Tuesday is another full day, and much of it is about the way Jesus manages the conflict with the authorities in the temple area. At least a third of the time on Tuesday is about Jesus talking with them about the destruction of the temple and the coming of the Son of God.[8] It is obvious that Jesus and the temple authorities have a different understanding of the place and current value of the way the temple is being run. The temple, in the time of Jesus, was much more than just a religious building on the corner of an important street in town. It was the center of the city. In fact, it had at least five different sections, each serving different needs and groups:

1. The Court of the Gentiles is where the non-Jewish population could pray. It was also where there was a market for sellers of animals for sacrifice, and the place where money could be exchanged. It was in this court that Jesus showed his anger about how what was going on hindered gentiles from praying.

2. There was a Court for Women where women and children could go to pray, and a setting in which there were four candelabra symbolizing a tree of life and God's unseen presence with light that shows the way.[9]

3. There was a Court of Israel where Jewish men brought their animals for sacrifice.

4. There was the Court of the Priests, where priests made their sacrifices.

5. And there was the Sanctuary, the Holy of Holies, symbolizing God's presence.

The religious leaders, and the Pharisees in particular, saw the temple as the center of their religious life, a setting in which they could be blessed by God as they studied the Torah. However, some of the common people would have viewed the temple as the place of power and a symbol of all that oppressed them. It is clear from the exchange Jesus had with the temple authorities that

7. Borg and Crossan, *Last Week*, 49–53.

8. See chapter 6 on the way this interaction about the destruction of the temple might be understood.

9. These candelabra had been present in earlier Jewish worship serving the cultic practices.

Jesus saw the temple as a sort of symbol of all that was wrong with Israel, and why he displays prophetic judgment on the temple.[10]

Most of the rest of Tuesday is spent in conversations with the disciples and with people in the temple. As they walk back from Bethany to the temple on Tuesday morning, Jesus reminds them of the lesson from the fig tree, and then they go directly to the outer court. As they enter this area, Jesus is confronted by the temple authorities and asked,

> "By what authority are you doing these things? Who gave you this authority to do these things?" Jesus said to them, "I will ask you one question: answer me, and I will tell you by what authority I do these things. Did the baptism of John come from heaven, or was it of human origin? Answer me." They argued with one another, "If we say, 'from heaven,' he will say, 'Why then did you not believe him?' But shall we say of human origin?" They were afraid of the crowd, for all regarded John as truly a prophet. So they answered Jesus, "We do not know." And Jesus said to them, "Neither will I tell you by what authority I am doing these things." (Mark 11:27–32)

It is an interesting exchange, and we observe how Jesus evades their trap and even makes them look a bit foolish. Indirectly, he is saying to them that his authority comes from God, even as John's ministry came from God.

Jesus goes on to teach the disciples and the many who have come to hear him throughout the day. Following the exchange with the temple authorities, he tells all those gathered around him a parable about the wicked tenants (Mark 12:1–12). It is a story about a man who planted a vineyard and then left the region, leasing the vineyards to a tenant. Following the harvest, the owner sends a servant to bring back the revenue from the tenant, but the servant is beaten up and sent away. The owner tries again, but again the servant is sent away empty-handed. Another representative of the owner is actually killed. Finally the owner sends his beloved son, thinking he will be respected. But he is recognized as the heir and one who has a rightful claim to the money, and he too is killed. The question arises about what the owner of the vineyard should do. The owner returns, sends the tenants away, and gives the vineyard to others. The temple authorities recognize that the parable is about them, and that they as tenants will lose the vineyard. They begin to plot how to arrest him, but they fear the crowd and leave.

---

10. A small, somewhat conservative book by Mike Beaumont entitled *The One-Stop Guide to Jesus* has some helpful details about the environment in which Jesus spends the last week of his life. The temple is described on page 17.

The interpretation of this parable about the greedy tenants has generally been understood as the way the author of the Gospel of Mark is speaking about the church becoming the new Israel based on the death of the Son of God and new beginnings. However, as Jesus told the parable, it would not have had this Christological meaning. A better interpretation of this parable told by Jesus is that Jesus is speaking about the present in his role as a Jewish prophet. He gives a warning that judgment is coming. It is likely that this parable is redacted from the original form and then recorded later with new theological meaning. But we should not neglect a more historical interpretation, one that reflects the actual teaching of the historical Jesus. I do understand and appreciate that the intention of the author of the Gospel of Mark is to guide the new Christian community, and of course the parable may be understood that way as well. Either way, the parable is direct and challenges the temple authorities.

The temple authorities ask Jesus another difficult question, and he is as equally adept in his answer as he was with the last question. It is the famous exchange about paying taxes to Caesar. Another group arrives, some Pharisees and Herodians,[11] to question Jesus and see if he might be tricked into saying something that would allow the authorities to arrest him. The question is this: "Teacher, we know that you are sincere, and show deference to no one; for you do not regard people with partiality, but teach the way of God in accordance with truth. Is it lawful to pay taxes to the emperor, or not? Should we pay them or should we not?" Jesus responds directly to them and calls them on their hypocrisy. He asks why they are putting him to the test. He then says: "'Bring me a denarius and let me see it.' And they brought him one. Then he said to them, 'Whose head is this, and whose title?' They answered, 'The emperor's.' Jesus then says, 'Give to the emperor the things that are the emperor's, and to God the things that are God's.' And they were utterly amazed at him" (Mark 12:13-17).

This passage has been discussed at length across the centuries. Some say that Jesus too easily endorses the rule of Rome by saying to pay Roman taxes, and that he should have taken a stand against an alien government ruling the affairs of Israel. Others use the account to argue that we should obey government authorities because God has placed them there. The question does raise very important issues, although I would like to stress that the obvious point of the response is to not allow the Pharisees and the Herodians to find a way to catch Jesus speaking against the current government

---

11. Herodians were those who lived near the geographical midpoint in Israel and Palestine. The Romans appointed Herod (from whom the title comes) as the head of the regional government. In the time of the public ministry of Jesus, Herod's four sons were appointed to regional posts.

structure. While a full discussion of this topic is outside the scope of this book, I think we can summarize the meaning of the passage as a way that Jesus did not allow himself to be drawn into a conflict and arrested. He makes a wise and thoughtful comment when he shows them the coin, saying that they should pay their taxes and give their alms. The passage does call our attention to the larger question of the conflict between the kingdom of God and the kingdom of Caesar, a topic that needs careful and extended attention. For our purposes, we leave it in the background as we trace the actions in the final week of the life of Jesus. The Pharisees and the Herodians are amazed by his wisdom, and there are more questions to come.

Another group of religious people, the Sadducees, who did not believe in an afterlife or resurrection, came with their question, also designed to catch Jesus off guard. They ask him about a person with seven brothers who die in succession and have no children who survive. They say that this man must accept and marry these brothers' wives who have been widowed. They quote the teaching of Moses that requires the surviving brother to marry these widows. They then come to the question of how the surviving brother will know which one is his true wife at the resurrection. Wisely, Jesus does not take the bait of this "what if" question and explains that there will be no marriage at the resurrection, quoting Moses in support of his answer. Again, Jesus honors the questions, even though the questions may be designed to trap him into saying something that might lead to his arrest. He knows that the question in this case is hypothetical and hypocritical, and that a long answer is neither wise nor necessary (Mark 12:18–27).

Jesus then launches into his role as a rabbi and displays his gifts as a charismatic teacher. There are many present on Tuesday in the temple that expect him to teach the great truths of Torah, not just respond to those who are threatened by him and want to trap him into a serious mistake. The Gospel of Mark does describe a question from a scribe that enables him to teach the people about the heart of the their faith.[12] He asks Jesus, "Which commandment is the first of all?" Jesus answers that the first commandment is to "love the Lord with all of your heart, with all of your soul, and with all of your mind, and with all of your strength." He goes on to say, "The second is this, 'You shall love your neighbor as yourself.'" The scribe has to say, "You are right, Teacher; this is much more important than all burnt offerings and sacrifices." Jesus answers him: "You are not far from the kingdom of God." Mark's Gospel concludes this conversation with the observation: "After that no one dared to ask him any question" (Mark 12:28–34). In this exchange,

---

12. These questions described in the Gospel of Mark may not have all occurred on Tuesday, although Mark uses this day-to-day design to explain the teaching of Jesus.

we observe Jesus as he summarizes the deep and profound character of his mission and message, that the love of God and one's neighbor is the essence of the spiritual life.

Mark does include more conversations and teaching on Tuesday in his account. There is a question about how the Messiah is related to King David and whether the messiah as a descendent of David is lower in status than his ancestor. Then they ask Jesus that if he is the messiah, shouldn't you pay homage to David. Jesus explains that even David calls the coming Messiah the Lord (Mark 12:3-37). There were other moments of teaching that day, one of which was to call attention to the hypocritical practices of the scribes "who like to walk around in long robes, and to be greeted with respect in the marketplaces, and to have the best seats in the synagogues and places of honor at banquets!" They are unkind to widows and like to say long prayers (Mark 12:38-40). He goes on to illustrate the true meaning of the spiritual life. As people listen to him, he points to those who are putting money into the treasury, some of whom are rich and make sizeable offerings. He then points out the poor widow who puts in two small copper coins worth a penny. He tells his disciples: "Truly I tell you, this poor widow has put in more than all those who are contributing out of their abundance; but she out of her poverty has put in everything she had, all she had to live on" (Mark 12:41-44).

As the day moves along, there is another topic of great interest to Jesus, his disciples, and his questioners and listeners (Mark 13:1-37). It comes up close to the end of the day as Jesus leaves the temple. As he and his disciples, standing on the temple platform, look back at this great building, one of the disciples exclaims, "What large stones and what large buildings." The temple then becomes the subject of discussion. As Jesus addresses this subject, he clearly becomes a prophet and speaks more about his message in his strategic mission in Jerusalem. It has to do with judgment and how there is a time coming when there will be great change. The first part of the discussion and teaching is in reference to their view of the temple. Initially Mark records Jesus as saying: "Do you see these great buildings? Not one stone will be left here upon another; all will be thrown down." After this comment, and as they move on and stop on the Mount of Olives opposite the temple, a small group of the disciples, Peter, James, John, and Andrew, ask him privately: "Tell us, when will this be, and what will be the sign that all these things are about to be accomplished?" Jesus gives them a partial answer and cautions them to be careful about what they might hear. He says: "When you hear of wars and rumors of wars, do not be alarmed; this must take place, but the end is still to come. For nation will rise up against nation, and kingdom against kingdom; there will be earthquakes in various places; there will be famines. This is but the beginning of the birth pangs" (Mark 13:1–12).

This explanation does not really answer the question about the timing of the judgment and the end times. Rather, he tells them that what we observe around us and what is happening in our world are not clear signs of the end. Others will point to these events and interpret them as signs of the end, but be cautious about this answer. It is wise counsel that Jesus gives to his disciples and one that should guide us in our time. Many who were present in the time of Jesus, because of the unrest against Rome, are pointing to these events and speaking of them as signs of the end times. Jesus says to them (and to us) not to pretend you know the time of the end. Rather, trust that God is sovereign. Even though there may be suffering as you continue the work and it feels like a sign of the end, trust God and do not worry about what to say if you are asked questions. Trust the Holy Spirit to guide you. So be alert. Above all, do not follow false messiahs and prophets.

The Gospel of Mark concludes this conversation and subject with a brief explanation by Jesus. Jesus teaches that the coming of the Son of Man will be foreshadowed by profound suffering. Jesus is quoted as saying:

> But in those days, after the suffering, the sun will be darkened, and the moon will not give its light, and the stars will be falling from heaven, and the powers of the heavens will be shaken. Then you will see the Son of Man coming in clouds with great power and glory. Then he will send out the angels, and gather his elect from the four winds, from the ends of the earth to the ends of heaven. (Mark 13:24–27)

This passage is and has been very difficult to interpret. As we make a modest effort, we should keep the following in mind:[13]

- This passage may not have been spoken by Jesus, although he was likely aware of the point of view prevalent in Second Temple Palestinian Judaism. I prefer the view that this passage is included in the Gospel because this kind of apocalyptic literature, drawn mostly from the second half of the book of Daniel, was present and available to the early Christian community.[14]

- The literature was used in reference to the seizure and desecration of the temple by the gentile emperor Antiochus Epiphanes two centuries earlier.

---

13. Borg and Crossan, *Last Week*, 79–83.

14. There was also the literature between the Old and New Testaments, included in some Bibles: Tobit, Judith, and First and Second Maccabees.

- The author of the Gospel of Mark may have used the language about the destruction of the temple in reference to the Roman attack of Jerusalem in the year 70 CE, a war that started in 66 CE, and when the Jewish revolts against Rome began.
- What we have in this passage, then, is less about what Jesus may have said in his conversations with his disciples and more about guiding the young Christian community in the time of the Jewish revolt against Rome.
- Jesus is clear that the way of nonviolence should be used in opposition to Rome. He stresses that there is one true kingdom, the kingdom of God, not two, and that the kingdom of Rome should be resisted.

Mark's section on understanding what might happen in the future concludes with two final issues. The first is to understand the lesson of the fig tree, that the current religious beliefs and practices are empty and there is a need for change (Mark 13:28–31). The second is the guidance to be wise and watchful. No one knows when the end might come. Keep awake and trust God (Mark 13:32–36). This counsel was wise and helpful to his disciples and should apply to our contemporary situation as well. We should be more trusting of God, and as we engage in social change and protest, we should do it in a nonviolent way.

Wednesday: A Day of Anticipation, Teaching, and Betrayal

Wednesday has the character of being a day of rest and reflection. However, there is a great deal going on behind the scene. The Gospel of Mark begins with the following description: "It was two days before the Passover and the festival of Unleavened Bread. The chief priests and the scribes were looking for a way to arrest Jesus by stealth and kill him; for they said, 'Not during the festival, or there may be a riot among the people'" (Mark 14:1–2). Mark lists two events that anticipate what is to come Thursday and Friday. The other Gospels speak of them as well, add helpful detail, and anticipate the coming death of Jesus.

The first recorded event on Wednesday in Mark's Gospel occurs not in the temple area of Jerusalem, but in the house of Simon the leper, in or near where Jesus and his disciples were staying in Bethany. As they were sitting at the table anticipating a meal, a woman approaches Jesus.

> While he was at Bethany in the house of Simon the leper, as he sat at the table, a woman came with an alabaster jar of very

> costly ointment, and she broke open the jar and poured the ointment on his head. But some were there who said to one another in anger, "Why was the ointment wasted in this way? For this ointment could have been sold for more than three denarii and the money given to the poor."[15] And they scolded her.

Jesus responds and says to those at the table,

> Let her alone; why do you trouble her? She has performed a good service for me. For you always have the poor with you, and you can show kindness to them whenever you wish; but you will not always have me. She has done what she could; she has anointed my body beforehand for its burial. Truly I tell you, wherever the good news is proclaimed in the whole world, what she has done will be told in remembrance of her. (Mark 14:3–9)

Mark describes this kind and somewhat innocent story as occurring on Wednesday of the last week of the life of Jesus. The story contains three critical concerns:

1. For the author of Mark, it is a way to provide a crucial transition to the events of Thursday and Friday. For Jesus, it is a day of transition, one to spend with friends and supporters. It is a time for him to be refreshed and gather strength for what he knows will be very difficult days to follow. In a community of support, Jesus gathers inner strength and recommits himself to his mission and message.

2. Perhaps there were moments of quiet reflection and prayer on Wednesday in preparation for the difficult days ahead. He has dinner with friends and uses the time to teach those around him and underline what he expects will happen. A woman enters the room with a deep desire to help Jesus and anoints him with oil. It was not an uncommon act in this setting as the day would be hot and dusty. There would be a need to be clean and refreshed. But what is most important in the story is that it became a symbolic act of preparing the body of Jesus for death. It was all that she could do, and she does it with great courage and love.

3. Jesus uses this extraordinary action of the woman to teach those around him. A few of those with Jesus at the table complain about this action because of the cost of the oil. In their judgment, the money to purchase the oil could have been used to help the poor. Jesus reassures them that it was both a loving and appropriate action to take. He

---

15. A denarius was worth approximately one day's pay for basic work.

expects that death is coming, and the use of the oil brings the reality of it front and center at the table. It was a spiritual moment, liturgical in character. She teaches all at the table that they should be prepared for the loss of their friend and teacher. Jesus honors her and underlines that his action will be part of the good news that will be proclaimed around the world. And he adds that she will be remembered.

While this meal and action were taking place, there was another part of the story unfolding. Judas was working behind the scenes to betray Jesus. Mark records what Judas was doing: "Then Judas Iscariot, who was one of the twelve, went to the chief priests in order to betray him to them. When they heard it they were greatly pleased and promised to give him money. So he began to look for an opportunity to betray him." That opportunity would come in the middle of the night on Thursday (Mark 14:10-11).

One of the questions—somewhat difficult to answer in reading this account of the betrayal—is why Judas was willing to betray Jesus. What was his motivation? As part of the inner groups of Jesus, Judas would have heard conversation about the possible arrest of Jesus as he came to Jerusalem to complete his mission. The fact that Jesus anticipated conflict and possible death was discussed among the disciples. Is it possible that these conversations gave Judas the idea of betrayal? As we explore this question, we cross over into events of Thursday, although Judas did begin the betrayal on Wednesday.

The Gospel of Matthew, in recounting the story of Judas, is quite direct in saying that Judas was motivated by money. Matthew's account says that when Judas went to the high priests, he asked them, "'What will you give me if I betray him to you?' They paid him thirty pieces of silver" (Matt 26:14-15). And later, on Friday, Judas repents of his action, returns the thirty pieces of silver, and says, "I have sinned by betraying innocent blood." As he receives the money back, Matthew says, "Throwing down the thirty pieces of silver in the temple, he departed; and he went and hanged himself" (Matt 27:4a-5). John's Gospel adds the more theological explanation that Judas was under the influence of the devil: "The devil had already put into the heart of Judas son of Simon Iscariot to betray him" (John 13:2).

Still another theory, although not fully developed in the biblical account, is that Judas was part of the Zealot movement and was disillusioned when Jesus did not actively resist the alien government of Rome. He may have hoped as he joined the movement with Jesus that it would lead to a military revolt and that Jesus as messiah would become a military leader like David and restore the kingdom. Perhaps we will never fully know why

Judas betrayed Jesus, but it is a very sad part of the narrative. Matthew records what occurred on the night when he was betrayed.

> While he was still speaking, Judas, one of the twelve arrived; with him was a large crowd with swords and clubs, from the chief priests and the elders of the people. Now the betrayer had given them a sign, saying, "The one that I kiss is the man; arrest him." At once he came up to Jesus and said, "Greetings, Rabbi!" and kissed him. Jesus said to him, "Do what you are here to do." Then they came and laid hands on him and arrested him. (Matt 26:47–50)

Thursday: The Events Leading to the Crucifixion

As we follow the account in Mark's Gospel, we read that Thursday is filled with events that lead to and anticipate the crucifixion of Jesus. Jesus and his followers were Jewish and would participate in the Jewish holiday of Passover. Early in the day, his disciples asked him about where they would go to celebrate the Passover. Mark records this conversation:

> On the first day of Unleavened Bread, when the Passover lamb is sacrificed, his disciples said to him, "Where do you want us to go and make preparations for you to eat the Passover?" So he sent two of his disciples, saying to them, "Go into the city, and a man carrying a jar of water will meet you; follow him, and wherever he enters, say to the owner of the house, 'The Teacher asks, where is my guest room where I may eat the Passover with my disciples?' He will show you a large room upstairs, furnished and ready. Make preparations for us there." So the disciples set out and went to the city, and found everything as he had told them; and they prepared the Passover meal. (Mark 14:12–16)

Note the following as we read this paragraph:

- Jesus and his disciples do participate in what may be the most important holiday in the Jewish calendar. Even in the rush and worry of this weeklong visit, they take time to honor their faith and history.

- It is also quite remarkable that Jesus had already found the time and a way to arrange for the Passover meal. Some of his disciples find the upper room and spend the day in preparation. Arranging for the meal would have taken them most of the day. It was done in secret as a measure of security.

- It is interesting that John's Gospel has different timing. Because the Passover meal is generally celebrated on Friday, John places it on Friday rather than Thursday. For Mark, Matthew, and Luke, it is an early Passover meal, or perhaps just a Last Supper. For John, the real Passover is the death of Jesus on Friday. The Thursday meal is a time of reflection, with John providing five chapters (13–17) of Jesus' so-called "Farewell Address." On the Christian calendar, Thursday is called Maundy Thursday, with Maundy being taken from a Latin word for "mandate," echoing the time when Jesus gives the disciples the mandate "to love one another, just as I have loved you" (John 13:34). It may have also been the time when Jesus washes the disciples feet, illustrating the practical nature of love.

The Last Supper has come down through Christian history charged with a range of meanings (Mark 14:17–25). The first of these was early in the meal. As Jesus and the disciples were eating, Jesus said: "'Truly I tell you, one of you will betray me.' They began to be distressed and to say to him, one after another, 'Surely not I?' He said to them, 'It is one of the twelve who is dipping bread into the bowl with me' . . . 'It would have been better for that one not to have been born.'" Later in the evening, Judas leaves the gathering to make arrangements for the arrest of Jesus. The event invited a reflection on what it means to be courageous and loyal in the most trying of circumstances. Each of the disciples said to Jesus in their own way that they would never be disloyal. Their faith commitment would be profoundly tested in the next several hours.

But perhaps the most important meaning of the meal is that it was acting out and anticipating in a symbolic way what was to come, the crucifixion of Jesus. The celebration of the meal (thanksgiving-Eucharist) has become an integral part of Christian worship. On a regular schedule, Christian churches have celebrated in gratitude that Jesus gave his life for the sins of the world. Using the bread as the symbol of his body, Jesus took the bread, broke it, and then gave it to his disciples, followed by the words "This is my body." Jesus is helping the disciples understand that there are crucial times when one must be willing to give one's life for truth and love. Jesus then took the cup, and "after giving thanks he gave it to them, and all of them drank from it. He said to them: 'this is my blood of the covenant, which is poured out for many. Truly I tell you I will never again drink of the fruit of the vine until the day when I drink it anew in the kingdom of God.'" Note here three critical points:

1. The meal will be continued in the Christian church and reenacted as a time of remembrance and gratitude. The event is a meal, and in the time of Jesus, the meal was often the most important part of the day; it was a time of coming together, sharing the day's activities, communication with loved ones, and giving and receiving empathy and understanding. It was a time for the family and extended family to be a community.

2. The theological meaning of the meal is that that death of Jesus was a sacrifice of love for the human family. For some, its meaning would have been that the death of Jesus was a blood sacrifice to pay for the sins of humankind. I understand this point of view, discussed by the apostle Paul and developed in a persuasive way by the Christian theologian Anselm (1033–1106 CE). There is an alternative meaning, one that maintains that Jesus died more because of our sins than for our sins.[16] Perhaps it is both.

3. The phrase "drink it anew in the kingdom of God" suggests that Jesus, or at least the early Christian community that records these events in print, continues to give eschatological meaning to his ministry. The statement may be saying that the kingdom or the reign of God will be realized by the action of God.

Mark's Gospel records that, following the meal, they sang a hymn and went out to the Mount of Olives. Mark records a conversation between Jesus and the disciples that there will be those who will desert him and their common mission. Peter rises to the occasion and says to Jesus, "Even though all become deserters, I will not." Jesus responds to Peter and tells him that "this night, before the cock crows, you will deny me three times" (Mark 14:26–31).

Near the Mount of Olives was a garden called Gethsemane, and Jesus tells his disciples to "Sit here while I pray." It is late in the evening, and the events and conversations in this garden echo across the centuries (Mark 14:32–42). As Jesus goes to pray, he invites Peter, James, and John to join him. Knowing that he is facing arrest and perhaps a sentence of death, he says to them: "I am deeply grieved, even to death; remain here, and keep awake. And going a little farther, he threw himself on the ground and prayed that, if it were possible, the hour might pass from him. He said, 'Abba, Father, for you all things are possible; remove this cup from me; yet not what I want, but what you want." In this passage, we begin to see how Jesus dealt with his coming death.

---

16. I will return to the meaning of the death of Jesus later in this chapter.

- He takes three of his closest friends, Peter, James, and John, with him as he goes to pray. He says to them, "stay with me." In our closing moments of life, we do need those who we love and who love us in return to be with us.
- Though deeply grieved, he prays honestly and courageously. He hopes that he might not need to die.
- But if it is not possible, he seeks his Father's will and not his. He uses the term "Abba," an Aramaic term for Father, as he prays. There is a kind of intimacy and deep love that Jesus has with his Father.

He returns to his disciples and finds them asleep. After all, it is in the middle of the night, and it has been a very long and stressful day. Gently he chides them: "Could you not keep awake one hour?" He says the same words to Peter, his special and unique disciple. These are difficult times, and he does know "that the spirit is indeed willing, but the flesh is weak." Jesus continues in his quiet spot for prayer, and then returns to find his dear friends asleep. After a third time, he wakes them again and says to them, "Get up, let us be going. See, my betrayer is at hand."

We shift now to the betrayal and arrest of Jesus (Mark 14:43–51). Some of the events were occurring in the early morning in our system of days ending at midnight. But it was still on Thursday (middle of the night) in the way time was understood by those engaged in this great drama. The day began at sunrise.

The next event, one about which we have already spoken, was when Judas greets Jesus and identifies him for the priests and soldiers with a kiss. One disciple, likely Peter,[17] draws a sword and strikes the slave of the high priest, cutting his ear. Jesus intervenes and says: "Put your sword back in its place; for all who take the sword will perish by the sword" (Matt 26:52). He goes on to question why priests and soldiers have come to arrest him in the middle of the night. "Have you come out with swords and clubs to arrest me as though I were a bandit? Day after day I was with you in the temple teaching, and you did not arrest me." At this point, the Gospel of Mark records the action of the disciples: "All of them deserted him and fled" (Mark 14:50). Mark adds a further note about one who had only a linen cloth for clothing, and it comes off and he runs away naked.

---

17. John 18:10.

Friday: The Trial and Crucifixion

Jesus is taken as a prisoner early on Friday morning to a meeting with the chief priests, the elders, and the scribes, although it was not a formal meeting of the Sanhedrin. Caiaphas, the high priest, was likely present (Mark 14:53–65). They were looking for evidence that would allow them to recommend a sentence that would put Jesus to death. Peter follows from a distance to listen to the questions that are posed to Jesus. Many people were willing to provide false testimony against Jesus, although there were conflicting accounts making these testimonies less persuasive. One person testified that Jesus had threatened to destroy the temple, a serious charge. Toward the end of this assembly, the high priest asks Jesus a central question, pointing to possible heresy: "Are you the Messiah, the Son of the Blessed One?" Jesus, referencing Daniel 7, said, "I am; and you will see the Son of Man seated by the right hand of Power and coming with the clouds of heaven." With this direct answer from Jesus, the high priest said they had heard blasphemy, and Jesus was condemned. The guards took Jesus aside and beat him.

One of the servant-girls of the high priest, seeing Peter listening from a distance, said to him that he was a follower of Jesus, noting his Galilean accent. Peter denied it, and as the conversation continued with others, he denied it twice more. In the early morning, Peter heard the cock crow and remembered what Jesus had said, and "he broke down and wept" (Mark 14:66–72).

Because the Sanhedrin did not have the authority to issue a death sentence, the chief priests held a consultation with the elders and the whole council, and decided to take him to the Roman authority, Pontius Pilate. As a Roman official, Pilate was more concerned about loyalty to Rome and possible insurrection than Jewish blasphemy, and asked Jesus: "'Are you the king of the Jews?' Jesus answered him, 'You say so.' Then the chief priests accused him of many things. Pilate asked him again, 'Have you no answer? See how many charges they bring against you.' But Jesus made no further reply, so that Pilate was amazed" (Mark 15:2–5).

Luke records one other stop in these early-morning conversations for Jesus. Learning that Jesus was a Galilean, Pilate sent him over to Herod, the regional ruler of the Galilean area, who was in Jerusalem at that time (Luke 23:6–12). Herod, who wanted to meet Jesus because he had become so well-known, questioned Jesus and listened to what the chief priests and scribes were saying. Herod made no formal judgment, but did allow his soldiers to treat Jesus with contempt and to mock him by putting an elegant robe on him. Herod then sent him back for the final phase of his trial, and with a trace of irony, "Herod and Pilate became fast friends with each other; before this they had been enemies" (Luke 23:12).

Jesus is taken back to Pilate, and Pilate was reluctant to sentence Jesus to death. In Luke's account, we read, "You brought me this man as one who is perverting the people; and here I have examined him in your presence and have not found this man guilty of any of your charges against him. Neither has Herod, for he sent him back to us. Indeed, he has done nothing to deserve death. I will therefore have him flogged and release him" (Luke 23:14–16). There was a custom to release a prisoner at the time of a holiday festival, and Pilate was inclined to release Jesus. But the crowd objects and says that Barabbas, also on trial, should be released. Finally, Pilate gives in to the crowd's cry of "crucify him," pointing to Jesus. Barabbas, on trial for insurrection, was released.

They led Jesus away, and the soldiers prepared Jesus for crucifixion (Mark 15:16–32). It is approximately nine o'clock in the morning. They ask a man standing by on the road to the cross, Simon of Cyrene, to help Jesus carry his cross. A great number of people follow, including devout women who had known Jesus and cry out in deep pain. The soldiers mock him, put a purple cloak on him, and a crown of thorns is placed on his head. All of this happens at the dreaded site of the crucifixion (Golgotha, meaning "the place of the skull"). The soldiers continued to mock him by saying "Hail, King of the Jews."[18] They offer him wine mixed with myrrh, and then cast lots for his clothes. There are two other men on crosses next to Jesus. According to Luke, one of the men joins in the mocking and says, "'Are you not the Messiah? Save yourself and us!' But the other prisoner rebukes him, saying 'Do you not fear God, since you are under the same sentence of condemnation?'" (Luke 23:40). At about three o'clock, Jesus dies on a skull-shaped hill in the darkened skies.

The Gospels, each with slightly different conclusions, record four additional events following the death of Jesus. The first one is the burial of Jesus, on which there is agreement in the Gospels. A member of the Sanhedrin Council, Joseph of Arimathea, one who had met Jesus and had become his disciple, approached Pilate and asked for the body (Mark 15:42–47). His request is granted, and the body of Jesus is "wrapped in linen cloth and laid in the tomb," and a large rock was rolled against the door of the tomb, a significant detail in reference to the belief in the resurrection of Jesus.

---

18. Note that the Romans crucify Jesus because of treason, as the "King of the Jews."

Saturday and Sunday: Grief and Resurrection

The next sections in each of the Gospels then speak about the resurrection of Jesus. Little is said about Saturday, although there are hints that those who followed Jesus were very troubled. It is a quiet Sabbath, but it all changed on Sunday morning. In Mark's account, one that is followed by Matthew and Luke, we read that early on Sunday morning, the women who were devoted to Jesus go to the tomb with spices to anoint his body. When they arrive, they discover that the tomb has been opened, and a young man in white robe greets them and says: "Do not be alarmed; you are looking for Jesus of Nazareth, who was crucified. He has been raised; he is not here. Look, there is the place where they laid him. But go, tell his disciples and Peter that he is going ahead of you to Galilee; there you will see him just as he told you.' So they went out and fled from the tomb, for terror and amazement had seized them; and they said nothing to anyone, for they were afraid" (Mark 16:6-8). Matthew adds to this account that the women actually encounter Jesus, and he says to them, "'Greetings!' And they came to him, took hold of his feet, and worshiped him. Then Jesus said to them, 'Do not be afraid; go and tell my brothers to go to Galilee; there they will see me'" (Matt 28:9-10). Luke speaks about the women being greeted by two men "in dazzling clothes" who say to the women, "Why do you look for the living among the dead? He is not here, but had risen" (Luke 24:4-5). The Gospel of John says that not only the women went to the tomb, but also Peter and "the disciple whom Jesus loved"; they found the tomb open and the burial wrappings laying empty. John writes that Mary Magdalene, in deep grief, enters the tomb and is met by two angels and comforted, and then encounters the risen Jesus. She is overwhelmed, and then goes to the disciples and says, "I have seen the Lord" (John 20:11-18).

Following the visits of the women and the disciples to the tomb and their discovery that Jesus is not there, the Gospels record a number of conversations with the risen Christ. Matthew places the emphasis on Jesus giving the disciples the Great Commission, urging the disciples to continue the work that has begun. The account reads as follows: "All authority in heaven and on earth has been given to me. Go therefore and make disciples of all nations, baptizing them in the name of the Father and the Son and the Holy Spirit, and teaching them to obey everything that I have commanded you. And remember, I am with you always, to the end of the age" (Matt 28:18-20). Mark's ending is somewhat problematic in that part of the ending of the Gospel was lost. A new section was added later, one that reflects the same message as Matthew, which instructs the disciples about the great commission (Mark 16:9-18). The Gospel of Luke adds the touching story of the resurrected Jesus meeting discouraged followers of Jesus on the road to Emmaus. An abbreviated account of this walk to Emmaus is in Matthew's account as well (Matt 16:12-13). They are returning to their village after the crucifixion and are discouraged by the death of Jesus. Jesus joins them and gives them hope in their new faith. Luke also adds the account of the disciples meeting the resurrected Jesus and having their faith restored (Luke 24:13-35). John adds the additional stories of the meeting of resurrected Jesus with his disciples. There is one account of Jesus giving general encouragement, and there are two other stories that describe the interaction of Jesus with two specific disciples. He invites Thomas, who doubts that Jesus has been resurrected, to place his "finger in the mark of the nails" to reassure him. Thomas, deeply moved, replies, "My Lord and my God." The resurrected Jesus also speaks with Peter about his love for Jesus, with Peter reassuring Jesus three times about the depth of his love (John 20:24-21; 21:18-19)

Following these accounts, the Synoptic Gospels speak of the ascension of Jesus. Luke's account says: "Then he led them out as far as Bethany, and lifting up his hands, he blessed them. While he was blessing them, he withdrew from them and was carried up into heaven" (Luke 24:50-51). Mark says that Jesus "sat down at the right hand of God" (Mark 16:19). These passages point to the belief on the part of the disciples and the early church that Jesus is with God.

The Quest for Meaning

There are many ways to understand the crucifixion of Jesus and the account of his resurrection. I want to use three strategies, one examining what Jesus said on the cross,[19] another looking at the various ways his crucifixion has been understood, and the third suggesting ways of thinking about the resurrection. We turn first to the last words of Jesus on the cross. As always, we are cautious about definitively saying that Jesus spoke these seven last words. There may have been others, and the ones we have were handed down in an oral tradition, used for guiding the young church, and later found their way into the Gospels. Not all of these seven last sayings are in one Gospel, but with these qualifications, I list them, suggesting what they

---

19. Again, we should be aware that the seven last words of Jesus that are recorded in the Gospels, and especially in the Gospel of Luke, have come through a historical process and then were put in writing several years later. We live with the historical questions.

might mean. I then explore how they add to our understanding of Jesus and his invitation to follow his way.

1. One of them comes to us in Aramaic, the language spoken by Jesus: "E'lī, E'līi, le-ma' sa-bach'tha-nī" (Matt 27:46). This verse is often translated as "My God, my God, why have you forsaken me." It is the first verse of Psalm 22, a passage that Jesus may have known well and was able to draw upon as a way of expressing his grief and suffering. Traditionally, Psalm 22 is thought to be a Psalm of David expressing his sense of being forsaken as he led the nation of Israel. If it is a later Psalm, it may express the sense of Israel feeling forsaken in the Babylonian captivity and the difficulty of restoring the nation with the constant presence of alien governments. Christian theologians have often read the passage as the time when Jesus was actually separated from God as he suffered an atoning death for the sins of humankind. The sentence "he died for our sins" expresses this point of view. I am open to this view, but also want to interpret the saying as a simple and honest expression of his suffering on the cross. It was a horrible death. There was the psychic pain of the end of his life and his loss of contact with those whom he loved.

2. A second saying of Jesus on the cross is about forgiveness: "Father, forgive them for they know not what they do" (Luke 23:34). While there is little detail given, I find it possible to believe that Jesus was keenly aware of and had empathy for those who were responsible for his crucifixion, and especially those who were implementing it. They were doing their duty and had little choice. If in fact this is an authentic saying of Jesus, it speaks of his inordinate love for those who are responsible for the crucifixion. This kind of unlimited love was the centerpiece of his remarkable ministry.

3. There is his comment to the prisoner next to him: "Truly, I tell you, today you will be with me in Paradise" (Luke 23:43). Once again, we observe the marvelous love Jesus had for those near him, even when he was experiencing the worst kind of pain and coming death. He took the time to listen to the one who was suffering next to him. With miraculous love, he answered him and reassured him that he will pass into the presence of a loving God and a state of uninterrupted bliss. The loving pastor gave comfort.

4. In John 19:26–27, we read: "When Jesus saw his mother and the disciple whom he loved standing beside her, he said to his mother, 'Woman, here is your son.' Then he said to the disciple, 'Here is your

mother." And from that hour the disciple took her into his own home." Once again, in the depth of pain and the reality of death, Jesus was able to rise above his own suffering, look down from the cross with deep love, and make sure that his mother would be cared for by his trusted friend, John.

5. In John 19:28, we read that Jesus says, "I am thirsty." Several hours had gone by since Jesus was arrested in the garden of Gethsemane. He has been questioned by the members of the Sanhedrin; sent to Pilate, who continued the questioning from a Roman perspective; moved on to Herod Antipas with more questions from still a different perspective; and then returned to Pilate who, after more questioning, sentences Jesus and turns him over to soldiers who take him to Golgotha. Jesus has been mocked and beaten and then nailed to a cross. Was there any time for a sip of water? We don't know for sure, but it is easy to hear Jesus groan from the cross, "I thirst." In response, the guards use a branch with an attached sponge full of wine and hold it up for Jesus. It was next to nothing—perhaps worse than nothing.

6. We read in Luke 23:46 the words of Jesus: "Father, into your hands I commend my spirit." As mid-afternoon approaches, Jesus sensed that the end was near. With the deep faith in God that has sustained him across the years, Jesus knew that death was approaching. The spoken words suggest that Jesus was at peace. He did not cry out in pain and anger, but sensed God's love and peacefully waited for the end to come.

7. And finally, in John 19:30, we hear Jesus say, "It is finished." This final saying has been interpreted differently, with some Christian theology maintaining that Jesus is saying that he has done all that was required to establish a new spiritual way for humankind. I understand this theological perspective, and even find it attractive if it is not exclusively understood as a substitutionary atonement. I also want to affirm that this final saying of Jesus is about how Jesus had no regrets, that he has lived his life with love and integrity, and that he is essentially saying that his life and work are "finished."

The crucifixion of Jesus has been central to the understanding of the Christian faith across the centuries. And from one period of time to another, it has been interpreted in slightly different ways. These ways are not necessarily in conflict, but more often supplement each other, although from time to time there have been divisions in the church caused by the different views. My tradition, the International Reformed Church, and its expression in the Presbyterian Church USA, is a Confessional communion, which means that it takes full advantage of the many Confessions of Faith (creeds) that have been developed across the centuries. The Reformed Churches have drawn wisdom from each of them and have understood that at different times there was a particular concern or belief that needed clarification for the believing community. The Confessions are normative for the Reformed Churches, even as they may reflect a point of view of a particular period of history. I have read (and studied) these creeds, and I find the one written for the United Presbyterian Church of America in 1967, called the Confession of 1967, to be helpful in its summary of the meaning of the crucifixion of Jesus. In a relatively short paragraph, the Confession speaks of "the Grace of Our Lord Jesus Christ" and addresses the reconciling act in Jesus Christ.

> God's reconciling act in Jesus Christ is a mystery which the Scriptures describe in various ways. It is called the sacrifice of the a lamb, a shepherd's life given for his sheep, atonement by a priest; again it is ransom for a slave, payment of a debt, vicarious satisfaction of a legal penalty, and victory over the powers of evil. These are expressions of a truth, which remains beyond the reach of all theory in the depths of God's love for man. They reveal the gravity, cost, and sure achievement of God's reconciling work.[20]

I want to briefly suggest the meaning of the images and metaphors used in this Confession that speak about the crucifixion of Jesus.

1. It is called the sacrifice of a lamb. Drawing upon the Hebrew Bible, the Confession speaks of the need to sacrifice a pure lamb as an offering to God. Often associated with the Exodus, the blood of the pure lamb represents what was put on the doorposts in the Passover as the Hebrew people were protected from the final plague in Egypt. It then becomes a feast of remembrance. The implication is that Jesus, as the pure lamb, emancipates us from all that would lead to bondage.[21] We are set free. There are additional meanings associated with "lamb," such as the quest for a just peace and a way of life that is simple and honest. I have a small plaque on my desk with a picture of a small pure lamb with the saying, "Our lamb has conquered; let us follow him." It is a metaphor about Jesus that invites us to a way of life that is pure, filled with love and truth, and in service to all who are in bondage.

2. The second image in the Confession is "a shepherd's life given for his sheep." In John 10:11, we read that Jesus says: "I am the good shepherd.

---

20. Office of the General Assembly, *Book of Confessions*, 254.
21. Exod 12:1–20.

The shepherd lays down his life for the sheep." Those who needed a good explanation for the death of Jesus would have immediately understood that Jesus was a good shepherd. It was a wonderful image used by Jesus in a culture in which the shepherd had the full responsibility for the safety and wellbeing of the sheep. Jesus, the good shepherd, gave his life for our safety and wellbeing.

3. A third image of the crucifixion compares it to an act of atonement by a priest. Deeply rooted in the faith of the Jewish people was the keen sense of God's righteousness and the call to live by the principles and dictates of Torah. The priest's role within this faith tradition was to take the infidelities of the people to God in the form of an offering, asking for God's forgiveness. It is to say that we are sorry, forgive us, and then do better in following Torah.

4. A fourth image of the crucifixion is to compare it to the ransom of a slave. Slavery was not uncommon in the time and place of Jesus; slavery would be understood in all of its abuse of human life. It was possible to pay a ransom as one had resources, often with money or property, to emancipate a slave. This image suggests that we are often in slavery—actual slavery in certain parts of the world, but also in slavery to self-destructive habits and a way of life that controls us rather than a way of life that we control. Jesus pays the ransom and sets us free (redeems us) from our slavery.

5. Still another image is the payment of a debt. Again, this image might be a reference to an actual debt, but it is more often spoken of as the misuse of our gifts and talents, using them for hurtful and harmful causes. Instead of being thankful to God for all that we have been given, we waste what we have and find ourselves "in debt" to God. The death of Jesus removes that debt, and we are free to start again and live a faithful spiritual life.

6. There is the image of how the crucifixion of Jesus is a vicarious satisfaction of a legal penalty. There are times when we break the speed limit and perhaps receive a traffic ticket with the penalty of $150. A parent or a friend comes to our aid and gives us the $150 to pay for our offense. The crucifixion of Jesus is that payment. The apostle Paul, as a Roman citizen, understood the Roman emphasis on law and order and the need for justice. Part of his theology is to understand Jesus in this legal frame of reference.

7. The final image (and perhaps there are others not mentioned in the Confession) is to liken the crucifixion of Jesus as a victory over the

powers of evil. One might, with a surface reading, say that Jesus lost his life because of the power of evil. Others (and I am among them) understand that Jesus' courage, integrity, and love as he faced the powers of evil won the day, and indeed all the days and eternity. Who remembers the names of the Roman ruler or the high priest that had a part in crucifying Jesus? Yet the name and life of Jesus are honored, and his teaching is followed by millions of people.

More could be and has been said and written about the death of Jesus. It became the central theme of the new movement that was to be called Christianity. It is an extraordinary and inspiring story, but much more than just a model of a heroic person. It is a narrative of one whose life, teachings, and death created a new religion. However, from the beginning of the Christian movement, his followers did not speak only of his death, but also of his resurrection. It was the capstone of Christian belief, and without this belief, the life of Jesus may have been worthy of remembrance as a courageous teacher and prophet, but not the foundation of a whole new worldview. The resurrection has anchored the Christian faith.

Yet those of us living on this side of the enlightenment, the birth of scientific understanding, and the development of critical historical study find the resurrection much more difficult to believe and understand than the courageous death of this great teacher and prophet. We may recite one or more of the classical creeds that mention the resurrection in our weekly worship, but if asked to speak on the topic of the resurrection of Jesus, we would find it hard to say much more than it happened. Even the historical creeds of the church, while placing the resurrection in a central place, do not always develop the theological meaning of the resurrection. For example, the Apostles' Creed (c. 180 CE) says: "The third day he rose again from the dead." The Nicene Creed (325 CE) affirms approximately the same belief: "On the third day, he rose again in accordance with the Scriptures."[22] The church has written many additional creedal statements across the centuries, some more expanded and others as brief as the Nicene and Apostles' creeds.

The Presbyterian Church's Confession of 1967 has a single sentence that says: "The risen Christ is the Savior of all men." A later Presbyterian Confession, called "A Brief Statement of Faith" (1993), provides some expansion: "God raised this Jesus from the dead, vindicating his sinless life, breaking the power of sin and evil, and delivering us from death to life eternal."[23] Again, there are libraries full of books about the resurrection of Jesus, but for our purposes, I want to look at it briefly from three positions.

---

22. Office of the General Assembly, *Book of Confessions*, 3, 7.

23. Office of the General Assembly, *Book of Confessions*, 267.

The first position, held by Christians across the centuries, is to affirm the reality of the resurrection of Jesus, much like it is described in the Gospels. It is the case that the early Christian community did believe that Jesus rose from the dead, and there are several accounts in the New Testament that speak about those who encountered the risen Christ. The apostle Paul lists them in 1 Corinthians 15. Even though such a belief goes against our experience and understanding, the vast majority of Christians still give the resurrection a foundational place in their faith. It is for them what the "Brief Statement of Faith" affirms:

1. Jesus rose from the dead.
2. The resurrection is the vindication of his sinless life.
3. It was the sign that Jesus was victorious over the great enemies of humankind, sin and death, "breaking the power of sin and evil."
4. And "delivering us from death to eternal life."

A second position, partially accepted by the more progressive wing of the Christian church, would say that the first generations of Christians were sincere in their belief, and there is some evidence such as the empty tomb and many reported sightings of the resurrected Jesus that support their belief. They might add, however, that it was the case that those who lived in the first century often used supernatural explanations for what they did not understand. For example, people at that time believed that storms came from the hand of God. A severe storm may even be a punishment. There is no reason to question the sincerity of those who believe in a literal reading of the Bible, and foundational beliefs such as the resurrection. But we now live in a time when there are credible explanations for occurrences that are unusual. One hermeneutical principle that we often use in understanding the Bible is to say that what the Bible says is true, but not all of the details are necessarily true in a literal sense.[24] We certainly read the creation story in that way. It didn't happen in six days, but it is true that God is the Creator of all and has created us to live in harmony with the divine will and way. We may say that the resurrection is true in the sense of Jesus being in the presence of God following his death.

There is a third position, one that is sometimes present, although quietly so, in the Christian community. It is present among Christians who fully live in the secular, postmodern world, and accept the understanding of reality from a scientific frame of reference. It is the view, expressed quite simply, that there was no resurrection, only people who thought there was

---

24. Borg, *Convictions*, 103.

one. The life and teachings of Jesus are admirable and noble, and to follow them is the essence of Christian faith.

As I have struggled with the questions of faith, I have reviewed these various views of the resurrection. I have always sensed the integrity of those who affirm them. The first option is basic Christian belief, and I find myself deeply rooted in the primary understanding of the Christian faith. But I would like to say why I listen carefully to the other positions.

1. They have the dimension of openness. They enable one to directly face the difficult intellectual challenges of belief. With openness, one does not have to be defensive or resort to "tribal certainty," because there is a built-in willingness to listen with respect and reflect honestly on other points of view. In this position, there is the hard work of integrating faith with a rational and scientific understanding of the world. We live in a postmodern world, and it is necessary to frame a new cosmology, different from the one on which classical Christian theology is based.[25]

2. They also provide the opportunity to help many in the Christian community affirm a faith that is not in opposition to the way the world and the larger cosmos are currently understood. This outlook does allow one to stay within the Christian family, even with genuine doubts. Ideally, one may have the desire and background to do the demanding work of integration, although not every one will have the background to do this complex work. The church at its best should be able to provide guidance for the integration of faith and science, as well as a haven of support and growth. The church at its best should be a base for those who are struggling to find a faith orientation that is credible.

3. In addition, as this more credible faith is articulated in thoughtful and persuasive ways, it will represent the Christian faith in a way that makes it a respected option for others from different religions and alternative worldviews. It should be able to provide ways for the church to be in partnership with other religious traditions in order to share the common quest for a more just and peaceful world. Further, it will be more difficult for "cultured despisers of religion" to write off Christian belief as an outlook that is uninformed and superstitious.[26] It will become harder for honest doubters to label the Christian faith as

---

25. See Delio, *Unbearable Wholeness of Being*, and Delio, *Making All Things New*. Dr. Delio bases her work on the writing of Pierre Teilhard de Chardin.

26. Friedrich Schleiermacher, a nineteenth-century German theologian, used the phrase "cultured despisers of religion" as he made a case for thoughtful religion.

fundamentalism or exclusively evangelical.[27] In addition, being open and yet still in the Christian family, one is able to genuinely respect those in the other categories and maintain that differences of belief should not fundamentally separate us. We are all pilgrims on the way. I have learned that it is possible to live with differences and even celebrate and learn from them. The third option enables one to affirm the Christian way by directly facing the difficult intellectual challenges of belief and continue to learn from others who have a different view of the resurrection of Jesus.

In short, the two positions that differ from the traditional Christian view allow one to stay in the Christian family, say yes to the invitation of Jesus, follow the Christian way of life, and accept and respect those with a different point of view. Deep in my heart, I know that there is a need for humility regarding questions of faith. In fact, all three positions may honor the reality that God, however understood, but also accept the truth that God is beyond our full comprehension. We know that a full understanding of God is beyond our reason, categories, and words. There will always be the temptation to bring God down to our level and exclusively to speak of the divine within our cultural categories. We so easily create God in our image. We must learn to live with our approximations, ones that can be expanded and deepened as we go through life and remain open to new insights into truth.[28]

Study Resources

Discussion Questions

1. Why do you think Jesus decided to go to Jerusalem to continue his mission, even though he knew it would be dangerous?
2. How would you describe the way that Jesus interacted with the people in the temple during the last week of his life?
3. Do you think that it was wise for Jesus to overturn the tables of the money-changers? Was it a good strategy?

---

27. I regret that we can no longer use the word "evangelical" (good news) as a general term. It continues to describe quite thoughtful conservative Christians, but more frequently it is the label for the ultra-conservative side of Protestant faith, once called fundamentalism.

28. I am persuaded that we must move beyond the magical and mythical projections of God. Nor should we rest easy with a rational and scientific worldview that simply rejects any notion of the divine.

4. How do you understand the crucifixion of Jesus? What image or metaphor do you think is the best way to describe the meaning of the crucifixion?

5. How do you interpret the Christian belief in the resurrection of Jesus?

Terms and Concepts

1. Atonement: The way in which the Bible describes how the crucifixion of Jesus overcomes the sinfulness of human beings and how reconciliation between God and humankind becomes possible.

2. The Court of the Gentiles: The area at the edge of the Temple where gentiles could go to pray and where the moneychangers and sellers of animals for sacrifice were located.

3. The Seven Last Words: Those sayings of Jesus recorded in the New Testament that he spoke while on the cross.

4. Last Supper: the meal (a Passover Meal) that Jesus shared with his disciples just before he was arrested. It is now the basis for the Christian celebration of communion.

5. Pontius Pilate and Caiaphas: Pilate was the Roman who was appointed prefect (in charge of the Roman occupation) in Judea and who ultimately condemned Jesus to death. Caiaphas was the high priest at the time of the sentence of Jesus and led the Sanhedrin.

Suggested Reading

Borg, Marcus J., and John Dominic Crosson. *The Last Week: A Day-to-Day Account of Jesus's Final Week in Jerusalem*. San Francisco: HarperSanFrancisco, 2006.

Bailey, Kenneth E. *Jesus Through Middle Eastern Eyes: Cultural Studies in the Gospel*. Downers Grove: IVP Academic, 2008.

Delio, Ilia. *The Unbearable Wholeness of Being: God, Evolution, and the Power of Love*. Maryknoll: Orbis, 2013.

Sanders, E. P. *The Historical Figure of Jesus*. London: Penguin, 1993.

Wright, N. T. *Jesus and the Victory of God*. Minneapolis: Fortress, 1996.

SECTION 4

The Difficult Decisions

How Do We Respond to the Invitation?

WE ARE EXPLORING TOGETHER how Jesus invites us to replace a self-centered approach to life with a God-centered orientation. We have maintained that this shift is radical in that we are asked to get control of our evolutionary and historical conditioning and inclinations to seek our own welfare and gratification. The invitation counsels us to resist all forms of self-aggrandizement and to seek first the kingdom of God. To accept the invitation will mean a fundamental shift in worldviews. It is radical in the sense of adopting a counterculture mode, going against the values and norms of our commodity culture, and one that invites us and almost compels us to spend our days seeking pleasure, possessions, and power. As we read the Gospels, Jesus asks us to live in a different way, to give ourselves to an ethical life in which we forgive enemies, give away our cloak, turn the other cheek, love those who insult us, walk an extra mile, get up and walk, go and sin no more, take no thought for tomorrow, and follow me.[1] We are asked to stop on the road to Jericho, like the Good Samaritan, and help the injured person who has just been robbed. Unlike the scribe and the priest, we take time to be compassionate. It is an invitation to leave behind one lifestyle and adopt another one—no easy shift! It would place us in a process of transformation, one that will guide us and

1. Eagleton, *Reason, Faith, and Revolution*, 364.

empower us to move toward becoming our true and best self. It will mean opening ourselves up to the redemptive presence of God's Spirit. In time we will find deep peace, begin to flourish as a person created in the image of God, and turn toward becoming a person for others. Filled with love and compassion, we dedicate ourselves to becoming all that God intends for us to be.

> Do not be conformed to this world, but be transformed by the renewing of your minds, so that you may discern what is the will of God—what is good and acceptable and perfect.
>
> Rom 12:2

10

The Place of Knowledge, the Place of Faith, and the Place of Action

WE HAVE BEEN CAREFUL to answer the preliminary questions that arise when we look at the radical invitation of Jesus. We first asked how it is possible to access the invitation in that it is contained in Gospels written nearly two thousand years ago, and many years after the life of Jesus. We urged a careful study of the historical records and of the Gospels. It is also very wise as we seek access to find our way through the maze of the teaching of the church about Jesus across the centuries, filled as it is with a mix of human brilliance and limitations. These strategies give us our frame of reference.

We must be serious about this quest in that it requires dedication and discipline. When we give it our best attention and concentration, we will then be able to answer the second question: What are the components of the invitation? Our answer is based on three components: his ethical teaching, our full acceptance of the reign of God in our lives, and how we manage the conflicts we may face in our choice. We then sought answers to a third question: What are the implications of accepting the invitation? As a way of expanding our answer to this question, we looked at the example of Jesus, from his birth to the last week of his life, and saw in his life and teaching the model of the way to say yes to his invitation. We now turn directly to our final question: How should we respond to the invitation? We will explore the place of knowledge, the place of faith, and the place of action in our response. We will then suggest strategies that may work for each of us; we will need to find our way.

The Place of Knowledge

As we contemplate the implications of the invitation, we find ourselves wanting to be sure that we accept it for good reasons. Yes, it is an act of faith and an entrance into a relationship. Because it has this character, there are many who have reservations about whether historical knowledge and thoughtful theological understanding are crucial to the acceptance of the invitation.[1] I do hear these voices, listen carefully, and accept and honor their point of view. Yet I remain persuaded that, while acceptance of the invitation is not primarily an intellectual assent to a series of theological propositions, it is still wisely accepted if our religious commitment is well grounded, credible, and trustworthy. Superstition and distortion are always in the background.

I am persuaded that religious faith can be very life-giving, nurturing, and fulfilling. But in part because of its power, religion can also be very dangerous and life-denying.[2] We have read about large groups of people having their lives destroyed because of a false religious outlook and commitment. While not everyone must become a religious studies scholar, it is still wise to base our life commitment on a trustworthy foundation and, as far as possible, what we think is true.

Truth has often been defined and described in three ways: (1) as that which actually is, not just an opinion growing out of our experience and cultural context; a statement or viewpoint that corresponds to reality; and (2) statements that have a coherent logic and are free from contradictions.[3] As we affirm the truth of a religious outlook, we want it, as far as possible, to describe what truly is and have internal consistency. (3) A third understanding

---

1. See, for example, Rohr, *Naked Now*. Father Rohr makes a good case for the personal character of our decision and provides a helpful corrective to the view that our response to God is exclusively intellectual. He argues for what he calls contemplative seeing, and I value his point of view. But I do not think that we need to give up our reasoned understanding of faith, although our direct linkage with God is relational rather than merely understanding intellectual and theological statements.

2. See my book *Exploring the Spirituality*, in which I look at many of the world's religions in terms of being life giving or life denying. Nearly all of them are both (Ferguson, *Exploring the Spirituality*, 7–10).

3. See the books by Oxford scholar Richard Swinburne, *Coherence of Theism* and *Faith and Reason* for a persuasive argument for a faith that is well-reasoned and coherent.

of truth is much more personal. It is to say that an outlook and commitment are true for me when they bring me health and happiness (blessedness) and guide me toward meaning and purpose.

Even with the assurance on these three aspects of truth, there will still be many unanswered questions. These questions will require a lifetime of study, and we may never answer them fully. Einstein left this earth with answers to some fundamental questions as he sought to find a way of understanding time and space in more accurate ways. Yet there were many unanswered questions for him. It is that way with a religious commitment; we want the foundation of our faith to be as trustworthy as possible, even if we have lingering questions. It is not possible at this point in our discussion to address all of the questions that will surface, in part because the subject is not the primary focus of this writing, and also because I still have too many questions, many which I cannot fully answer. I want to suggest that our best strategy is to ask two foundational questions and reflect on what might be trustworthy answers. In answering them, we will need to have a starting point in order to find answers to other questions.

Perhaps the most fundamental of these questions is whether there is a God, or at least another layer of transcendence.[4] And if there is a God or cosmic principle of order, how do we gain an understanding of the divine will and way of this ground of being as a guide for life? Many of the religions of the world are based on a belief in God, although Buddhism and its cousins, Hinduism and Taoism, speak about transcendent and universal realities rather than about a personal God.[5] Looking back upon my personal history in reference to these questions, I discovered that I have taken several steps, not necessarily in a straight path, but nevertheless helpful in finding a place to rest and approach these and other questions. They were and are:

1. I first found some trustworthy people who were persons of faith and who were kind and patient with me about my questions and faith journey. I sought their wisdom. They were not necessarily scholars of religion, yet very helpful. They did represent a conservative branch of one religion: Protestant Christian, with a moderate evangelical orientation and an emphasis on the cultivation of the spiritual life. They were kind people, although looking back, they were limited in their outlook by

---

4. I have read dozens of books that seek to answer this most fundamental question. I have found Küng, *Does God Exist?*, published in 1980, to be an excellent guide in the quest to find answers.

5. Heehs, *Spirituality Without God*, suggests that the word "God" implies consciousness, and that impersonal references to what is beyond such as the ground of being are not references to God.

their commitment to a distinctly American and conservative version of Christianity. But it worked for them, and it did for me for a few years. I remain grateful to them for their patience and understanding of my journey. I am grateful as well for the community of faith in which they participated and invited me to join. It was also supportive of my desire to grow and deepen my spirituality.

2. As I finished my university education, I had a number of questions about faith, and found that I could continue in my faith journey even with questions. They were existential and personal, and became a part of the journey. I branched out to some degree in my seminary education, continued to explore answers to the many questions during my years in campus ministry, and then faced them more squarely in my doctoral studies. Across the years of teaching, I continued my explorations, was pleased that they did not become disruptive and remained interesting, and continued to be of great value in my growth. But many of the questions remained.

3. In these final years of my journey, I have continued to probe the issues of religious faith and to seek trustworthy foundations of faith. It has become a way of life. My quest might be summarized in the following way:

- I have found some degree of comfort in the unique way that personal faith, coupled with reason and scholarship, interact and contribute to finding a place to stand and be. All three have been important, and I continue to think that it is not necessary to set one over against the other. Rather, it is wise to integrate them and have them complement one another.

- I have engaged in carefully reading the challenges to faith. For example, I have exposed myself to rationalism and a scientific outlook in the writings of people such as Spinoza, Hume, and Darwin. I have explored the view that we create God out of our needs and experience by looking at the writing of Feuerbach, Nietzsche, and Freud. In addition, I studied the ways that religion may be a product of our social context as described, for example, in the thought of Auguste Comte and Karl Marx. I was exposed in my graduate education to twentieth-century philosophers who spoke about belief in God and asked whether "God talk" had any meaning. Bertrand Russell made a case for atheism, and Ludwig Wittgenstein and the logical positivists who followed him maintained that God talk was essentially meaningless. There are contemporary authors

THE PLACE OF KNOWLEDGE, FAITH, AND ACTION   193

who ask hard questions and maintain an atheistic point of view, two of whom I have studied with some care: Richard Dawkins and Edward O. Wilson.[6] Their views demanded a thoughtful response. I have reviewed the point of view in postmodern thought that suggests that every worldview has historical roots and is relative, a point of view that may lead to nihilism. Postmodern thought argues that we come closer to the truth when we deconstruct both historical and contemporary worldviews. I have found the "hermeneutics of suspicion" to be very informative and helpful. My exposure to these perspectives have pushed me to study carefully, think deeply, and find ways of treating these points of view with understanding and respect. It has not been easy.

- I have arrived at the position that no point of view regarding one's belief in God can be proved in the sense of a scientific proof. God is not an object "out there" to study like a bright star. But there is a rational and trustworthy way to engage in the life of faith while at the same time keeping the questions in mind as a check on the truthful and trustworthy character of my religious faith and spiritual path.

- I have chosen the Christian way, influenced profoundly by Jesus, shaped by the excellent theological work that has been done by Christian thinkers across the centuries, and because it has "worked" for me. In choosing to follow the Christian way, I am not saying that other ways are false or of little value. In fact, as I have observed them and talked with their adherents, I have learned that they can be very truthful and life-giving. Yet Christianity has given me meaning (a way of being grounded in a trustworthy faith) and purpose (a life of compassionate service) to love others, relieve suffering, and seek justice. I can follow Jesus while I ponder ontological questions. As I do, I am fully aware that other great teachers and religions have taught a similar pathway.

- I have focused my attention more recently on studying the life and teachings of Jesus as an example of what it means to be a person of faith, one who is committed, compassionate, and has integrity. I have made the study of Jesus an important dimension of my professional life and taught several courses on the life and teaching of Jesus.[7] But my commitment is much more than profes-

6. Dawkins, *God Delusion*; Wilson, *Meaning of Human Existence*. I have also read Christopher Hitchens's *God Is Not Great* and Sam Harris's *End of Faith*. David Bentley Hart's book, *Experience of God*, provides good counterarguments.

7. This book is a product of this emphasis, as was my *Radical Teaching of Jesus*.

- High on my list of subjects to continue to study in more depth is the ways in which the understanding of God grows out of the cosmology, the historical circumstances, and the cultural norms of a particular time and place. We do partially create God in our own image, out of our language, cultural assumptions, and out of our needs. Therefore, the understanding of God or ultimate reality is constantly evolving. In response to this evolutionary pattern of understanding God, I am giving particular focus to the writing of Pierre Teilhard de Chardin who sought to integrate a scientific outlook with Christian thought. In particular, I am been drawn to his concern to find a way to understand Christian faith by integrating faith with modern science and evolution in particular. I am persuaded that we do need to explore ways of understanding God as being "in creation" rather than only and primarily being above and behind it. This view has been called panentheism, not pantheism (God is nature) or a God that occasionally shows up from beyond to engage in the human drama (traditional theism). Pierre Teilhard de Chardin believed in and wrote about the God of love who is in creation and moving the cosmos forward toward what he called the cosmic Christ.[8]

I have used years of study, knowledge, and reason in my faith journey. It has been my lane. These dimensions are not contrary to faith, but undergird faith. They do not necessarily take me to a dualistic orientation if the integrative work is done. This outlook is the heart of my spiritual life and continues to be the way I pursue a life of faith.

The Place of Faith

An initial definition of faith is in order as we explore the life of faith. I draw upon the Bible as a resource for articulating this definition. There are many words used in the Bible for faith, each with a slightly different connotation. There are also many cognates for faith such as "trust," "fidelity," and "belief." One primary word for faith in the Hebrew Bible is *'aman*, a term that

---

8. The books of Ilia Delio and Matthew Fox have been especially helpful in framing and applying the views of Teihlard de Chardin in the contemporary setting. The philosophical works of Georg Wilhelm Friedrich Hegel and Alfred North Whitehead, each in different ways, have been in the background in terms of their understanding of the divine presence within the historical process.

essentially means to accept what is true (or thought to be true), to be faithful to this personal truth, and to live with fidelity in reference to it's inherent ethical norms.[9] Abraham is often thought of as the prototype of the person of faith. He represents the model of faith in the three major monotheistic religions: Judaism, Christianity, and Islam. Abraham left his home with his family and possessions on faith to travel to a new land, an extraordinary undertaking in the ancient world. "Now the Lord said to Abraham, 'Go from your country and your kindred and your father's house to land that I will show you.'" It was a tremendous act of faith in that he left without knowing where they were going (Gen 12). Abraham trusted what he understood as the command of God based on a covenant that God would protect him and a promise that he and his many descendants would be blessed. "And he believed the Lord; and the Lord reckoned it to him as righteousness" (Gen 15:6).

Moses was called upon to have *'aman* in reference to the Exodus. The life of Moses was filled with challenge and change. He was born to a Hebrew mother who was a slave, and who sought to give him a better life than one that was possible for a slave to provide. She left him on the shore of the Nile River in the hope that he would be rescued and cared for by an Egyptian family. He was found and adopted by the daughter of Pharaoh, and he grew up as a royal child. In time, identifying and in solidarity with the Hebrew people, he killed an Egyptian soldier who had beaten a Hebrew slave. He fled to Midian, a region east of Egypt, and became a farmer. In time, he felt called to return to Egypt to free the Hebrew slaves. The calling came in the form of a burning bush in which he heard the command of God. "Then the Lord said, 'I have observed the misery of my people who are in Egypt; I have heard their cry on account of their taskmasters . . . So come, I will send you to Pharaoh to bring my people, the Israelites, out of Egypt'" (Exod 3:7, 10). With reluctance, Moses accepted the responsibility. The story continues: "Then the Lord said to Moses, 'Now you shall see what I will do to Pharaoh: Indeed, by a mighty hand he will let them go; by a mighty hand he will drive them out of this land'" (Exod 6:1). Moses on faith accepted the challenge of God to set the Hebrew people free. When he returned to Egypt, he spoke boldly to Pharaoh, saying: "Let my people go." Pharaoh refuses. There are plagues, the Passover for the Hebrew people, and the great Exodus, a foundational event that has given Jewish people across the centuries courage, faith, and hope.[10] It was an extraordinary act of faith on the part of Moses.

9. Other important words in the Hebrew text that are related to faith are *ruach* (often translated as "spirit") and *hesed* (often translated as "steadfast love"), which point to and undergird our commitment to a trustworthy God and the divine way.

10. Christians, Muslims, Jews, and many marginalized people have found guidance

Both Abraham and Moses believed (had faith) that they heard the voice of God, and that God was in these great endeavors. God was trustworthy.

The Greek word for faith in the New Testament, *pistis*, has similar meaning to the Hebrew words. The persons of faith are those who trust what God has done in and through the life and teachings of Jesus, and who place their faith in the God whom Jesus followed. There are so many dimensions of the life of Jesus that are exemplary, and most of them are the way he acted with integrity on what he faithfully believed was the will of God. In faith, at about the age of thirty, he leaves his home in Galilee and goes south to Judah to be with and learn from his cousin John. Jesus observes John as a prophet, and expands his understanding of and deepens his commitment to his vocation. He senses that God is guiding him in faith. Following a retreat in the wilderness, he returns to Galilee and begins his public ministry of teaching, healing, and prophetic action. In time, his deeds and words become a serious challenge to the religious leaders. He is arrested, charged, and suffers death on the cross. We do not have all the information we would like to have about the life and teaching of Jesus, but there is sufficient information to see this remarkable human being as a model of faith (and much more!).

At the end of his life, Jesus was with his disciples in the garden of Gethsemane. They knew the end was near. In this moment of crisis, Jesus left them to pray. The record we have reports that he asked: "Father, if you are willing, remove this cup from me; yet not my will, but yours be done" (Luke 22:42). His faith in God and his deep commitment to follow the will of God gave him the strength and courage to face his arrest and likely crucifixion. We see in Jesus that in these last hours of his life and also across the time of his public ministry, he was true to his belief that he was doing the will of God. It was an extraordinary act of faith.

The word "faith" appears frequently in the writings of the apostle Paul as he describes the life of a new believer in the Christian movement. It is a way of saying yes to the way of Jesus and the reign of God; one lives by faith. We read in Paul's letter to the Romans 10:17: "So faith comes from what is heard, and what is heard comes through the word of Christ." He writes as well in the Galatian epistle: "But now that faith has come, we are no longer subject to a disciplinarian, for in Christ Jesus you are all children of God through faith" (3:25–26). He writes in his closing remarks of 1 Corinthians: "Keep alert, stand firm in your faith, be courageous, be strong. Let all you do be done in love" (16:13–14).

From these examples, I want us to explore the several dimensions of faith. Let me suggest four aspects of human experience that are integrated

---

and hope in the story of Moses and the Exodus.

into what we mean by faith. The first dimension of faith, although not necessarily the most important one, is that faith is based on knowledge and understanding. We give ourselves to what we hope is an authentic view of God. Our belief does not encompass a comprehensive understanding of God, nor does this knowledge become the primary connection with God. But it is where we start, as do people of faith from other traditions. There is the belief that we encounter the Infinite; that God is there, or more accurately, God is here. Most religious traditions point out that it is an encounter and union, not just an acceptance of a set of theological propositions. There is the deep belief that they do make contact with God, who is present in some sense.

We might initially think of God in reference to the statements in the New Testament that begin with "God is . . ." Nearly all of the images used for God in both the Old and New Testaments are metaphorical in character, as, for example, God is like a King (Ps 47:7), the Lord is my shepherd (Ps 23:1), and God will judge the world with righteousness (Ps 96:13). In the New Testament, there are also metaphorical and analogical ways of speaking about God. Yet there are some more descriptive statements that begin with "God is . . ." For example, we read in 1 John that God is love: "Whoever does not love does not know God, for God is love" (1 John 4:8). In the same letter, 1 John 1:5, we read that "This is the message we have heard from him and proclaim to you, that God is light and in him there is no darkness at all." Light in this passage is metaphorical in character, and makes the direct statement that God is light, the ground of truth, and shines in a way that empowers us to see and understand. God is light, which means that God is Truth. Still another image of God, using the "God is" language, is found in John 4:24: "God is spirit, and those who worship him must worship in spirit and in truth." The word "spirit" (*pneuma*) in this context speaks about the presence, even omnipresence of God; it is like the wind that always surrounds us (John 3:8). We might say that we begin our faith journey with the knowledge that God is love, light (truth), and spirit (ever present). We are loved unconditionally, given the light to see God clearly, and surrounded by God's redemptive presence.

Secondly, faith is a relationship. In this understanding, we do learn from the pious and mystical traditions of the church. We discover that God is not an idea or an object, but personal, and has qualities that we are able to understand in that we experience them. For example, God is love, and as we mature, we discover the true meaning of selfless love and begin to know that we are truly loved by God. God forgives, and as we mature, we discover the importance of forgiveness in our lives and in our relationships. We gain a deep understanding that God is a loving parent who guides our lives, giving us meaning and direction as we make our way in a confusing environment.

Essentially, it is the acceptance of the affirmation that we are created in the image of God and therefore can relate to God in an understandable and authentic way. We are able to form a relationship with God based on love and trust. We open our hearts to the very presence of God, and in our silence and prayers we sense God's presence and feel as if we are one with God. In recent years, I have given more emphasis in my life of faith to the identification and union with God. I understand my prayers as less about asking God for favors and more about changing me.[11]

Third, faith is learning how to be faithful and trustworthy. It is how, as we begin to know and personally understand the will and way of God, we find ourselves choosing to be in the center of God's will and way. It is as if God's presence and will, as the author of John's Gospel says, are like the wind, gently blowing in way that brings comfort. The wind is always there, we feel it, and we choose to allow the wind or energy and presence of God to guide us and empower us. In those moments, when we feel no "wind" because of fatigue or a sense of failure, we dig deeply into the foundation of our faith and depend on what we have learned about finding the way. We learn how to seek and be responsive to the will and way of God, even in our struggles and doubts. I may not always feel love for another person for a variety of reasons, but I can choose to be trustworthy and show acceptance and respect. I find that I experience this situation when I am around a person who has hurt me in some fashion. It is why the teaching of Jesus to love our enemies is so radical and difficult.

A fourth component of faith, as we have already implied, is an active way of life that puts God first and accepts and receives the reign of God for empowerment and guidance. Or to say it in a slightly different way, we act faithfully and are led by the Spirit of God. It is a point that needs some expansion, and we now turn to exploring the meaning of the place of action in the life of faith.

The Place of Action

We gain some knowledge and understanding of the life of faith. It is a marvelous starting place for our spiritual journey. We give ourselves in faith to God, who we understand to be love, light, and spirit, as well as much more. How does this understanding influence the contours of our life? What is it that we have done by accepting the invitation of Jesus to a life that is

---

11. There are times when I drift away. It is to acknowledge what Mother Teresa said about her experience, that she did not always feel the closeness to God. At these times, it is more what I will to do than what my feelings motivate me to do.

God-centered rather than self-centered? What is now expected of us? We begin our trek of faith with the knowledge that there will be implications from this commitment. We have spoken of them earlier in section 2, and outlined some of the demands that are now present. We spoke of the ethical demands of the reign of God, the ways we manage conflict and change, and explored the model of Jesus as a charismatic teacher, compassionate healer, and a radical prophet. We noted the fundamental values of love and compassion, truth and integrity, and peace and justice. But how do we begin to act in reference to our acceptance of the radical invitation of Jesus, filled as it is with a design for action?

One way is by learning what Jesus meant when he named the people who followed him as disciples. The biblical narrative called those who followed Jesus and his design for action disciples. It is a term that meant follower, learner, or pupil. Initially, his followers were learners, listening to their masterful teacher and watching him as he taught all who came to hear him, healed the sick, and sought the common good by working for justice and peace. He gathered this group of learners around him in order to carry out his mission. He had a special group of people within his inner circle who were called apostles, and they traveled with Jesus and learned what was expected of a disciple daily. He also spent time with several people who were intimate friends, shared meals with them, and gave them comfort and counsel. His strategy for his mission, then, was relatively simple, to gather disciples around him, teach them by word and example, and use them in his ministry of teaching, compassion, and healing. In a sense, he is today still calling disciples to join him in the work of the kingdom of God, sharing the good news of transformation for individuals and joining in the quest to make life better for all people.

A disciple's life is relatively easy to understand, but more difficult to implement. There is the cost of discipleship, underlined by Dietrich Bonhoeffer in his classic study.[12] As he taught his disciples, Jesus said that they must "strive first for the kingdom of God and his righteousness, and all these things will be given to you as well" (Matt 6:33). He urges them not to be totally preoccupied with food and clothing, but to focus on the reign of God. He also taught the subtle truth that "Those who find their life will lose it, and those who lose their life for my sake will find it" (Matt 10:33). The true meaning of discipleship is to put the will and way of God first in one's life, and to trust that the basic needs of life will be graciously provided. It is to give up one's personal quest to succeed and gain power (to find one's life) and to lose one's life by following the way of Jesus.

12. Bonhoeffer, *Cost of Discipleship*.

Finding Our Way

The goal of the disciple is to put the will and way of God first. Each of us will need to do it in a way that matches who we are and how we work it out in our context. An essential plank in our action platform is that we will need to acknowledge that we cannot do everything, yet can do something. We need to discern what we are ideally suited to do in expanding the kingdom of God. We are distinctive individuals living at a certain time, in a particular place, with a unique set of circumstances and a range of gifts and talents. Jesus understood this reality and guided his disciples in a way that was distinctively designed for each of them. The apostle Paul, in writing about differences, often used the metaphor of the human body in speaking about how we find our way as faithful followers of Christ. He wrote to the gifted Corinthian Church: "Now concerning spiritual gifts, brothers and sisters, I do not want you to be uninformed . . . Now there are varieties of gifts, but the same Spirit; and there are varieties of services, but the same Lord; and there are varieties of activities, but it is the same God who activates all of them in everyone. To each is given the manifestation of the Spirit for the common good" (1 Cor 12:1, 4–6). Paul then uses the metaphor of the body to describe how different parts of the body function in harmony with other parts of the body. "Indeed, the body does not consist of one member but of many. If the foot would say, 'because I am not a hand, I do not belong to the body,' that would not make it any less a part of the body" (1 Cor 12:14). There are those with wisdom, those with knowledge, those who can heal, and those who are able to discern. He goes on to say that all should strive for "a still more excellent way" which is the gift of love. "And now faith, hope, and love abide, these three; and the greatest of these is love" (1 Cor 13:13). We are to exercise our gifts and talents in the spirit of faith, hope, and love.

The Common Good

And to what cause do we give ourselves? There are so many causes that need attention! In general, we are to be led by the Spirit of God to use our gifts and talents in the sprit of faith, hope, and love to serve the common good (1 Cor 12:7). Step one in serving the common good is to discern and serve the will and way of God in our immediate environment. There are urgent needs wherever we are located. So, regardless of the nature of our talents and where we live, there is an abundance of work to do for the common good. There are those who are unemployed and homeless; those who have limited education and need more targeted programs and tutoring; those who are aging and need assistance in managing the daily tasks of life; those who are without sufficient resources to buy food; those without transportation to receive medical attention and buy basic necessities; those who are marginalized, perhaps because of the subtle injustice of local laws and customs; and those who are seriously ill who need healing and guidance as they face the end of life.

In our small community on Whidbey Island, just a few miles north of Seattle, there are over a dozen nonprofit service organizations serving the common good. There is a range of governmental services available to this well-educated and aging community, but some needs are not addressed by these services. Thoughtful and gifted people have stepped up to serve the common good by creating a broad range of helpful organizations that complement government services. Most of them are based on volunteer leadership and rely on local fundraising. They are designed to meet the many needs that exist. My wife and I are grateful for these services, support them, and often volunteer to serve.

The common good is local, and as we observe the life of Jesus, we see how sensitive he was to those in his circle of nearness. He reached out with compassionate caring and gave himself to those with the basic needs of healing, sustenance, and empathic care. He counseled the woman at the well, healed the leper and the demoniac, allowed the children to come to him, and fed the five thousand. He challenged local laws that were unjust and reinterpreted them in a way that would serve the common good. Indeed, he interpreted Torah as teaching wise compassion and justice for all. He confronted the religious leadership that was self-serving and unresponsive to the spiritual needs of the people. Again and again, he targeted the hierarchical pattern of power that preserved the status quo, one that kept those at the top in power and with access to the wealth of a region. As it was with Jesus, we need not travel far to serve the common good.

Many of the same concerns are present in the larger region in which we live, such as a state or particular section of the country. For example, California must deal with the reality of climate change and address the tragedies of forest fires. The Southwest must address the limitations of water supply and provide a high quality of life for an expanding population. In the region of the Puget Sound where we live, we must be concerned with the health of the Sound, a huge body of water that shapes our pattern of life. Annually, right on our island, there is a conference with outstanding resources that is attended by hundreds of people eager to learn how they can contribute to the health of the Sound. Among the wide range of concerns is the challenge of sustaining the natural rhythms of the life of salmon and whales. In addition, across the Northwest, there is the continuing concern about the ways that Native Americans are treated with justice within the compromise system of reservations. In Seattle, there is a rapid expansion of huge corporations such as Amazon and Microsoft, and a significant challenge of controlling housing costs and facilitating transportation systems that serve the employees. I suspect that in nearly every region of the United States there are a range of problems related to infrastructure and insufficient funds to address them.

Of course, we do not control the decision-making in both government agencies and private business, but we do have the right to vote and be engaged in solving problems through volunteer services in ways that improve equal opportunity for citizens, protect them from unjust practices, make possible a good education, provide an opportunity for meaningful work, and create an income that enables a relatively normal life. Once again, as we look across the geographical region in which we live, we can look to Jesus as a model. He cared for the region now called Israel and Palestine, engaged in practices that served the common good, and challenged the abusive laws and vested interests that resulted in an unjust social order. He spoke directly and acted courageously as he encountered those who had control of the religious and social life of Judea and Galilee. Where there was injustice, hypocrisy, and the protection of vested interests and the abuse of power, he spoke and acted in the role of a prophet calling for change and the common good.

In our time and place in human history, we must also be concerned about the overwhelming national and global problems, and we should note that Jesus looked beyond his region and challenged the alien Roman government. He worked diligently for the kingdom of God, often over against the kingdom of Caesar. We carry his example with us as we observe the continuing tension, unrest, and violence in several parts of the world. I think of the Middle East in particular as I continue to engage in the quest for securing a just peace in Israel and Palestine. There are pockets of famine, lack of pure water, and unstable government structure on nearly every continent. How do we find better ways to more equally share the wealth and to provide enough food for the starving? There is enough to go around if only we could find systems of distribution. Coupled with these problems is the flow of immigrants, people who for a variety of reasons are leaving their countries to find settings that promise a better life. As I write, a large "caravan" of immigrants from Central America is arriving at the US border, and our President's policy is less than welcoming. The systems to process this group of people are inadequate, problematic, and causing great suffering.

Perhaps the most threatening problem of all is climate change. Global warming and the deterioration of the environment are present now, not coming some time in the future. In November of 2018, a report issued by thirteen federal agencies and mandated by Congress warned that there will be serious consequences if major steps are not taken to rein in global warming and carbon emissions. Among the consequences will be the major reduction of the economy of the United States. In addition, there will be increasing fires such as the ones in California, crop failures in the Midwest, and the exacerbation of the crumbling infrastructure in the south. Global warming will cause agricultural yield to fall, disrupting exports and supply chains. Warming will increase rising ocean waters that will impact several coastal locations. The irony above all ironies is the Trump administration's continuing attempt to allow more planet-warming pollution from vehicle tailpipes and powerplant smokestacks, reopening coal mines, and removing the United States from the Paris agreement, under which nearly every other nation pledged to cut carbon emissions. President Trump, in what he considers a way to expand the economy, continues to mock climate change, pointing ignorantly to cold snaps in the Northeast and the Midwest.[13]

We often feel helpless as individuals in addressing such serious problems as global warming. It is so easy to just return to the routines of our daily lives and hope that someone else will take care of these problems. We may help those with needs in our local region, but we often feel helpless in dealing with the serious problems that are national and international in character. If there is some encouragement and hope, it is the way that thousands of people have responded in protest and challenge to the leadership of local, state, and national governments and their agencies. It happened in reference to the election in 2018 at nearly every level. We are seeing democracy at work on a number of fronts. We can make a difference. We are able to use our gifts and talents in a wide variety of ways to address the overwhelming problems we face, not the least of which is to be sure to vote for candidates who are ideally suited to make a difference and who care deeply about improving the life of those whom they serve. It is also possible to influence major corporations in one's region and to encourage the use of the extraordinary wealth of individuals. In our region, we are grateful that Bill and Melinda Gates have founded one of the largest and most lucrative private foundations in the world. They have used their personal wealth

---

13. The report is now available (see a summary at Intergovernmental Panel on Climate Change, "Global Warming"). I have based these few summary remarks on several articles about the report, including Bush, "From Skiing to Salmon Runs." In addition to these reports, there are many books addressing the problem of climate change. Dunne and Coleman, *Ecology, Ethics, and Interdependence*, is a series of essays by leading thinkers on climate change with the Dalai Lama, and has helped me to better understand environmental issues.

and private foundation to address many of the world's most threatening problems.

Jesus not only cared for people in Bethlehem and Capernaum, but traveled to Jerusalem as well. There he took on the role of the Hebrew prophet, speaking and acting boldly at the center of power in his Palestine, but he also did not flinch in his encounters with what was then the primary global power, the Roman government. His invitation is for us to follow in his way, to use our gifts and talents in working for a more just and humane world. As we Christians are led by the Spirit of God, and then join with others from all across the world with different challenges, religious traditions, and a range of governmental systems, we are wise to trust and follow the guidance of Acts 1:8: "But you will receive power when the Holy Spirit has come upon you; and you will be my witnesses in Jerusalem, in Judea and Samaria, and to the ends of the earth." To be a witness is to embrace the model of Jesus, be empowered by God's power and presence, and go into the world with faith, hope, and love to be peacemakers, protect the good creation, and be advocates for justice across the globe. This challenge is fundamental to the invitation of Jesus.

Study Resources

Discussion Questions

1. Do you think that Jesus is a good model for us to follow in our faith journey as we face contemporary problems, or was his situation quite different than ours, and therefore his teaching and actions have little relevance for us?
2. What is the place of reason and knowledge in our faith journey?
3. What is the meaning of faith? What are its many dimensions? Is it a crucial part of being a healthy and productive person in the contemporary world?
4. In what ways should our faith journey involve us in serving the common good?
5. How do you define the word "God"? And how does the understanding of God differ among the many religions? How has the meaning of God changed in the religions of monotheism over the centuries?

Terms and Concepts

1. Truth: the meaning of truth has three related components: a) what exists, what is present, what actually happened; b) an understanding that is coherent and has a logical structure; c) what is an authentic experience and life-giving for us.
2. The Common Good: actions and policies that relieve suffering and contribute to the welfare of the all beings, and especially human beings.
3. Faith: A life commitment and direction that is based on: a) a trustworthy account or narrative; b) a relationship with God or a divine being; c) an ethical way of life that seeks a more just and humane world.
4. Disciple: One who follows a wise teacher, a learner or student, one who seeks to follow the actions of a thoughtful and ethical person.
5. *Weltanshuuang*: a German word that is a compound term meaning "worldview," "perspective on life," or "a way of understanding reality."

Suggested Reading

Delio, Ilia. *The Unbearable Wholeness of Being: God, Evolution, and the Power of Love.* Maryknoll: Orbis, 2013.
Fox, Matthew. *Creation Spirituality: Liberating Gifts for the People of Earth.* San Francisco: HarperSanFrancisco, 1991.
Küng, Hans. *Does God Exist? An Answer for Today.* Translated by Edward Quinn. Garden City: Doubleday, 1980.
Teilhard de Chardin, Pierre. *The Hymn of the Universe.* New York: Harper & Row, 1969.
Wilber, Ken. *Integral Spirituality: A Startling New Role for Religion in the Modern and Postmodern World.* Boston: Integral Books, 2006.

Bibliography

Airey, Tommy. *Descending Like a Dove: Adventures in Decolonizing Evangelical Christianity*. Ypsilanti, MI: Kardia Kaiomone, 2018.
Allison, Dale C., Jr. *Constructing Jesus: Memory, Imagination, and History*. Grand Rapids: Baker Academic, 2010.
Bailey, Kenneth E. *Jesus Through Middle Eastern Eyes: Cultural Studies in the Gospel*. Downers Grove: IVP Academic, 2008.
Beasley-Murray. G. R. *Jesus and the Kingdom of God*. Grand Rapids: Eerdmans, 1986.
Beaumont, Mike. *The One-Stop Guide to Jesus*. Oxford: Lion, 2010.
Benefiel, Margaret. *The Soul of a Leader: Finding Your Path to Fulfillment and Success*. New York: Crossword, 2008.
Bernstein, Richard. *Beyond Objectivism and Relativism: Science, Hermeneutics, and Praxis*. Philadelphia: University of Pennsylvania Press, 1983.
Berry, Thomas. *The Great Work: Our Way into the Future*. New York: Three Rivers, 1999.
———. *The Sacred Universe: Earth, Spirituality, and Religion in the Twenty-First Century*. New York: Columbia University Press, 2009.
Bonhoeffer, Dietrich. *The Cost of Discipleship*. Translated by Reginald Fuller. New York: Touchstone, 2014.
Borg, Marcus J. *Convictions: How I Learned What Matters Most*. New York: HarperCollins, 2014.
Borg, Marcus J., and John Dominic Crosson. *The Last Week: A Day-to-Day Account of Jesus's Final Week in Jerusalem*. San Francisco: HarperSanFrancisco, 2006.
Bourgeault, Cynthia. *Centering Prayer and Inner Awakening*. Lantham: Cowley, 2004.
Brown, Raymond F. *The Birth of the Messiah: A Commentary on the Infancy Narratives in Matthew and Luke*. Garden City: Doubleday, 1977.
Brueggemann, Walter. *Gift and Task: A Year of Daily Readings and Reflections*. Louisville: Westminster John Knox, 2017.
Bultmann, Rudolf. *Jesus and the Word*. Translated by Louise Pettibone Smith and Erminie Huntress Lantero. London: Collins, 1958.
———. *Kerygma and Myth by Rudolf Bultmann and Five Critics*. Edited by Hans Werner Bartsch. New York: Harper & Row, 1961.

Burckhardt, Jacob. *The Civilization of the Renaissance in Italy*. Translated by S. G. G. Middlemore. Revised and edited by Irene Gordon. Mentor Book MT321. London: Phaidon, 1960.

Bush, Evan. "From Skiing to Salmon Runs, the National Climate Report Predicts a Northwest in Peril." *Seattle Times*, November 24, 2018. https://www.seattletimes.com/seattle-news/environment/national-climate-assessment-paints-grim-picture-for-northwest/.

Carroll, John T. *Jesus and the Gospels: An Introduction*. Louisville: Westminster John Knox, 2016.

Charlesworth, James H. *Jesus within Judaism: New Light from Exciting Archaeological Discoveries*. New York: Doubleday, 1988.

Chilton, Bruce. *Rabbi Jesus: An Intimate Biography*. New York: Doubleday, 2000.

Collingwood, R. G. *The Idea of History*. London: Oxford University Press, 1961.

Conzelmann, Hans. *Jesus: The Classic Article from RGG Expanded and Updated*. Translated by J. Raymond Lord. Philadelphia: Fortress, 1973.

Crossan, John Dominic. *The Historical Jesus: The Life of a Mediterranean Jewish Peasant*. San Francisco: HarperSanFrancisco, 1991.

———. *How to Read the Bible & Still Be A Christian*. New York: HarperOne, 2015.

Dawes, Gregory W., ed. *The Historical Jesus Quest: Landmarks in the Search for the Jesus of History*. Louisville: Westminster John Knox, 2000.

Dawkins, Richard. *The God Delusion*. 1st Mariner Books ed. New York: Houghton Mifflin, 2006.

Delio, Illia. *Making All Things New: Catholicity, Cosmology, and Consciousness*. Maryknoll: Orbis, 2015.

———. *The Unbearable Wholeness of Being: God, Evolution, and the Power of Love*. Maryknoll: Orbis, 2013.

Dodd, C. H. *The Founder of Christianity*. London: Collins, 1970.

Dunne, John, and Daniel Goleman, eds. *Ecology, Ethics, and Interdependence: The Dalai Lama in Conversation with Leading Thinkers on Climate Change*. Sommerville, MA: Wisdom, 2018.

Eagleton, Terry. *Reason, Faith, and Revolution: Reflections on the God Debate*. New Haven: Yale University Press, 2009.

Edersheim, Alfred. *The Life and Times of Jesus the Messiah*. 2 vols. Grand Rapids: Eerdmans, 1950.

Ehrman, Bart D. *Jesus: Apocalyptic Prophet of the New Millennium*. New York: Oxford University Press, 1999.

Farrar, Frederic W. *Life of Christ*. New York: Burt, 1896.

Ferguson, Duncan S. *Biblical Hermeneutics: An Introduction*. Atlanta: John Knox, 1986.

———. *Exploring the Spirituality of the World Religions*. New York: Continuum, 2010.

———. *Lovescapes: Mapping the Geography of Love*. Eugene, OR: Cascade, 2012.

———. *The Radical Teaching of Jesus*. Eugene, OR: Wipf & Stock, 2016.

Fiorenza, Francis Schussler. *Foundational Theology: Jesus and the Church*. New York: Crossroad, 1986.

Forsyth, P. T. *The Person and Place of Jesus Christ*. London: Independent Press, 1909.

Fowler, James W. *Stages of Faith: The Psychology of Human Development and the Quest for Meaning*. San Francisco: Harper & Row, 1981.

Fox, Matthew. *Creation Spirituality: Liberating Gifts for the People of Earth*. San Francisco: HarperSanFrancisco, 1991.

Fredriksen, Paula. *Jesus of Nazareth: King of the Jews*. New York: Vintage, 1999.

Funk, Robert W. *Honest to Jesus: Jesus for a New Millenium.* San Francisco: HarperSanFrancisco, 1996.
Gadamar, Hans-George. *Truth and Method.* Translated by Joel C. Weinsheimer and Donald G. Marshall. New York: Crossroads, 1965.
Goleman, Daniel. *Emotional Intelligence: Why It Can Matter More than IQ.* New York: Bantam, 1995.
———. *Social Intelligence: The New Science of Human Relationships.* New York: Bantam, 2006.
Grant, Michael. *Jesus: An Historian's Review of the Gospels.* New York: Scribner, 1977.
Grant, Robert M., and David Tracy. *A Short History of the Interpretation of the Bible.* 2nd rev. ed. Philadelphia: Fortress, 1984.
Gushee, David P. *Still Christian: Following Jesus out of American Evangelicalism.* Louisville: Westminster John Knox, 2017.
Holladay, Carl. "Biblical Criticism." In *Harper's Bible Dictionary*, edited by Paul J. Achtemeier, 129–33. San Francisco: Harper & Row, 1985.
Harris, Sam. *The End of Faith: Religion, Terror, and the Future of Reason.* New York: Norton, 2005.
Hart, David Bentley. *The Experience of God: Being, Consciousness, Bliss.* New Haven: Yale University Press, 2013.
Harvey, A. E. *Jesus and the Constraints of History.* Philadelphia: Westminster, 1982.
Heehs, Peter. *Spirituality Without God: A Global History of Thought and Practice.* London: Bloomsbury Academic, 2019.
Helmick, Raymond G., and Rodney L. Peterson, eds. *Forgiveness and Reconciliation: Religion, Public Policy, & Conflict Resolution.* Philadelphia: Templeton Foundation, 2001.
Hitchens, Christopher. *God Is Not Great: How Religion Poisons Everything.* New York: Twelve, 2007.
Holmes, George. *The Florentine Enlightenment 1400–50.* New York: Pegusus, 1969.
Intergovernmental Panel on Climate Change. "Global Warming of 1.5°C." https://www.ipcc.ch/site/assets/uploads/sites/2/2018/07/SR15_SPM_version_stand_alone_LR.pdf.
Jasper, David. *A Short Introduction to Hermeneutics.* Louisville: Westminster John Knox, 2004.
Johnson, Elizabeth A. *Consider Jesus: Waves of Renewal in Christology.* New York: Crossroad, 1990.
Johnson, Jerah, and William Percy. *The Age of Recovery: The Fifteenth Century.* Ithica: Cornell University Press, 1970.
Kähler, Martin. *The So-Called Historical Jesus and the Historic Biblical Christ.* Translated by Carl E. Braaten. Philadelphia: Fortress, 1964.
Keck, Leander E. *Who Is Jesus? History in Perfect Tense.* Minneapolis: Fortress, 2000.
Kirkpatrick, Thomas G. *Communication in the Church.* Lanham: Rowman & Littlefield, 2016.
Küng, Hans. *Does God Exist? An Answer for Today.* Translated by Edward Quinn. Garden City: Doubleday, 1980.
Ladd, George E. *The Blessed Hope.* Grand Rapids: Eerdmans, 1956.
Lahaye, Tim, and Jerry B. Jenkins. *Left Behind.* 16 vols. Wheaton: Tyndale, 1995–2007.
Lindsay, Hal, and Carole C. Carlson. *The Late Great Planet Earth.* Grand Rapids: Zondervan, 1970.
Lohfink, Gerhard. *Jesus of Nazareth: What He Wanted, Who He Was.* Translated by Linda M. Maloney. Collegeville: Liturgical, 2012.

Meier, John P. *A Marginal Jew: Rethinking the Historical Jesus.* Vol. 1, *The Roots of the Problem and the Person.* New York: Doubleday, 1991.
Merton, Thomas. *Love and Living.* New York: Bantam, 1965.
———. *New Seeds of Contemplation.* New York: New Directions, 1962.
Meyers, Isabel Briggs, and Peter B. Meyers. *Gifts Differing.* Palo Alto: Consulting Psychologists, 1980.
Meyers, Robin R. *Saving Jesus from the Church: How to Stop Worshiping Christ and Start Following Jesus.* New York: HarperOne, 2009.
Moltmann, Jürgen. *Theology of Hope: On the Grounds and Implications of a Christian Eschatology.* Translated by James W. Lietch. New York: Harper & Row, 1967.
Muggeridge, Malcolm. *Something Beautiful for God: Mother Teresa of Calcutta.* San Francisco: HarperOne, 1971.
Murphy, Frederick J. *The Religious World of Jesus: An Introduction to Second Temple Palestinian Judaism.* Nashville: Abingdon, 1991.
Newbigin, Lesslie. *Honest Religion for Secular Man.* Philadelphia: Westminster, 1966.
Niebuhr, Reinhold. *Moral Man and Immoral Society: A Study in Ethics and Politics.* New York: Scribner, 1960.
Nolan, Albert. *Jesus Before Christianity.* Maryknoll: Orbis, 1978.
Nouwen, Henri J. M. *The Wounded Healer: Ministry in Contemporary Society.* Garden City: Image, 1972.
Office of the General Assembly, Presbyterian Church (USA). *The Book of Confessions.* Louisville: Office of the General Assembly, 2002.
Ottati, Douglas F. *Theology for Liberal Protestants: God the Creator.* Grand Rapids: Eerdmans, 2013.
Palmer, Richard E. *Hermeneutics: Interpretation in Schleiermacher, Dilthey, Heidigger, and Gadamer.* Evenston: Northwestern University Press, 1969.
Pickus, Robert, and Robert Woito. *To End War: An Introduction to the Ideas, Books, Organizations, and Work that Can Help.* New York: Harper & Row, 1970.
Ratzinger, Joseph (Pope Benedict XVI). *Jesus of Nazareth: The Infancy Narratives.* New York: Image, 2012.
Renan, Ernest. *The Life of Jesus.* London: Watts, 1935.
Reventlow, Henning Graf. *The Authority of the Bible and the Rise of the Modern World.* Translated by John Bowden. Philadelphia: Fortress, 1985.
Robinson, James M. *A New Quest of the Historical Jesus.* Naperville, IL: Allenson, 1958.
Robinson, John A. T. *Honest to God.* London: SCM, 1963.
Rogers, Jack B., and Donald K. McKim. *The Authority and Interpretation of the Bible.* New York: Harper & Row, 1979.
Rohr, Richard. *The Naked Now: Learning to See As the Mystics See.* New York: Crossroad, 2013.
Salzberg, Sharon. *Real Love: The Art of Mindful Connection.* New York: Flatiron, 2017.
Sanders, E. P. *The Historical Figure of Jesus.* London: Penguin, 1993.
———. *Jesus and Judaism.* Philadelphia: Fortress, 1985.
Schweitzer, Albert. *The Mystery of the Kingdom of God.* Translated by Walter Lowrie. Reprint, London: A. & C. Black, 1956.
———. *The Quest of the Historical Jesus: A Critical Study of Its Progress from Reimarus to Wrede.* Translated by W. Montgomery. New York: Macmillan, 1948.
Sonderegger, Katherine. *Systematic Theology.* Vol. 1, *The Doctrine of God.* Minneapolis: Fortress, 2015.

BIBLIOGRAPHY

Spong, John Shelby. *Unbelievable: Why Neither Ancient Creeds Nor the Reformation Can Produce a Living Faith Today*. San Francisco: HarperOne, 2018.

Stevenson, Bryan. *Just Mercy: A Story of Justice and Redemption*. New York: Spioegel & Grau, 2014.

Swinburne, Richard. *The Coherence of Theism*. 2nd ed. Oxford: Oxford University Press, 1993.

Tatum, W. Barnes. *The Quest of Jesus*. Nashville: Abingdon Press, 1999.

Teilhard de Chardin, Pierre. *The Hymn of the Universe*. New York: Harper & Row, 1969.

Theissen, Gerd, and Annette Mertz. *The Historical Jesus: A Comprehensive Guide*. Translated by John Bowden. Minneapolis: Fortress, 1996.

Theissen, Gerd, and Dagmar Winter. *The Quest for the Plausible Jesus: The Question of Criteria*. Translated by M. Eugene Boring. Louisville: Westminster John Knox, 2002.

Vermes, Geza. *Jesus in His Jewish Context*. Minneapolis: Fortress, 2003.

Weber, Max. *The Protestant Ethic and the Spirit of Capitalism*. Translated by Talcott Parsons. New York: Scribner, 1958.

White, L. Michael. *From Jesus to Christianity*. San Francisco: HarperOne, 2005.

Wilber, Ken. *Integral Spirituality: A Startling New Role for Religion in the Modern and Postmodern World*. Boston: Integral Books, 2006.

———. *The Religion of Tomorrow: A Vision for the Future of the Great Traditions: More Inclusive, More Comprehensive, More Complete*. Boulder: Shambhala, 2017.

Wilson, Edward O. *The Meaning of Human Existence*. New York: Liveright, 2014.

Wright, N. T. *Christian Origins and the People of God: The New Testament and the People of God*. Minneapolis: Fortress, 1992.

———. *Jesus and the Victory of God*. Minneapolis: Fortress, 1996.

Zeitlin, Irving M. *Jesus and the Judaism of His Time*. Cambridge: Polity, 1988.

Index

Abba Father, 82, 172–73
Abraham, 117, 118, 195–96
action, moral. *See* justice, equality; moral action, ethics
Acts 1, and the invitation of Jesus, 204
agape (love), 59–64, 73. *See also* compassion, mercy; love
Allison, Dale C. Jr., 38n7, 87n16
alms, 70–71, 73, 84–85
"already-not yet" perspective on the second coming, 89, 89n22
'aman (faith as trust in God), 194–96
anointment
    and the "anointed one" as messiah, 129–31, 129n6, 133
    of Jesus prior to death, 167–68
Anselm, 172
Antiochus Epiphanes, 166–67
aphorisms, 35, 142, 145–48, 155
apocalyptic, defined, 91
apostles, 78, 199. *See also* disciples, discipleship
Apostles' Creed, 182
atheism, 193
atonement
    crucifixion as, 181
    defined, 186
    and sacrifice, 160
    substitutionary, 179–80
attitudinal preunderstanding, 38
Augustine
    credo ut intelligam, 26

    hermeneutical approach to Scripture, 43–44
    linking of experience with faith, 44
    prayer, 58
authority. *See* conflict; power and authority

Babylonian captivity/exile, 49, 73, 79, 178. *See also* Second Temple Palestinian Judaism
baptism, Jesus's, 127–28
Barth, Karl, 47n15, 120n4
basileia (kingdom), as a term, 75n2
Beaumont, Mike, 162n10
Benefiel, Margaret, 97n5
Bernstein, Richard J., 25n10
Berry, Thomas, 14
Bethany, Jesus's community at, 158–59, 167, 177
Bethlehem
    Jesus's birth in, 3–4, 117, 121
    Jesus's ministry in, 204
Beyond Objectivism and Relativism (Bernstein), 25n10
the Bible. *See also* hermeneutics; historical Jesus; the Gospels; the Hebrew Bible; oral traditions
    application of scientific methods to, 45
    Augustine's views on Scripture, 43–44
    autonomous interpretations, 45

the Bible (*continued*)
   and the field of hermeneutics, 37, 43
   and function of specific interpretations, 39–40
   as God-inspired and literal, inerrant source, 7–10, 90, 182
   and God's entry into human history, 9–10, 12, 20, 42, 76, 87–88, 118, 194n8
   historical-critical interpretations, 45–48
   hope as central theme in, 90
   importance of careful scholarship, 23–24, 47, 51, 192–93
   inconsistencies in language use, 8, 82
   as metaphorical truth, 75n2, 85, 118, 123–24
   nineteenth century interpretations, 7–8, 19
   possible sources for, 8, 14, 18, 20, 22, 72, 117, 123–24, 127
   and the term *basileia* (kingdom), 75n2
   traditional views of, 8–9
   violence and nonviolence in, 147–48, 148n18
   and the wisdom from parables and stories, 99–100
   words for faith in, 194–96
   as written by humans over time, 8, 12, 46, 88n18
biographical approach to life and teachings of Jesus, 46
birth/infancy of Jesus
   accounts of, beauty and meaning in, 123–24
   emphasis on inclusiveness and messianic prophecy in Luke, 122–23
   questions raised by scholars about, 118–19
   story of, in the Gospels of Matthew and Luke, 116–24
The Birth of the Messiah: A Commentary on the Infancy Narratives in Matthew and Luke (Brown), 116n1
blessedness, in Matthew 5:8, 145
the body, as metaphor used by Paul, 200
Bonhoeffer, Dietrich, 199
Borg, Marcus, 157n2
Brown, Raymond E., 4n1, 116n1
Bultmann, Rudolf
   on the essence of the gospel message, 10
   hermeneutics of, 120n4
   on knowing the truth about the historical Jesus, 11
   vorverständnis (preunderstanding), 25

Caiaphas, 126, 174, 186
Calvin, John, 13
Cana, wedding at, 139–40
candelabra, in the temple, 161, 161n9
Capernaum, Jesus's ministry at, 136
Carlson, Carole C., 58n2
carpentry, Jesus's work at, 30–31
Carroll, John T., 21n6
Chalcedonian Creed, 43
Christian faith *See also* the Bible; hermeneutics; love; the God-centered life; moral action
   articulating, challenges of, 183–84
   and biblical studies as foundational for, 9, 37, 47
   centrality of the crucifixion to, 179
   diversity of beliefs and practices, 36
   historical development of, 26, 179
   holistic understanding in the modern context, 13, 120n4
   integrating with scientific understanding, 184–85, 185n28
   and love for God and other humans, 59–60
   making relevant in the modern world, xix-xx
   panetheist perspective, 14
   partnerships with other religious traditions, value, 184
   progressive approach, 26–27, 26–27n15
   and subjective interpretations, 12

as underlying author's worldview,
26, 26n14
Christian Origins and the Question of God (Wright), xiiin2
Christmas story, 3–4. *See also* birth/infancy
Christ of faith/Jesus Christ. *See also* historical Jesus; kingdom of God; messiah
  distinguishing from the historical Jesus, xi, xin1, 17, 48
  as God's reconciling act, 180
  historical Jesus as underlying, xxiin2, 18–19
  and Jesus as the incarnation of God, 119
  and Jesus's healing miracles, 6, 15, 47, 47n15
  and Jesus's messianic ministry, 81–83, 85, 89, 89n22, 109, 116, 135
  and the need to redeem the Jewish people, 32, 85–86, 100–101, 149, 152
  and the resurrection, 85, 164–65, 176–77, 180–184
  as seated at the right hand of God, 85, 174, 177, 183
  and the second coming, 87–89, 87n16, 88n18, 89n22, 91
church history/tradition. *See also* the Bible; creeds and confessions
  acceptance of Jesus as incarnation/expression of God, 118–19
  and Confessions of Faith, 179
  and the creedal councils, 43
  efforts to develop, and the writing of the Gospels, 7, 21–22, 115–16, 152, 177
  emergence of after Jesus's death, 78–79
  focus on the resurrection, 182
civil disobedience, 99, 111. *See also* moral action, ethics
cleansing of the temple incident, 84–85
climate change, working to address, 201–3, 203n13
common good, working for, 14, 200–205. *See also* love; moral action, ethics

Communication in Church (Kirkpatrick), 97n4
compassion, mercy. *See also* love; moral action, ethics
  as characteristic of the God-centered life, 67, 187–88
  and giving/generosity, 71
  Jesus's displays of, 28–29, 62–63
  Jesus's emphasis on, 50, 67–68, 101–2, 107–11, 115, 140–42, 143, 153–54
  as Jesus's guiding value, 98
  and love for self and others, 14, 60, 61–62, 140
  as non-exclusive, 144
Confession of 1967 (United Presbyterian Church of America), 180–82
Confessions (Augustine), 44
Confessions of Faith, 179
conflict
  and the domain of human relationships, 106–11
  and the domain of power and authority, 95–100
  and the domain of values, 100–106
  handling conflicts in values, 100
  Jesus's refusal to be drawn into, 163–64
  and living the God-centered life, 94–95
  resolving, nonviolent approaches, 98, 98n6, 147–48, 148n19, 166–67, 173
Constraints of History (Harvey), 5n3
Constructing Jesus: Memory, Imagination, and History (Allison Jr.), 38n7, 87n16
consumerism. *See* materialism
contemplative seeing, 190n1
Conzelmann, Hans, 11n11
1 Corinthians
  concept of faith in, 196
  and the path of discipleship, 200
  and Paul's list of encounters with the risen Christ, 193
cosmology, understandings of, implications for faith, 184–85, 194

Court for Women (the temple), 161
Court of Israel (the temple), 161
Court of the Gentiles (the temple), 161, 186
Court of the Priests (the temple), 161
creeds and confessions
    the Apostles Creed, 182
    believability of and contemporary faith, xii-xiv
    Caledonian and Nicene, 43
    Confession of 1967 (United Presbyterian Church of America), 180-82
    and early Christian views of the Hebrew Bible, 42
    emphasis on the truth of the resurrection, 182
    International Reformed Church, 179
    as reflective of the Spirit of God as revealed in the Bible, xx
    understanding and integrating, xi-xii, xin1
critical history. *See also* historical Jesus; worldview
    and awareness of one's personal worldview, 24-25
    and the Gospels as sermons vs. biography, 124
    and interpreting the larger story of the resurrection, 182
    as a modern construct, 15
    nineteenth and early twentieth century approaches, 19-22
    overview, 23
    and preunderstanding, 24-26
    and the processes of textual and source criticism, 21
    and questions raised about the birth of Jesus, 51, 118-19
    and the search for the historical Jesus, 15
Croesan, John Dominic, 22-23, 148n18, 157n2
crucifixion. *See also* historical Jesus
    accounts of in the Gospels, 31, 175-179
    interpretations, 180-81

Daniel, Book of,
    Jesus's reference to during his trial, 173
    link to Jesus's return, 86
    vision of the "son of man" (*ben'adam*), 83
David, King of Israel
    idealized memories of, 116
    Jesus's parallels to, 81
    Jesus's references to during final days, 165
    role in Jesus's genealogy, 117, 118
Dawkins, Richard, 192-93
deconstruction, and the hermeneutics of suspicion, 37n5
Delio, Ilya, 184n25, 194n8
the devil (*diabolis*, evil one)
    body-inhabiting demons, 155
    and Jesus's handling of temptation, 104-5
    and Jesus's preparations for the ministry, 131n10
    Satan as, 133
disciples, discipleship
    the apostles, 78, 199
    costs associated with, 199
    defined, 199, 205
    desertion of Jesus, 173
    Jesus's choice of, 136, 136nn5-6
    Jesus's conversations with following resurrection, 176-77
    and Jesus's pastoral ministry, 140
    Judas Iscariot, 169
    and serving the common good, 200
dispensationalism, 58
Dodd, C. H., 88, 88nn18-19

ego, "I" identity. *See* self-centeredness
Einstein, Albert, 191
Elizabeth, 121-22, 133
end times, judgment. *See also* kingdom of God
    Jesus's comments about, 82
    pointers to in the Gospels, 87
    timing of, Jesus's comments on during his final days, 165-66

INDEX

enemies, Jesus's commandment to love, 61–62
the Enlightenment, 7–8, 46
epistemology, defined, 37
eschatology, defined, 91
ethics, ethical teachings. *See* moral action, ethics; the Law (Torah)
the Eucharist
    and accounts and meaning of the Last Supper, 170–72
    role of the priest in inviting people to receive, 39n11, 139
evangelicals, 185, 185n27
evil, crucifixion as victory over, 9, 180–82. *See also* moral action, ethics; the devil; sin
experience, Augustine's emphasis on, 44

faith journey. *See also* Christian faith; Christ of faith, Jesus Christ; compassion, mercy; the God-centered life; historical Jesus; love
    becoming faithful and trustworthy, 198
    and believability of creedal statements, xi–xiv
    definitions, 205
    and establishing a relationship with God, 166–67; 191–93, 197–98
    and handling struggles and doubts, 114, 198, 198n11
    and humility, 14, 19, 26, 87, 185
    and the importance of action, 198–99, 201–2
    and integrating science and faith, 13, 194
    Jesus's teachings as guide to, xiii, xviii–xix, 156–57
    and opening to an understanding of the Gospels, 34, 52, 189, 190–94, 190n1, 197
    restatement of, to fit needs of specific historical periods, 12–13
    and serving the common good, 200–204
    and spiritual healing, 150
    as unique and personal, 191–93
fig tree, barren, lessons from, 159, 162, 167
final week, 159–85
First Temple period, 73
forgiveness
    and Jesus's final words, 178
    Jesus's teachings on, 61–62, 61n10, 141
    and moral action, 61–62
Forgiveness and Reconciliation (Helmick and Peterson), 62n11
form criticism, 21–23
"forty," as a metaphorical number, 104n13, 131n10
Founder of Christianity (Dodd)`, 88n18
Fowler, James, 77–78n6, 120n4
Fox, Matthew, 194n8
Funk, Robert W., 35, 35n1

Gabriel, angel, 121
Galilee. *See also* historical Jesus; Second Temple Palestinian Judaism
    diversity of peoples in, 30
    life in, during first century CE, 124
    as location for Jesus's ministry, 32, 80, 135–37
generosity, giving, Jesus's teachings on, 70–71. *See also* compassion, mercy; the poor
Gerasene demoniac, healing of, 150–51
Gethsemane, Jesus's prayers and arrest at, 147–48, 172–73
Gifts Differing (Meyers and Meyers), 98n6
God. *See also* Christian faith; God-centered life
    coming judgment of, Jesus's prophecy concerning, 163
    as the creation of humans, 198
    as the creator of humans, 198
    devotion to, as most important, 68–69
    entry into human history through Jesus, 9–10, 12, 42, 76, 87–88, 118, 194n8

God (*continued*)
    existence of, pathway to affirming, 191–93
    human inability to control, 104–5
    Jesus as seated at the right hand of, 85, 174, 177, 183
    as love, radical implications, 59–61, 90–91, 156–57, 194, 197
    metaphorical images for, 197
    presence in the life of the historical Jesus, xi-xii, xin1, xxiin2, 18–19, 36, 48, 88, 88n18, 97–98, 105–6, 115, 119, 122, 127, 129, 196
    trust/faith in, as *'aman*, 194–95
    understanding through knowledge, 197
the God-centered life. *See also* compassion; love; moral action
    abundance and joy from, 103
    and acceptance of/respect for the other, 108
    and applying Jesus's teachings about the Law, 67
    challenges and conflicts associated with, 60–61, 94–95, 103–5, 105n14, 114, 131–32
    characteristics, 97–98, 113, 120n4, 153–54, 187–88
    and communities of faith, 11, 153–54, 194–98
    and discipleship, 199–200, 205
    and the double-love commandment, 60, 76–78, 79n7, 90–91, 143, 145–47, 164–65
    and integrity, honesty, 67–68, 71–72, 98, 152–53, 188, 198
    Jesus's modeling of, 48, 93–94, 115, 138, 143–45, 165, 187–88
    John the Baptist's modeling of, 127–29
    and the kingdom of God as metaphor for, 138
    living, as Jesus's radical invitation, 153–54
    meditative practice, 145
    and openness to healing, 149–50
    and repentance, 135
    role of ethical action, 68 100, 103, 198–99
    role of knowledge and understanding, 11, 190–94, 197
    servanthood, serving the common good, 105–6, 200–204
    and understanding and trusting the divine in Jesus's teachings, 119–20, 166–67
    wealth as impediment to, 69
Golgotha, Jesus's crucifixion at, 175
good Samaritan parable, 142–43
the Gospels. *See also* the Bible; Christ of faith; hermeneutics; historical Jesus; the Hebrew Bible *and specific Gospels*
    and determining what is being said, 37
    differences in related to the timing of Jesus's ministry, 135
    integrating differing accounts in, 19, 135
    difficult teachings in, ways of approaching, 50–52
    and efforts of the Jesus Seminar to determine authentic passages in, 35
    eschatological language, 82
    events in, as true, premodern explorations of, 19
    identifying sequence of writings included in 20–21, 20n6
    and Jesus as a compassionate healer, 28–29
    and Jesus's respect for the Hebrew Bible in, 41
    narrative criticism approach, 22
    premodern studies, 19
    Q source, 20
    as record of the spirit and intent of Jesus's incarnation, 34–35
    role in development of early Christian church, 18, 124, 157–58n3
    as sermons, testimonies of faith, 14–15
    sociological approaches, 22–23

possible sources, 8, 14, 18, 20, 22,
    72, 117, 123–24, 127
  studying and understanding, as
    basis for faith journey, 189
  textual interdependence, 20
  and the timing of Jesus's ministry,
    135–36, 136n4
  as written record of the historical
    Jesus, 14, 18
Greek philosophy/culture
  application to Jesus's divine and
    human natures, 119n3
  and the Enlightenment, 45
  incorporation with early Christian
    hermeneutics, 43

Harvey, A. E., 5n3
healing
  and compassion, 28–29
  importance of faith, 149–50
  and Jesus's emphasis on health and
    well-being, 96. 101, 148–51
  Jesus's gift for, xiii, 28–29, 31, 63,
    66–67, 80–81
  and miracles, 6, 15, 47, 47n15
  whole-person healing, 98
heart, in Matthew 5:8, 59
Hebrew Bible (the Pentateuch). *See also*
    the Bible; the Law (Torah)
  and accounts of the Maccabees,
    80n9
  as basis for the Law (Torah), 64, 111
  challenge of integrating into
    Christian faith, 42
  concept of 'aman, 194–96
  descriptions of the Babylonian exile,
    79
  and the forty-day formula, 104n13
  as foundational for the Christian
    faith, 8–9, 41–42
  Paul's interpretation of, 42
  as ritualistic, 86
  sacrifice in, and Jesus's crucifixion as
    metaphor for, 180
  words related to faith, 195n9
  writing of overextended time
    period, 8

Hegel, Georg Wilhelm Friedrich, 194n8
Helmick, Raymond G., 62n11
hermeneutics
  application to difficult teachings, 55
  and approaches to understanding
    Jesus's invitation, 113
  biographical approach to the life and
    teachings of Jesus, 46
  and changing concepts of faith
    during the Enlightenment, 46
  defined, 36, 53
  the hermeneutical task, 36–37
  hermeneutics of suspicion, 37–38,
    37n5, 51–52, 53, 193
  and interpretations of the Hebrew
    Bible by the early Church
    fathers, 42
  and interpretations of the
    resurrection as metaphorically
    true, 183
  and personal prejudices/worldviews
    and needs, 24, 37, 37n5, 39–41,
    64–65
  self-awareness needed for, 38, 51–52
  and types of preunderstanding,
    38–39
Herod Antipas, 136–37n
Herodians, 163n11
Herod the Great
  background, family origins, 137
  and the conviction of Jesus for
    treason, 82
  decapitation of John, 128
  leadership role, 163
  questioning of Jesus, 174–75
  response to learning of Jesus's birth,
    117–18
  role in service to Rome, 31
historical-critical method. *See also*
    hermeneutics
  applications to studies of the
    Gospels, 19n5
  efforts to address limits of, 47
  emergence during the
    Enlightenment, 45
  and the importance of historical
    context, 37
  limitations, 47

historical Jesus. *See also* Christ of faith; healing; invitation of Jesus; messiah; ministry, Jesus's
  accessing life of, challenges of, 7, 14–15
  baptism, 126–28
  betrayal and arrest, 169–71
  biographical approach to understanding, 11, 46
  as both human and divine, 119n3
  as both pastor and priest, 139
  breadth of travels by, 148–49
  call for moral action, 201–2, 204
  and challenges of accessing life and teachings of, 1–2, 107
  challenges of understanding, 18, 24, 24n9
  challenges to traditional law and authority, 48, 66–67, 81, 83–86, 95–102, 159–60
  as a charismatic teacher, xiii, 28, 31, 62, 99–100, 125–28, 142
  conception, birth and early life, 3–4, 30, 116–18, 116n1, 120–22, 124–26
  emphasis on compassion and mercy, 50, 67–68, 101–2, 107–11, 115, 140–42, 143, 153–54
  emphasis on love, 59–60, 59n5, 76, 96, 98–99, 108, 115, 156–57, 164
  ethical teachings, context, 28, 41, 57, 66, 74
  final week, 157–78, 177n19
  as first-century Palestinian Jewish prophet, xiii, 10–11, 29–31, 48–49, 64–65, 82, 82n11, 113
  foundational values, 68–72
  genealogy, 117
  God's presence in life and teachings of, xi–xii, xin1, xxiin2, 18–19, 36, 48, 88, 88n18, 97–98, 105–6, 115, 119, 122, 127, 129, 196
  as the good shepherd, 180–81
  the Gospels as source material, 9–10, 3418, 20–21, 20n6, 34
  handling of temptation by, 103–5, 104n12
  healing skills, xiii, 28–29, 31, 63, 66–67, 80–81
  historical Jesus, 122–23
  historiological approaches to understanding, 20–22
  humility, 82, 105–6, 128
  inclusiveness of teachings, 78
  and the Last Supper, 170–71
  maturing interest in religious heritage, 126
  as model for living a God-centered life, 28, 32, 93n1, 119, 153, 189–90, 193–94
  modern approaches to understanding, 47–48
  neoorthodox understandings, 10
  personal poverty, 70
  popularity and appeal, 41, 81, 126, 137, 152
  premodern historical and language studies of, 19
  preparation for coming death, 159, 167–68, 172–73, 179
  as a real person, importance of understanding, 4–5, 5n3
  religious training, respect for the Hebrew Bible, 30, 41, 65–66, 76, 80–81, 152
  self-view as servant of God, 129n6, 130–31
  sociological approach to understanding, 22–23
  as the Son of Man, 83
  and teachings about forgiveness, 61–62, 61n10, 141, 178
  and teachings about poverty, sharing, 23, 28–29, 69–71, 102, 126, 128–29, 168
  trial, crucifixion, and burial, 173, 175–76
  understanding of the "kingdom of God," 75–78
The Historical Jesus: The Life of a Mediterranean Jewish Peasant (Crossan), 22–23
history, as a field of study. *See also* hermeneutics; worldview (*Weltanshuuang*)

challenges associated with, 4–5,
    14–15, 17
and critical history approaches, 5,
    5n4
defined, 53
as a modern construct, 15
and the process of interpretation,
    5–6
religious history, 6
and underlying assumptions and
    biases, 5–6, 15
Holistic-Integral outlook, 14n15
Holy Spirit, trust in, as basis for faith,
    166–67
Honest Religion for a Secular Man
    (Newbigin), xixn3
Honest to Jesus: Jesus for a New
    Millennium (Funk), 35n1
hope
    as central theme of the Bible, 90
    defined, 91
    and Jesus's messianic ministry, 81–
        83, 85, 89, 89n22, 109, 116, 135
    and the promise of a better future,
        79, 90–91
    and the second coming, 86–89,
        87n16, 88n18, 89n22, 166
"Hosana," defined, 158
hypocrisy, Jesus's condemnation of, 29,
    71–72, 152–53, 163, 165, 202

ideological preunderstanding, 38–39
informational preunderstanding, 38
inspiration, defined, 16
integrity, honesty
    and effective conflict resolution, 99
    as fundamental value, 67–68, 71–72
    and Jesus's criticism of hypocrisy,
        29, 71–72, 152–53, 163, 165, 202
    and living a God-centered life, 98,
        188, 198
International Reformed Church,
    confession and creeds, 179
invitation of Jesus. *See also* faith
    journey; God-centered life;
    kingdom of God
accepting and responding to, xiii,
    xviii-xix, 114, 115, 199–204
accessing through studying the New
    Testament and the historical
    Jesus, 113
analyzing the components of, 113
contemporary understanding of, xii
and creating a relationship with
    God, 97–98, 194–98
difficult teachings, ways of
    approaching, 50–52
ethical guidelines, 58, 63–64
and integrating knowledge with
    faith, 190–94, 197
and living a God-centered life, 86,
    93, 153–54, 187–88
and living for others rather than
    oneself, 94
and relationship with money and
    material well-being, 102–3
selecting teachings, reasons for,
    55–56
and serving the common good,
    156–57, 200–204
showing compassion, 111
as ubiquitous and extended to all,
    113
and work towards peace and social
    justice, 50
Irenaeus, 42
Isaiah, Book of, and linking of Jesus
    with King David, 8
Israel, restoration of, 76, 81–82, 83n12.
    See also messiah; Second Temple
    Palestinian Judaism

Jerusalem
    as center of the Jewish faith, 126
    Jesus's entry into during final week,
        82, 158–59
    Jesus's family's visit to for Passover,
        125
    Jesus's ministry in, purpose, 157–58,
        160
    temple in, 126, 161
Jesus (Conzelmann), 11n11
Jesus and Judaism (Sanders), 83n12

INDEX

Jesus and the Gospels (Carroll), 20n6
Jesus Seminar, 35–36
Jews, Jewish people/ *See also* Judaism, mainstream; Second Temple Palestinian Jews
  Jesus's focus on ministry to, 32, 137
  Palestinian, diversity among, 30
  and the desire for a Messiah, 49, 79, 90–91, 116
John, Gospel of
  account of the cleansing of the temple, 84–85, 84n13
  account of Jesus's final words and death, 178–79
  account of Jesus's resurrection, 176
  account of Judas's betrayal, 169
  account of the Last Supper, 171
  account of the Samaritan woman, 109
  account of the wedding at Cana, 139–40
  account of the woman caught in adultery, 140–42
  and Jesus as voice for God's word, 10
  and Jesus's clarifications of Mosaic Law, 100–101
  and Jesus's "Farewell Address," 171
  metaphorical images for God, 197
  and the temptations of worldly attractions, 105n14
  and the timing for Jesus's ministry, 135–36, 136n4
John the Baptist
  baptism of Jesus, 126–28
  commitment to Jewish traditions, 49
  decapitation, 128
  emphasis on moral behavior, 126–28
  God-centered life, 128–29
  Jesus's studies with, 30–32, 128
  ministry of revival, 129
  parents and vocation, 133
  role in Jesus's genealogy, 121–22
Joseph (Jesus's father), 117
Joseph of Arimathea, burial of Jesus's body, 175–76
Judaism, mainstream. *See also see also* the Hebrew Bible; the Law (Torah); Pharisees; Second Temple Palestinian Judaism
  authorities in Jerusalem, 31
  commitment to the Law (Torah), 66
  conflicts with emerging Christian church, reflections of in the Gospels, 157–58n3
  importance of the temple, 83–84, 83n12, 161
  Jesus's criticisms of, 86, 159–60
  Jesus's effort to bring new life and purpose to, 32, 66, 85–86, 100–101, 141, 149, 152, 164
  and Jesus's respect for the Law, 30, 41, 65–66, 76, 80–81, 100, 126, 152
  and the rebuilding of Jewish traditions, 49
Judas Iscariot, 169–71
Judas Maccabee, 80
judgment day. *See* end times, judgment; kingdom of God
justice, equality. *See also* moral action; nonviolence; the poor
  desire for, as Christian value, 79n7
  as focus in Jesus's teachings, 23, 115, 142, 153–54
  and Jesus's efforts to reduce human suffering, 29
  the Law as basis for, 66–67
  and postmodern understanding of the historical Jesus, 50
  and resistance, protest, 79
  working towards, importance, 48, 61–62, 71, 79, 198–99, 201–2

kingdom of God
  as central to Jesus's ethical teachings, 75
  defined, 91
  and God's primary authority, 76, 89–91, 97, 160
  Jesus's ethical teachings, 57–58
  Jesus's proclamation of (the "good news"), 75–76, 81, 86, 89, 97, 122, 137–38, 152, 168–69; 185n27, 199

limitations of, as a term, 75
and the meaning of the word
    "kingdom," 59n4
meaning/scope of, debates about,
    76, 81, 87
as metaphor for the God-centered
    life, 76, 138
opening to, as part of *metanoia*,
    93–94
Paul's views on, 78–79
and the primacy of love and faith, 69
and the restoration of Israel, 78–79,
    81
as a term, Jesus's use of, 75–76
universality of, 160
Kirkpatrick, Thomas G., 97n4
knowledge. See faith, faith journey;
    historical Jesus; history, as a field
    of study

language
    eschatological, in the Bible, 82
    inconsistent, in scriptural accounts,
        8, 82
    use of in the Gospels, and
        understanding the historical
        Jesus, 19
Last Supper, accounts and meaning of,
    170–72, 186. See also historical
    Jesus; the Eucharist
Late Great Planet Earth (Lindsay and
    Carlson), 58n2
the Law (Torah)
    and concepts of "clean" vs.
        "unclean," 66
    and concepts of justice and mercy,
        66, 144
    defined, 111
    Jesus's respect for teachings in, 30,
        41, 65–66, 76, 80–81, 100, 126,
        152
    Jesus's call for new interpretations
        and practices, 32, 66, 85–86,
        100–101, 141, 149, 152, 164
    Jesus's emphasis on human need
        over obedience, 66–67

Pharisee knowledge of and
    commitment to, 59, 73
scope of, 64
leper, compassionate healing of, 62–63
Leviticus 19, and loving one's neighbor,
    60, 60n6
liberal, defined, 16
liberation theology, 23, 50
light, God as, 197
Lindsay, Hal, 58n2
literary criticism, application to Gospel
    studies, 19n5
logos (word), meaning of, 10
Lord's Prayer, forgiveness and, 61–62
love. See also the God-centered life
    challenges and conflicts associated
        with, 94–95
    as focus of Jesus's teachings, 59–60,
        59n5, 76, 96, 98–99, 108, 115,
        156–57, 164
    and the God-centered life, 188
    and giving/generosity, 70–71
    God as, 59–61, 90–91, 156–57, 194,
        197
    Jesus's expressions of during his
        crucifixion, 172, 178–79
    loving-kindness, 29n16
    and loving one's enemies, 61
Luke, Gospel of
    account of discovery of Jesus's
        resurrection, 176
    account of healing the paralyzed
        man, 96
    account of Herod's questioning of
        Jesus during trial, 174–75
    account of Jesus birth, infancy, and
        youth 116, 120–22, 124–25
    account of Jesus's ascension, 177
    account of Jesus's baptism, 126–28
    account of Jesus's crucifixion, 175
    account of Jesus's dinner with the
        Pharisees, 107
    account of Jesus's experience in the
        wilderness, 130
    account of Jesus's final week, 157–
        58, 171, 174–78
    account of Jesus's healing during the
        Sabbath, 66–67

Luke, Gospel of (*continued*)
    account of Jesus's return to Galilee, 124–25
    account of the cleansing of the temple, 84
    account of the healing of a woman on the Sabbath, 101
    account of the healing of the Gerasene demoniac, 150–51
    account of the walk to Emmaus, 176–77
    authorship and dating of, 120
    on breadth and inclusiveness of Jesus's ministry, 122, 136n4
    concept of faith in, 196
    discussion of Jesus's authority in, 97
    on Jesus's devotional life, 135
    Jesus's sayings about the temple, 51
    oral traditions underlying, 123
    and the parable of the Good Samaritan, 142–43
    possible sources for, 20, 125
    on the scope Jesus's ministry, 137
    as sermon vs. biography, 124
    story of Mary and Martha, 109–11
Luther, Martin, 13

Maccabees, resistance by, 80, 80n9
Marcion, 42
Mark, Gospel of
    account of Jesus's baptism, 127
    account of Jesus's experience in the wilderness, 130, 130n8
    account of Jesus's final days, 158–68
    account of Jesus's trial and verdict, 173
    account of Judas's betrayal, 169
    account of the cleansing of the temple, 84, 165
    account of the healing of a Syrophoenician woman, 148–49
    account of the healing of the Gerasene demoniac, 150–51
    account of the healing the leper, 62–63
    account of the rich man seeking redemption, 102–3
    account of the risen Christ's conversations with the disciples, 176
    account of the woman at Jesus's tomb, 176
    closing verses, redaction of, 22
    dependence of later Gospels on, 20, 120
    description of Jesus's ministry, 31n17, 80–81, 134, 136n4
    Jesus as prophet in, 159
    Jesus in, Wrede's account, 11
    and Jesus's role in expanding the reign of God, 75
    Jesus's statements about love in, 59n5
    Jesus's statements about resurrection, 164–65
    Jesus's teachings on Law and authority in, 66, 163
    parable of the greedy tenants, 162–63
    proclamation of the Kingdom of God in, 82, 86
    references to King David in, 165
Mary, Virgin Mary
    care for the young Jesus, 126
    conception, pregnancy, 117, 121
    relationship with Elizabeth, 121
    relationship with Joseph, 117
Mary and Martha, story of, 109–11
Mary Magdalene, 176
materialism. *See also* God-centered life; moral action; the poor
    challenges of shifting away from, 187–88
    defined, 112
    emphasis on in Western society, 156
    as form of negative love, 60
    Jesus's teachings related to, 68–69, 105–6, 159–60
    and worldly pleasures, 112
    worry, anxiety associated with, 102–3
Matthew, Gospel of. *See also* Sermon on the Mount
    acceptance of the power and reign of God, 74

account of Jesus's crucifixion, 178
account of Jesus's baptism, 127
account of Jesus's birth and infancy, 116–17, 122
account of Jesus's final week, 85, 157–58, 169–70, 173
account of Jesus's healing during the Sabbath, 66–67
account of Jesus's resurrection and return, 86
account of Jesus's sojourn in the wilderness, 104n12
account of Jesus's wilderness sojourn, 129–31
account of the cleansing of the temple in, 84
account of the communication of Great Commission, 176
account of the healing of a Syrophoenician woman, 148–49
account of the healing of the Gerasene demoniac, 150–51
affirmation of nonviolence in, 147
authorship and dating of, 116–17, 117n2
description of Jesus's ministry, 134, 136, 136n4, 137
and the God-centered life, 58, 93–94, 93n1, 145–46
Jesus's criticisms of the Pharisees, 72
Jesus's teaching about authority, 152–54
Jesus's teachings about ethics, 41
Jesus's teachings about forgiveness, 61, 61n10
Jesus's teachings about love, 59–61, 59n5
Jesus's teachings about wealth, 102–3
and proclamation of the Kingdom of God, 81
and the parable of the mustard seed, 83
parable of the Pharisees and the grain field, 66
possible sources for, 20
linking of Jesus with King David, 8
on responsibilities of disciples, 199

the Sermon on the Mount, 145
Maundy Thursday, 171
mental illness, 150–51. *See also* the devil (*diabolis*, evil one)
mercy. *See* compassion, mercy
messiah. *See also* Christ of faith/Jesus Christ; kingdom of God; ministry, Jesus's; resurrection
the "anointed one," 129–31, 129n6, 133
defined, 133
desire for among Second Temple Palestinian Jews, 49, 79, 90–91, 116
identification of Jesus as, 81–82, 123, 129n6
Jesus's avoidance of self-identification as, 82, 129n6, 130–31
view of Jesus as, in accounts of his birth, 122
metanoia (conversion), 93, 93n1, 111
metaphorical truth. *See also* miracles
and the Confession of 1967, 180–83
and directional metaphors, 77n5
and hermeneutics, 4
and imagery in the Gospels, 75n2, 85, 118, 123–24, 127, 197, 200
and Jesus's parables, examples, 109
and Jesus's struggle with temptations, 130–32, 130n9
and the kingdom of God, 75, 75n2, 138
and myth, 16
in stories of healing, miracles, 151
methodological preunderstanding, 39
Meyers, Isabel and Peter, 98n6
Mindful Spirituality (Ferguson), 76n5, 138n10
ministry, Jesus's
as both pastoral and priestly, 139, 141–42
and choice of disciples, 136, 136nn5–6
eschatological meaning, 172
focus on healing and the Law, 80–81
focus on others, 135, 139–40

ministry, Jesus's *(continued)*
   Jesus's preparations for, 103–5, 104n12, 126–27, 130–31
   and Jesus's self-awareness, 82, 158
   and Jesus's travels to distant places, 148–49
   and maintenance of humility, 106
   as messianic, 81–83, 85, 88–89, 89n22, 109, 116, 135
   principle themes, 134, 138
   social unrest associated with, 81
   start and length of, differences found in the Gospels, 135–36
   teaching as component of, 142
   as threat to people in power, 96
   use of parables/metaphors, 99–100, 142–43, 162–63
   wide impact of, 137
miracles. *See also* healing
   belief in, xiv, 47, 47n15
   as metaphorical truth, 6, 15, 140n14
   and the temptations facing Jesus, 104
moneychangers, 84n13, 159
moral action, ethics. *See also* compassion; the God-centered life; justice; love
   call for love and compassion, 58–64, 145–46
   civil disobedience, 99, 111
   challenges, 58, 74
   and the God-centered life, 89, 100, 103, 198–99
   Jesus's life and teachings as guide to, 28–29, 48, 68, 89
   and the kingdom of God, 75, 79, 79n7
   and the Law (Torah), 65
   nonviolence, 147–48, 166–67, 173
   and the progressive Christian perspective, 27
   and working for the common good, 14, 89–90, 200–205
   and working for social justice, 79, 198–99, 201–2
Moses. *See also* the Law (Torah)
   'aman shown by, 195–96
   hope brought by, 196n10
   law given by, 42, 101
the Mount of Olives, Jesus's final interactions with disciples at, 165, 172–73
mustard seed parable, 83
Myers-Briggs Inventory, 98n6
Mystery of the Kingdom (Schweitzer), 57–58n1
myth, defined, 16. *See also* metaphorical truth

narrative criticism, 20–22
Nazareth
   Jesus's early life in, 30–31
   Jesus's return to, 32, 118, 121–22
neoorthodoxy, 9–12, 11n11
Newbigin, Lesslie, xixn3
New Testament. *See also* the Bible; the Gospels; the Hebrew Bible
   and accounts of the resurrection, 183
   concept of *pistis*, 195–96
   development over time, 7–8, 19
   and identifying the most accurate texts, 20–21, 59n5
   interpretation of the Hebrew Bible in, 41
Nicene Creed, 43, 182
Niebuhr, Reinhold, 89, 89n23
nonviolence, Jesus's teachings on, 147–48, 148n19, 166–67, 173
Nouwen, Henri J. M., 79n7

oaths, promises, Jesus's cautions about, 41, 68, 71–72
objectivity, 25–26, 25n10, 53
The One-Stop Guide to Jesus (Beaumont), 162n10
oral traditions. *See also* the Gospels *and specific Gospels*
   and differences in Gospel accounts, 104n13, 110
   repurposing to support church communities, 7, 21–22, 115–16, 152, 177
   as source for Scripture, 14, 18, 22, 72, 117, 123–24, 127

Origin, 13
orthodox, orthodoxy, 16
the other, caring for, 60–64, 140. *See also* compassion, mercy; forgiveness; love

Palestine. *See also* Second Temple Palestinian Jews
    Jesus's origins in, 30
    Persian rulership, 80
    Roman rulership, 32, 137
    unrest in during Jesus's lifetime, 31–32
panentheism, 14, 14n15
parables
    as effective teaching tools, 99–100
    parable of the good Samaritan, 142–43
    parable of the greedy tenant, 162–63
parousia, defined, 91
pastor
    defined, 155
    and Jesus's pastoral ministry, 139–40
    role of, 138–39, 138n10
Paul, the apostle
    body metaphor for discipleship, 200
    on the gift of faith, 17
    hermeneutical approach to the Hebrew Bible, 41
    on Jesus's death as expiation for human sins, 172
    and living in God's presence, 58
    restatement of the parameters of faith, 13
    and the Roman emphasis on law and order, 181
    on the second coming, 88–89
    words used for "faith," 196
    Wright's study of, 25n12
Persia, rule over Palestine, 80
Peter
    betrayal of Jesus, 173
    expression of love for the resurrected Jesus, 177
    Jesus's exchange with during trip to Jerusalem, 158
    restatement of the parameters of faith, 12–13
Peterson, Rodney L., 62n11
Pharisees. *See also* Judaism, mainstream
    challenges to Jesus's authority and teachings, 66–67, 96–97, 108
    condemnation of as hypocritical, 29, 71–72, 152–53, 163
    defined, 73
    focus on the Law, 65–66
    Jesus's complex relationship with, 99, 99n8
    as representative of mainstream Judaism, 59, 72
    social position and behaviors, 107–8
    view of the temple, 161
pistis (faith), 195–96
Pontius Pilate
    authority given by Romans, 31, 186
    and Jesus's trial and conviction, 82, 85–86, 173–75, 175n18
    reluctance to execute Jesus, 175
the poor
    extreme poverty vs. temperate behavior, 103
    Jesus's advocacy and support for, 23, 28–29, 126, 128–29, 168
    Jesus's identification with, 50, 70, 154, 165
    Jesus's teachings about wealth, 69–71, 102
postmodern understanding of the historical Jesus, 50, 193
power and authority. *See also* conflict; kingdom of God
    of the church, Enlightenment challenges, 45
    defined, 111
    external, impacts on our lives, 95
    Jesus's handling of, 95–100, 131, 159–61, 162–63
    negative, self-serving, 93
    of the Sanhedrin and the Romans, 21, 31–32, 31n19, 79
    traditional, Jesus's challenges to, 66–67, 96–97, 108, 159, 167, 174
prejudices, personal. *See* preunderstanding; worldview

premodern, defined, 16
preunderstanding (*vorverständnis*). *See also* worldview
  and accuracy when interpreting biblical texts, 38
  attitudinal, 38
  defined, 25, 33
  functional impacts of scriptural interpretations, 39–41
  ideological, 38–39
  importance of identifying, 25–26
  informational, 38
  methodological, 39
priest
  defined, 155
  and Jesus's ministry, 140–42
  role, 138–39, 181
progressive Christianity, 12–13, 26–28, 26–27n15, 33
prophecy. *See* ministry, Jesus's
prophet, defined, 155
Psalms
  as guide for living a God-centered life, 76n5, 145
  and Jesus final words about being forsaken, 178
  metaphorical images for God, 197
Ptolemaic (Egyptian) Empire, 80

quelle (Q source). *See also* historical Jesus; oral traditions *and specific Gospels*
  defined, 53
  and oral traditions, 18, 20
  and the quest for the historical Jesus, 35
The Quest for the Historical Jesus (Schweitzer), 10, 57–58n1

rabbi. *See* teaching(s)
The Radical Teaching of Jesus (Ferguson)
  and the challenges of accessing Jesus's life and teachings, 1
  focus on Jesus as a teacher, 134, 134n1
  on Jesus's multiple roles, 138n9
  original scope, xiii
  themes addressed in, 28–29
realized eschatology, 88, 88n18
Real Love: The Art of Mindful Connection (Salzberg), 60n7
reason
  Aquinas's emphasis on, 44
  and modern approaches to the historical Jesus, 47–48
redaction criticism, 21–22, 33
Reformed Church
  importance of Confessions, 180
  tenets of, as part of the author's worldview, 27
reign of God, as term, 75. *See also* kingdom of God
religion
  benefits of, 184
  as both life affirming and denying, 190
  and the process of spiritual growth as a process, 76, 76n5
The Religion of Tomorrow: A Vision for the Future of the Great Traditions (Wilber), 76–77n6
religious practice. *See also* faith, faith journey
  importance of honesty and integrity, 72
  and receiving the power and presence of God, 74
repentance, 33, 77, 93, 126. *See also* faith, faith journey; forgiveness; sin
respect for others. *See also* compassion; love
  and the God-centered life, 144, 146, 184–85, 193, 198
  and the Golden Rule, 146
  Jesus's, 99, 99n8, 108
Restoration period, 80, 80n8
resurrection. *See also* God; kingdom of God
  accounts of in the Gospels, 176–77
  as basic tenet of Christian belief, 182–83
  Jesus's statements about, 85, 164–65
  meaning of, discussions about, 180–84

Rohr, Richard, 190n1
Roman authorities
    choice of Herod as ruler of Palestine, 137
    control over Palestine, 31–32
    and impacts on the lives of the Palestinians, 79
    Jesus's challenges to during final week, 160–61
    resistance and revolts against, 79
    taxes by, Jesus's comment on, 163
    trial and conviction of Jesus, 82, 85–86, 173–75, 175n18
Romans, Book of, and transformation through faith, 114, 187–88, 196

the Sabbath, laws governing, 66–67, 101–2. *See also* the Law (Torah)
sacrifices
    as atonement, 160
    Jesus's crucifixion as, 172, 180
    as part of temple life, 84–85
Sadducees, questioning of Jesus, 164
Salzberg, Sharon, 60n7
Samaritans
    the Good Samaritan, 142–43
    the woman at Jacob's Well, 109
Sanctuary (the temple), 161
Sanders, E. P., 83n13
Sanhedrin. *See also* Pharisees
    and Jesus's trial, 173–74
    mistrust of, 79
    rulership and authority of, 31n19
Satan (evil one), temptation of Jesus, 131–33. *See also* the devil (*diabolis*, evil one)
Schleiermacher, Friedrich, 184n26
scholastics, scholasticism, 44
Schweitzer, Albert, 10–11, 57, 57–58n1
science, integrating with faith, 9, 45, 184, 185n28, 194
scientism, 9
scribes. *See also* Pharisees
    defined, 73
    hypocritical practices, Jesus's denunciation of, 152–53, 165

second coming of Jesus (parousia). *See also* kingdom of God; messiah; resurrection
    "already-not yet" perspective, 89, 89n22
    as apocalyptic, eschatological, 87, 87n16
    as immanent, living in preparation for, 88–89
    and the realized eschatology viewpoint, 88, 88n18
Second Temple Palestinian Judaism. *See also* Judaism, mainstream
    as the context for Jesus's life and teachings, 23–24, 49–50, 113
    defined, 73
    hope and need for a messiah, 49, 88, 116, 166
    Jesus's honoring of, 65
    and the re-establishment of Judaism following the Babylonian captivity, 49
self-awareness, consciousness
    and accepting responsibility for one's behavior, 146–47
    and accurate interpretations of Scripture, 38
    importance when interpreting difficult passages, 51–52
    and incorporating teachings of compassion and justice, 102
    Jesus's humility and maintenance of role as God's servant, 106
    and living a God-centered life, 187–88
    and preunderstanding/prejudices, 39–41
    and self-love, 60, 60n7
self-centeredness
    ego, "I" identity, 93–94, 105–6
    vs. God-centeredness, 93–94, 135
    negativity associated with, 94
    self-love vs., 60, 60n7
Sermon on the Mount
    applicability of, Schweitzer's view, 57
    and Jesus as emphasis on ethics, integrity, 41, 71

Sermon on the Mount (*continued*)
  and Jesus's cautions about oaths and promises, 71–72
  and living the God-centered life, 69, 93–94, 145
sermons, as type of literature, 124
Seven Last Words, 186
Simon, apostle, 107–8, 123
sinfulness, sins. *See also* God-centered life
  and baptism, 129
  and forgiveness, 61–62, 96–97, 107–8, 126
  as innate to humans, 172
  and Jesus's crucifixion, 14, 44, 169, 171–72, 178, 186
  and Jesus's resurrection, 182–83
slave ransom, crucifixion as, 181
social action. *See* justice; equality; moral action
social sciences, sociology, 22–24
Son of Man, 83, 86–87, 166
The Soul of the Leader (Benefiel), 97n5
source criticism, 21
Spirit of God, 43–44, 197
Spirituality Without God (Heehs), 191n5
spiritual journey, faith pilgrimage. *See* faith journey; the God-centered life
Spong, John Shelby, xii
Stages of Faith (Fowler), 76–77n6
Synoptic Gospels. *See* the Gospels
Syria (Seleucid dynasty), rule over Judea, 80

Tatum, W. Barnes, 23
teaching(s). *See also* faith, faith journey; invitation of Jesus
  goals, 17–18
  Jesus's charismatic approach to, xiii, 28, 31, 62, 99–100, 125–28, 142
  parables, 99–100, 142–43, 162–63
  selecting, reasons for, 55–56
  as a spiritual gift (*pneumatica*), 28
  understanding, approaches to, 50–52

Teilhard de Chardin, Pierre, 13–14, 120n4, 194
the temple
  differing views of, 161–62
  and Jesus's cleansing of, 84, 159–60
  Jesus's sayings about, 51, 83–84
  Jesus's views on corruption of, 161–62
  multiple functions and activities in, 84, 84n14, 161
  and the parable of the greedy tenants, 162–63
  place in Jewish life, 83n12
  seizure and destruction, 166–67
temptation. *See also* the devil (*diabolis*, evil one)
  Jesus's handling of, 103–5, 104n12, 129–31
  of Jesus, as real or metaphorical, 130–32, 130n9
Tertullian, 42
textual criticism, 21, 33
1 Thessalonians, on the second coming, 88–89
thirst, Jesus's during the crucifixion, 179
Thomas, apostle, 177
Thomas Aquinas, 44
Torah. *See* the Law (Torah)
treason, Jesus's trial for, 31, 31n18, 175, 175n18
truth, 190–91, 205

Unbelievable: Why Neither Ancient Creeds Nor the Reformation Can Produce a Living Faith Today (Spong), xii
United Presbyterian Church of America, Confession of 1967, 180
universe, cosmos, panentheist view, 14

vocation, Christian, defined, 133
voting, importance of, 203

war, preventing, 148n19
water, living, as metaphor for faith, 109

wealth, material possessions, teachings related to, 68–70, 102–3. *See also* materialism; the poor
Whitehead, Alfred North, 194n8
whole-person healing, 98
Wilber, Ken, 14n14, 76–77n6, 120n4
wilderness, Jesus's sojourn in, 129–31
Wilson, Edward O., 192–93
wise men (magi), 117
worldview (*Weltanshuuang*). *See also* preunderstanding (*vorverständnis*)
  and the altering of Biblical text to reflect, 21–22
  and approaches to understanding reality, 15
  and being open to others' perspectives, 36
  Christian, as starting point for reading the Gospels, 29
  defined, 33, 205
  and exploration of Christian faith in the modern context, xix-xx
  in the Gospels, integrating into historical understanding, 18
  Jesus's life and teachings as guide to progressive Christianity, 28
  personal, importance when making historical assumptions, 24–27
  and the purpose of the Gospels, 18
  as a term, limits, 75n1
  and *vorverständnis* (preunderstanding), 25
worry, anxiety
  and clarifying priorities, 70
  and the self-centered life, 94
Wrede, Wilhelm
  essay on Jesus in the Gospel of Mark, 11
  as a first-century Palestinian prophet, 10
Wright, N. T.
  acceptance of miracles, 47n15
  Christian Origins and the Question of God, xiiin2
  examination of preunderstanding and starting points by, 25, 25n12

Zachariah (father of John the Baptist), 121–22
Zealots
  advocacy of violence, 79
  speculation about Judas's participation with, 169

www.ingramcontent.com/pod-product-compliance
Lightning Source LLC
Chambersburg PA
CBHW051635230426
43669CB00013B/2317